Book Bands

for Guided Reading

Organising
Key Stage One Texts
for the Literacy Hour

Produced by the
U.K. Reading Recovery
National Network

This publication builds on a database of titles used in the Reading Recovery Programme. It could not have been produced without the expertise and effort of Tutors and Teachers in the U.K. Reading Recovery National Network.

Editorial Committee: S. Baker, S. Bickler, A. Hobsbaum, A. Kotler and J. Prance.

ISBN 0 85473-564 X

Produced by Reprographic Services
Institute of Education University of London
20 Bedford Way, London WC1H 0AL

Printed by Orchard Publishing
Longfield, Kent, DA3 7QA

May 1998

The purpose of this book guide is to assist teachers to audit, organise and supplement a school's existing reading materials at Key Stage 1 for Guided Reading.

Ten bands have been identified to produce a gradient of difficulty for more than 3,000 texts:

Working Towards Level 1	2 bands
Working Within Level 1	3 bands
Working Towards Level 2	2 bands
Working Within Level 2	2 bands
Working Towards Level 3	1 band

The learning focus of each band is described, along with characteristics of typical texts. Benchmark books are listed as exemplars. There is also a full alphabetic listing of the titles.

This is not a list of recommended texts.
Nor is it exhaustive.
Where titles are missing, teachers should make provisional decisions based on the suggested benchmark texts and confirm or change the banding as experience dictates. Out-of-print texts and series have been omitted, as have unpunctuated texts. No judgements have been made regarding the literary quality of the titles listed.

Reading Recovery Tutors and Teachers have used the majority of these books with a wide variety of children and reached general agreement about the level of challenge they provide. However, a number of new series have recently appeared on the market, and as many as possible have been included here. These books need to be trialled with groups of children and adjustments made where the banding seems inappropriate.

No book guide can take the place of an individual teacher's experience and knowledge about the choice of book for a particular group of children.

Using the National Literacy Strategy Framework for Teaching Reading

The intellectual challenge for children learning to read:

> *Reading, like thinking, is very complex. When you think, all you have to do is produce responses from within you. When you read you have to produce responses which interpret what the author wrote: you have to try to match your thinking to his.*
>
> Marie M. Clay 1991
> (*Becoming Literate*, p.320)

Inexperienced readers must learn to use their knowledge of books and reading behaviours, an understanding of the world and control over oral language together with growing expertise in all aspects of print information in order to re-create an author's message in their own minds.

A balanced class reading programme consists of a variety of reading experiences, levels of support and methods of instruction to foster this expertise.

During **whole-class Shared Reading** sessions, children participate in the collaborative act of fluent, expressive reading, and are taught to attend to formal elements at the text, sentence and word levels.

In **Guided Reading**, children put into practice their developing expertise at an appropriate level in a structured situation. The teacher differentiates the instructional reading programme and guides children to develop independent reading strategies on new, increasingly challenging texts.

When **working independently**, children return to familiar texts, re-reading and strengthening their control over the reading process. They also carry out activities designed to direct their attention more closely to specific aspects of reading and writing.

Some Important Distinctions between Shared, Guided and Independent Reading

	SHARED READING	GUIDED READING	INDEPENDENT READING
Grouping of Pupils	WHOLE CLASS: mixed ability.	SMALL GROUP: usually 3-8 selected pupils.	INDIVIDUALLY or in small groups.
Text	LARGE PRINT: one text for whole group (or copy of text per child). Text re-read aloud repeatedly until well known.	SETS of texts with one copy for each group member. One lesson only on unfamiliar text or section of text.	VARIETY of texts from Shared and Guided reading, library books, games, activities, book-tapes, environmental print, instructions, recipes etc.
Text Level	RICH CHALLENGING text beyond the current ability of most of the class.	INSTRUCTIONAL LEVEL i.e. each member of group able to read and readily comprehend text at above 90% accuracy.	EASY LEVEL i.e. each child able to read and readily comprehend texts at above 95% accuracy.
Performance	HIGH LEVEL OF SUPPORT within a collaborative social framework of explicit teaching and oral response.	LOWER LEVEL OF SUPPORT. Teacher structures the task and then calls for individuals to apply strategies already introduced and practised in Shared Reading.	LITTLE/NO TEACHER SUPPORT. Pupils work independently or with others to practise reading in a variety of contexts, or respond to reading. Adults may organise and supervise certain activities.
Teaching Style	TEACHER-LED, with formal, pre-planned teaching objectives.	PUPILS expected to take the initiative and read to themselves following an introduction, with TEACHER facilitating.	PUPILS monitor their own activities. Assist and work with others within classroom organisation where expectations are clear and routines well established.
Focus	INTRODUCING AND PRACTISING planned objectives at the word, sentence and/or text levels.	REINFORCING AND EXTENDING strategies and/or objectives already taught in Shared Reading.	ACHIEVING FLUENCY AND FLEXIBILITY at current level of control. RESPONDING personally to text.

The goal of Guided Reading is for children to read to themselves accurately and with enjoyment, putting into practice appropriate reading skills and strategies while thinking about the content and implications of the text.

Organising Children for Guided Reading

For Guided Reading to be successful at Key Stage 1, the teacher needs to structure the membership of each group carefully so that the children are working at a similar level of control of the reading process.

With beginner readers, this will entail periodic alphabet and high-frequency word checks, along with observations of early reading behaviours, in particular one-to-one matching.

Subsequently teachers will carry out observations on text reading, most commonly by taking running records. Where children are working towards and within Level 1 (Bands 1-5), they will need to have some familiarity with a text before an assessment is made. The teacher may choose a text that the child has encountered previously in Guided Reading, or the teacher may introduce a text which is similar to one already mastered by the child.

Previously unseen texts are appropriate for assessment purposes once a child has reached Band 6 (Working Towards Level 2). However, an opportunity should be given for the child to look through an unfamiliar book, read the blurb where there is one, and comment on aspects of the layout and illustrations prior to reading.

Success in text reading is crucial for sustained progress. A child should not experience difficulty with more than one word in every 15-20. Where the accuracy rate falls consistently below 90% (more than one error in every 10 words), the reader no longer has control of the reading process.

Teachers using running records regularly to monitor progress are able to adjust the composition of the groups sensitively. Guided Reading then enables all the children to enjoy books and work at solving problems for themselves, taking pleasure in their own progress as readers.

Carrying Out Guided Reading

PRIOR TO THE LESSON:

Planning

— The teacher decides on specific learning objectives for a particular group.
— A text is chosen which the teacher anticipates will be within the control of the group, yet contains some challenge and suitable learning opportunities.
— The teacher reads the whole text, plans a careful introduction and teaching points, and any follow-up activities.
— Wherever possible, a copy of the text is provided for every child.

Introducing the new book

— The teacher usually reads the title and may give a very brief overview of how the text has been written eg. 'In this book, Jan is telling us what happened when she fell off her bike.'
— The children are invited to contribute their own experience and understanding to a brief discussion based on illustrations and the main ideas in the text. The teacher guides their language and observations as they leaf through the book so that each child is prepared to read this particular text independently, and at times with a specific feature in mind.
— In the case of a non-fiction text, each member of the group may be directed to read different sections in preparation for further discussion.

Reading the new book

— Each child then reads quietly or silently to themselves.
— After a satisfactory introduction, pupils will have a sense of how the text is structured and be familiar with the main ideas and any unusual vocabulary, names and sentence patterns.
— The teacher may listen in to monitor and/or work with one child and then another, supporting where necessary. If the child is reading silently, the teacher will signal to the child to read aloud from the point reached in the text.

The teacher's role in Guided Reading is to prompt a child to use prior knowledge together with print information, following the language syntax as s/he re-constructs the author's meaning. Prompts may help a child use a fuller range of information and keep track of their own reading, for example:

- Did that make sense?
- Good. You were thinking about the story, but does that look like 'happy'?
- Can we say it like that? Go back to the beginning of the sentence, listen to yourself and look more carefully.
- Do you know a word like that?
- What could you try?

Returning to the Text

This first reading is often followed by a brief teaching session to reinforce the lesson focus eg. deepening comprehension; or making links with appropriate word, sentence or text level work already introduced in Shared Reading.

Children may be asked to return to specific parts of the text to justify their responses or to frame questions for themselves arising from the text.

Follow-up

An independent activity based on the text may follow this first reading.
Copies of this text now join other familiar texts to be re-read independently in or out of the classroom.

Organising Texts for Guided Reading

Books vary in many dimensions:

- amount of print on the page

- size of font used and the spacing between words

- range and familiarity of vocabulary

- extent to which the language follows spoken or literary conventions

- extent of repetition in various forms including vocabulary, story structure

- extent to which illustrations support the text

- variety and familiarity of sentence structure

- predictability of the story line

- length and complexity of the story or book

- formality of language and layout used

- extent to which children are familiar with the text genre

It is the complex interactions between these and other features, together with each child's personal experience, which help to determine whether a particular child will be able to read a specific text successfully first time round.

The skill with which a teacher is able to give a group of children access to a particular text and to anticipate and deal in advance with difficulties may also determine the success of a first reading.

Over time, experienced Key Stage 1 teachers using the same texts for Guided Reading with many different children are able to reach a consensus about the relative challenge provided by a wide variety of books.

Certain books come to be regarded as typical or benchmark texts for each band. As new books come on the market, teachers provisionally assess and grade them against these benchmark texts, try them out with children, and confirm or modify the classification.

Making Use of This Publication

The daunting task for a teacher carrying out Guided Reading is to choose texts at an appropriate level for different groups of children so that the first reading of that text is successful, yet provides some challenge. This book guide represents the combined expertise of teachers who have used these texts or ones similar in this country and elsewhere with individuals and groups at Key Stage 1.

It has been impossible to be fully comprehensive, with publishers producing new materials at an unprecedented rate. Series are included if they are known to exist in large quantities in schools. Familiar texts eg. Not Now, Bernard, and small versions of Big Books are classified as though previously unseen.

Some non-fiction texts have been included, but the banding of these has been somewhat tentative. Non-fiction tends to be less accessible than fiction to inexperienced readers because of the formality of sentence structure and specialised vocabulary. For this reason, these are included at higher bands than similar fiction texts and may require fuller introductions.

Guide to the Book Bands

Bands	National Curriculum Levels	Suggested Colour Coding	Equivalent Reading Recovery Levels
1	Working Towards Level 1	Pink	1/2
2	Working Towards Level 1	Red	3-5
3	Working Within Level 1	Yellow	6-8
4	Working Within Level 1	Blue	9-11
5	Working Within Level 1	Green	12-14
6	Working Towards Level 2	Orange	15/16
7	Working Towards Level 2	Turquoise	17/18
2C*	Working Within Level 2	Purple	19/20
2B*	Working Within Level 2	Gold	21/22
2A*	Working Towards Level 3	White	23/24

These bands have been labelled to correspond with National Curriculum English Reading SATs levels.

Working Towards Level 1: Learning Focus

- Locate title.
- Open front cover.
- Turn pages appropriately.
- Understand that left page comes before right.
- Understand that we read print from left to right.
- Match spoken word to printed word (one-to-one corresponding).
- Locate familiar words and use them to check own reading.
- Use the meaning of the text.
- Use language patterns (syntax).
- Predict the story line and some vocabulary.

TEXT CHARACTERISTICS

- natural language following children's speech patterns
- a short, simple, highly predictable text involving familiar objects and actions
- repetitive sentence structures including high frequency words
- illustrations that provide full and direct support for the text
- reasonably large print size with clear spaces between words
- fully punctuated text in same position on each page

Benchmark texts

Me	PM Instant Readers/Nelson
The Farm Concert	Storychest/Kingscourt
Yuk Soup	Sunshine /Heinemann
Cat on the Mat	Brian Wildsmith/Oxford University Press
Weather	Jan Pienkowski/Picture Puffin
Getting Fit	Wonderworld NF/Badger Books

SERIES	PUBLISHER	SET (OR AUTHOR)	TITLE	BAND
All Aboard	Ginn	Easy Start Patt & Rhyme	Bat in a Hat	1
			Stars and Spots	1
		Easy Start Sam & Rosie	Balloon, The	1
			Bubbles	1
			Friends	1
			Hide and Seek	1
			Lollies	1
			Nog	1
			Pizza	1
			Play Tunnel, The	1
			Rosie's Family	1
			Sam Went In	1
			Sam's Family	1
			Shopping	1
		Stage 1 Intro Sam & Ro	Grandad's Balloon	1
			Parrot, The	1
			Rosie and the Dinosaurs	1
		Stage 1 Pattern & Rhyme	My Pet	1
		Stage 1 Sam & Rosie	Swimming	1
All Aboard Non Fiction	Ginn	Stage 1	Swimming	1
		Stage 1 Intro	This Week	1
			Bigger and Biggest	1
			Clever Clowns	1
			Feelings	1
			What Happens Next?	1
		Stage 2	Toys Now and Then	1
Book Project	Longman	Beginner Band 1	Can You Do This?	1
			Come In!	1
			I Am Red	1
			I Like Green	1
			Where Is My Ball?	1
			Who Am I?	1
Cambridge Reading	CUP	Begin to Read Stage A	Entering the Ark	1
			Hunting in the Marshes	1
			January	1
		Begin to Read Stage B	My Pet	1
Discovery World	Heinemann	Stage A	Choosing Cards	1
			Day and Night Animals	1
			Seasons	1
			Shapes	1
			Shopping	1
			Special Clothes	1
			Which is Alive?	1
		Stage B	Animal Legs	1
			My History	1
Foundations for Reading	Folens	Level 1 Emergent	Big and Little	1
			Eating	1
			Garden, A	1
			I Love My Family	1
			Making a Salad	1
			Mother Hippopotamus	1
			Mr Bumbleticker	1
			My Bike	1
			My Fish Bowl	1
			My Ride	1
			Packing	1
			Shopping at the Supermarket	1
			Splash!	1

SERIES	PUBLISHER	SET (OR AUTHOR)	TITLE	BAND
Foundations for Reading	Folens	Level 1 Emergent	Toys	1
			What Can I See?	1
			What Can This Animal Do?	1
		Level 2 Emergent	Birthdays	1
			Camping	1
			Can You Fly?	1
			Fitness	1
			Hair	1
			Hot Potato and Cold Potato	1
			In the Park	1
			Making Pictures	1
			Moving Day	1
			My Shadow	1
			River, The	1
			Sun, A Flower, A	1
			We Like	1
			When I Look Up	1
			When it Rains	1
			Who Ate the Pizza?	1
Link Up	Collins	Starter Books	Children	1
			People at Work	1
			Pets	1
			Playing	1
			Things at Home	1
			Things in the Street	1
			Things on Wheels	1
			Things to Eat	1
			Things We Read	1
			Wild Animals	1
		Starter Build-Up	Drivers	1
Literacy Links Plus	Kingscourt	Emergent A	Circus, The	1
			Farm, The	1
			Fruit Salad	1
			Let's Build a Tower	1
			Miss Popple's Pets	1
			Scrumptious Sundae, A	1
			Tommy's Tummy Ache	1
			Toy Box, A	1
			What Are You?	1
			Wheels	1
			Who Likes Icecream?	1
			Who's Coming for a Ride?	1
			Zoo, A	1
		Emergent B	Don't Wake the Baby	1
			I Paint	1
			Look Out!	1
			What has Spots?	1
		Emergent C	Climbing	1
			Yellow	1
One, Two, Three & Away	Collins	Pre-reader 1-4	Blue	1
			Brown	1
			Red	1
			Yellow	1
		Pre-reader 5b-8b	Eight, Nine, Ten, Eleven, Twelve	1
			Four, Five, Six	1
Open Door	Nelson	Red Fun Books	Help	1
			No	1
			Wake Up	1

SERIES	PUBLISHER	SET (OR AUTHOR)	TITLE	BAND
Oxford Reading Tree	OUP	Stage 1 First Words	Floppy Floppy	1
			Fun at the Beach	1
			Good Trick, A	1
			Pancake, The	1
			Six in a Bed	1
			Who is it?	1
		Stage 2 More Wrens	Journey, The	1
			Making Faces	1
		Stage 2 Wrens	Fancy Dress	1
			Headache, The	1
			Pet Shop, The	1
Oxford RT Branch Library	OUP	Wildsmith Bks St 1A	Apple Bird, The	1
			Nest, The	1
			Trunk, The	1
			Whose Shoes?	1
		Wildsmith Bks St 2A	Cat on the Mat	1
Pathways	Collins	Stage 0 Set A	New Glasses	1
			S Book, The	1
			What is This?	1
		Stage 0 Set B	How Many Candles?	1
			Who Did That?	1
		Stage 0 Set C	Juggler, The	1
			Look Out!	1
			My Jigsaw	1
			Traffic Lights	1
			Weather Forecast, The	1
		Stage 0 Set D	Apple On The Bed	1
			Woof!	1
		Stage 1 Set A	Magic Trick, A	1
			Up and Down	1
		Stage 1 Set C	Ghost Train	1
PM Storybook Starters	Nelson	Set 1	At the Zoo	1
			Big Things	1
			Climbing	1
			Dad	1
			Dressing Up	1
			Go Cart, The	1
			House, A	1
			In The Trolley	1
			Little Things	1
			Look at Me	1
			Me	1
			Mum	1
			Mums and Dads	1
			Pets	1
			Playing	1
			Shopping Mall, The	1
			Skier, The	1
			Way I Go to School, The	1
			We Go Out	1
		Set 2	At The Library	1
			Ball Games	1
			Ben's Red Car	1
			Can You See The Eggs?	1
			Cat and Mouse	1
			Farm In Spring, The	1
			Fishing	1
			Four Ice Creams	1

SERIES	PUBLISHER	SET (OR AUTHOR)	TITLE	BAND
PM Storybook Starters	Nelson	Set 2	Looking Down	1
			My Accident	1
			My Little Dog	1
			Out In The Weather	1
			Packing My Bag	1
			Pencil, The	1
			Rock Pools, The	1
			Sally's New Shoes	1
			Stop!	1
			We Can Run	1
			We Like Fish!	1
			Where are the Babies?	1
Reading 360	Ginn	Level 1	Help	1
			Lad	1
			Look	1
		Magic Circle Level 1	Bumbershoot, The	1
			Walk, Robot, Walk	1
			We need a bigger Zoo	1
		Magic Circle Level 3	Look	1
Reading 360 Upstarts	Ginn	Introductory	Race, The	1
			There's Paul	1
Reading World	Longman	Level 1 Pack A	Sandwich, The	1
Ready to Read	Nelson	Emergent Set A	All Kinds of Things	1
			Boat, The	1
			Boots for Toots	1
			Busy Bird	1
			I Can Read	1
			Off We Go!	1
			Wild Bear	1
		Emergent Set B	Lights at Night	1
			Mouse, The	1
			My Chair	1
			New Cat, The	1
			Where is Lunch?	1
		Emergent Set C	Dog	1
			In the Dark Forest	1
			It's My Bread	1
			Our Rocket	1
			We All Play Sports	1
		Emergent Set D	Elena Makes Tortillas	1
			What Does Greedy Cat Like?	1
Story Chest	Kingscourt	Get-ready Set A	Ghost, The	1
			Go, Go, Go	1
			If You Meet a Dragon	1
			In the Mirror	1
			Party, The	1
			Tree-House, The	1
		Get-ready Set AA	Brenda's Birthday	1
			Shoo, Fly!	1
			Surprise, The	1
			Swing	1
		Get-ready Set B	Night-time	1
		Get-ready Set BB	Chick's Walk	1
			Gotcha Box, The	1
			Mrs Wishy-Washy's Tub	1
			Salad	1
		Get-ready Set C	Clown and Elephant	1
			Going to school	1

SERIES	PUBLISHER	SET (OR AUTHOR)	TITLE	BAND
Story Chest	Kingscourt	Get-ready Set CC	Halloween	1
			Mouse Train	1
		Get-ready Set DD	Tick-Tock	1
		Large Read-tog Set 2	Farm Concert, The	1
		Ready-set-go Set A	Who's Going to Lick the Bowl?	1
Storyworlds	Heinemann	Stage 2 Animal World	Big Surprise, The	1
Sunrise	Heinemann	-	At School	1
			Barbecue, The	1
			Birthday Party, The	1
			Books	1
			Building With Blocks	1
			Dressing Up	1
			Faces	1
			Getting Dressed	1
			Give me a Hug	1
			I am...	1
			I Like...	1
			Just Look at You!	1
			Look...	1
			My Family	1
			My Shadow	1
			Run!	1
			Shopping	1
			Space Journey	1
			To School	1
			What's in this Egg?	1
			Come On	1
			I go, go, go	1
			Storm, The	1
			What's that?	1
Sunshine	Heinemann	Level 1 Set A	Baby Gets Dressed	1
			Birthday cake, The	1
			Dinner!	1
			Down to town	1
			Huggles' breakfast	1
			Huggles can juggle	1
			Huggles goes away	1
			I can fly	1
		Level 1 Set B	Little brother	1
			Major Jump	1
			Yuk soup	1
			Long, long tail, The	1
			My Puppy	1
Sunshine New	Heinemann	Level 1 Set A	Face Sandwich, The	1
			Jumpers	1
			My Book	1
			New House, The	1
			Paint the Sky	1
		Level 1 Set B	Going in the Car	1
			Helping Dad	1
			Super Hero	1
		Level 1 Set C	Snap! Splat!	1
			Spots	1
			Stepping Stones	1
		Level 1 Set D	Where is my Bone?	1
Sunshine Spirals	Heinemann	Set 1	Balloons, The	1
			Juggler, The	1
			Storm, The	1

14

SERIES	PUBLISHER	SET (OR AUTHOR)	TITLE	BAND
Sunshine Spirals	Heinemann	Set 1	Watching TV	1
			Where is My Dad?	1
		Set 2	Dinnertime	1
			I Can Climb	1
			Sausage, The	1
Sunshine Spirals Starters	Heinemann	Set A	Christmas	1
			Clown, The	1
			Farm, The	1
			Going to School	1
			Little Seed, A	1
			Snowman, The	1
			Time for Dinner	1
			Treasure Hunt, The	1
			Weather, The	1
			What a Mess!	1
		Set B	Books	1
			Dressing up	1
			Greedy Monster	1
			Holidays	1
			Hungry Bear	1
			In Trouble	1
			Model, The	1
			Naughty Kitten	1
			Socks	1
			Time for Bed	1
		Set C	Amazing Race, The	1
			Bath, The	1
			Be Quiet!	1
			Dinosaur Party	1
			My Box	1
			On Safari	1
			Robber, The	1
			Spots	1
			We Like Animals	1
		Set D	Cat, The	1
			Giant's Day Out, The	1
			In the Bathroom	1
			Jigsaw, The	1
			Lost	1
			My Planet	1
			On the Beach	1
			Robot, The	1
			What Did Ben Want?	1
			Where is my Pet?	1
Wonder World	Badger	Set 1	Basketball	1
			Getting Fit	1
			Getting There	1
			Nests	1
			Seed, The	1
			What Season is This?	1
		Set 2	Bathtime	1
		Set 4	Cleaning Teeth	1
			My Story	1
			Sometimes	1
			Whiskers	1
Individual Titles	Collins Pict Lions	Aruego, Jose	Look What I Can Do	1
	Methuen	Bruna, Dick	In My House	1
	Lothian	Campbell, Rod	Look Inside	1

SERIES	PUBLISHER	SET (OR AUTHOR)	TITLE	BAND
Individual Titles	Picture Puffin	Carle, Eric	Do You Want to be my Friend?	1
	Picture Puffin	Ginsberg, Mirra	Have You Seen My Duckling?	1
	Picture Puffin	Maris, Ron	My Book	1
	Picture Puffin	Pienkowski, Jan	Colours	1
	Picture Puffin	Pienkowski, Jan	Farm	1
	Picture Puffin	Pienkowski, Jan	Food	1
	Picture Puffin	Pienkowski, Jan	Homes	1
	Picture Puffin	Pienkowski, Jan	Numbers	1
	Picture Puffin	Pienkowski, Jan	Shapes	1
	Picture Puffin	Pienkowski, Jan	Sizes	1
	Picture Puffin	Pienkowski, Jan	Weather	1
	Picture Puffin	Pienkowski, Jan	Zoo	1
	Collins Pict Lions	Powling, Chris	Hot Dog	1
	Victor Gollancz	Pragoff, Fiona	Growing	1
	Picture Hippo	Sharratt, Nick	Ketchup on your Cornflakes	1
	Sainsbury	Sharratt, Nick	Monday, Fun Day	1
	OUP	Wildsmith, Brian	Circus, The	1

Working Towards Level 1: Learning Focus

- Locate and recall title.
- Have secure control of one-to-one matching.
- Use known words to check and confirm reading.
- Start to read more rhythmically or use phrasing while maintaining track of print.
- Repeat words, phrases or sentences to check, confirm or modify own reading.
- Predict from meaning, syntax and print to solve new words.

TEXT CHARACTERISTICS

— slightly longer, highly predictable text involving familiar objects and actions

— repetitive sentence/phrase patterns including high frequency words

— language short, clear and straightforward following children's speech patterns

— illustrations provide full and direct support for the text

— simple story development (fiction text)

— more than one source of print information (non-fiction text)

— reasonably large print with obvious spaces between words

— full range of punctuation

Benchmark Texts

Brown Bear, Brown Bear, what do you see?	Bill Martin/Picture Puffin
Sam's Mask	Ready to Read/Nelson
Ghost, Ghost, are you scared?	Reading World/Longman
Roller Coaster	Pathways/Collins
Chairs	All Aboard NF/Ginn
The Giant's Breakfast	Literacy Links Plus/Kingscourt

SERIES	PUBLISHER	SET (OR AUTHOR)	TITLE	BAND
All Aboard	Ginn	Easy Start Patt & Rhyme	Birds	2
			Fast Asleep	2
		Stage 1 Intro Patt & Rh	Bug in a Mug	2
			Dolly Dot	2
			Flower Pots and Forget-me-nots	2
			Tap Tap Tap	2
			Where's the Fox?	2
			Wizard, The	2
		Stage 1 Intro Sam & Ro	Jabeen and the New Moon	2
			Nog's Dinner	2
			Pancakes	2
		Stage 1 Pattern & Rhyme	Late At Night	2
			Tick Tock	2
			Washing	2
		Stage 1 Sam & Rosie	Jack in the Box	2
			Mum and Dad Went Out	2
			No Lunchbox	2
			Park, The	2
			Play, The	2
			Rosie and the Wasp	2
			Rosie Wanted to Play	2
		Stage 2 Booster Bks	Dirty Car, The	2
			Woof! Woof!	2
		Stage 2 Sam & Rosie	Dinosaur Jumper, The	2
			Ghost Train, The	2
			I Want A Go!	2
			Let's Play Monsters	2
			No Sam!	2
			One Sock	2
			Terrible Fright, The	2
		Stage 2 Set A Patt & Rh	Clouds	2
All Aboard Non Fiction	Ginn	Stage 1	Chairs	2
			Hats	2
			Honeybee	2
			Places We Visit	2
			What Do We Drive?	2
		Stage 1 Intro	In the Morning	2
		Stage 2	Weather	2
			When Gran Was A Girl	2
Book Project	Longman	Beginner Band 1	Can I Play?	2
			I Can Make You Red	2
			I Want A Red Ball	2
			I Want To Be	2
			In The Box	2
			In The Toy Shop	2
			What's That?	2
			Where Is The Snake?	2
Book Project Fiction 1	Longman	Band 1 Read On	Come Back, Teddy!	2
			Mai Ling In The Toy Shop	2
			Mai Ling's Friend	2
			Snail Song	2
			Wiggle, Waggle	2
		Band 1 Read On Specials	Ben Biggins' playtime	2
			Ben Biggins' socks	2
			Ben Biggins' week	2
			Garden friends	2
			Mai Ling plays monsters	2
			Mai Ling's castle	2

SERIES	PUBLISHER	SET (OR AUTHOR)	TITLE	BAND
Book Project Fiction 1	Longman	Band 1 Read On Specials	Monkey's banana	2
			Playtime	2
			Teddy liked the little one	2
			Teddy plays hide and seek	2
			What's the time, Mai Ling?	2
			Norma's Notebook	2
		Band 1 Read On	Ben Biggins' tummy	2
			Not yet! Ben Biggins said	2
		Band 2 Read On	Dad	2
Bright and Early Books	Collins	Berenstain, Stan & Jan	Bears In The Night	2
Cambridge Reading	CUP	Begin to Read Stage A	Fishy Numbers	2
			Hey Diddle Diddle	2
			Hickory, Dickory, Dock	2
			Humpty Dumpty	2
			Incy Wincy Spider	2
			Jumping	2
			Looking For Dragons	2
			Picnic, The	2
			Two Babies	2
			Very Hot Day, A	2
			Walking in the Jungle	2
			What's In The Box?	2
		Begin to Read Stage B	Blowing Bubbles	2
			Dirty Dog	2
			Five Green Monsters	2
			Guess Who I Am!	2
			I Went to School This Morning	2
			One Teddy All Alone	2
			That's Me	2
			Three Spotty Monsters	2
			What For?	2
			Where's Woolly?	2
Discovery World	Heinemann	Stage B	Homes	2
			Just Add Water	2
			My Body	2
			Sizes	2
			What did I use?	2
Foundations for Reading	Folens	Level 3 Emergent	Baby in the Trolley	2
			Beep, Beep, Beep	2
			Breakfast	2
			Grandma's Letter	2
			Happy Face, Sad Face	2
			My Nest is Best	2
			Picnic in the Sky, The	2
			Pizza, The	2
			Riding	2
			Running	2
			Snowman, A	2
			What Are You Doing?	2
			What do You Like to Eat?	2
			What's Inside?	2
			Where is My Grandma?	2
			Where Will You Sleep Tonight?	2
		Level 4 Emergent	At the Pool	2
			Boxes	2
			Fast Machines	2
		Level 5 Emergent	Hiding	2
			I Wonder Why?	2

SERIES	PUBLISHER	SET (OR AUTHOR)	TITLE	BAND
Foundations for Reading	Folens	Level 5 Emergent	Mother Hippopotamus Goes Shopping	2
			Turtle, The	2
		Level 6 Early	Scratch My Back	2
Journeys in Reading	Schofield & Sims	Level 1	Look At Me	2
Link Up	Collins	Starter Books	Things in School	2
		Starter Build-Up	Hill Street	2
			Police Car The	2
Literacy Links Plus	Kingscourt	Early A	Legs	2
			Monkey's Friends	2
			Row Your Boat	2
			Talk,Talk,Talk	2
			Wrinkles	2
		Emergent A	Blue Day	2
			Buffy	2
			Dancing Shoes	2
			Dressing Up	2
			Getting Ready for the Ball	2
			Ouch!	2
			Sharing	2
			Signs	2
			Sometimes	2
			Teeny Tiny Tina	2
			Too Many Clothes	2
		Emergent B	Ants Love Picnics Too	2
			Bike Parade, The	2
			Birthday Cake, The	2
			Hat Trick, The	2
			Hello, Goodbye	2
			Here's What I Made	2
			I Spy	2
			Kittens	2
			Koalas	2
			On the Farm	2
			Our Baby	2
			Our Garden	2
			Water	2
			Who Made These Tracks?	2
		Emergent C	Chew, Chew, Chew	2
			Dear Santa	2
			Giant's Breakfast, The	2
			Guess What!	2
			Have You Seen?	2
			I Like	2
			In My Bed	2
			In My Room	2
			Our Dog Sam	2
			Pet Parade, The	2
			Sunrise	2
			Surprise Cake	2
			What Goes in the Bathtub?	2
			What is Red?	2
			Woof!	2
		Emergent D	All Join In	2
			In Went Goldilocks	2
			Puppet Show, The	2
			Shopping	2
			What Did Kim Catch?	2
One, Two, Three & Away	Collins	Blue Platform 1-6	Big Dog and the Little White Cat, The	2

SERIES	PUBLISHER	SET (OR AUTHOR)	TITLE	BAND
One, Two, Three & Away	Collins	Blue Platform 1-6	Little Old Man and the Donkey, The	2
			Little Old Woman, The	2
			Old Blue Bus, The	2
			Rip's Bath	2
		Introductory A-D	Billy Blue-hat	2
			Johnny and Jennifer Yellow-hat	2
			Roger Red-hat	2
		Introductory I-L	Jennifer Yellow-hat went to Town	2
			Roger and Mrs Blue-hat	2
		Introductory M-P	Donkey went to Town, The	2
			Percy Green	2
		Pre-reader 1a-4a	Green	2
			Red, Green, Blue, Yellow and Brown	2
			Roger and the Ball	2
			Roger and the Bus	2
		Pre-reader 1b-4b	Billy Blue-hat and the Snowman	2
			Jennifer Yellow-hat and the White Cat	2
			Jennifer Yellow-hat and Mr Brown's Goat	2
			Roger Red-hat and Mrs Green's Hat	2
		Pre-reader 5-8	Big and Little	2
			Houses	2
			One, Two, Three	2
			Roger, Billy, Jennifer and Johnny	2
		Pre-reader 5a-8a	I see Green!	2
			Jennifer and the Little Yellow Cat	2
			No! Percy Green	2
			Yellow Cat and the Brown Dog, The	2
		Pre-reader 5b-8b	Big Man and the Little Mouse, The	2
			Seven Geese	2
		Pre-reader 9-12	Billy went to School	2
			Cat and the Mouse, the Dog and the Frog	2
			Jennifer went to School	2
			Little Yellow Cat & the Little Brown Mouse	2
		Pre-reader 9a-12a	Alex at the Fair	2
			Billy's Picture	2
			Stop it! Percy Green	2
		Pre-reader 9b-12b	Billy Blue-hat and the Red Mask	2
			Roger and the Frog	2
Open Door	Nelson	Blue Fun Books	Elephants Going to Bed	2
			One Jumping Kangaroo	2
			Out of the House	2
			Up the Wall	2
		Green Fun Books	Bear in a Hole, A	2
			Bill had a Bus	2
		Red Fun Books	Look At Me	2
		Yellow Fun Books	Cat and a Fiddle, A	2
			Longer, Faster and Bigger	2
Oxford Reading Tree	OUP	Stage 2 More Wrens	Goal!	2
			Shopping	2
			What a Mess!	2
			Who Did That?	2
		Stage 2 Storybooks	New Dog, A	2
			Toy's Party, The	2
		Stage 2 Wrens	At the Park	2
			Good Old Mum!	2
			Push!	2
		Stage 3 More Wrens	Band, The	2
			Little Dragon, The	2

SERIES	PUBLISHER	SET (OR AUTHOR)	TITLE	BAND
Oxford Reading Tree	OUP	Stage 3 More Wrens	Lost Puppy, The	2
			New Trees	2
			Up and Down	2
			What is it?	2
		Stage 3 Storybooks	Nobody Wanted to Play	2
		Stage 3 Wrens	Creepy Crawly	2
			Hey Presto!	2
			It's the Weather	2
			Monkey Tricks	2
			Naughty Children	2
			Sinking Feeling, A	2
Oxford RT Branch Library	OUP	Wildsmith Bks St 1A	Toot Toot	2
		Wildsmith Bks St 2A	All Fall Down	2
			Frog and the Fly, The	2
			Island, The	2
			My Dream	2
Pathways	Collins	Stage 0 Set A	Raft Ride	2
			Splish, Splash	2
		Stage 0 Set B	Deema's Dragon	2
			I Can	2
		Stage 0 Set C	Dragon at the Pool	2
			Sandwich, The	2
		Stage 1 Set A	What Am I?	2
		Stage 1 Set B	Animal Homes	2
			You Can Eat My Bicycle	2
		Stage 1 Set C	Brother & Sister	2
			Grandpa's Chair	2
			Pop!	2
		Stage 1 Set D	Roller Coaster	2
		Stage 2 Set A	Monsters	2
			What's There?	2
PM Storybooks	Nelson	Red Set A	Baby Lamb's First Drink	2
			Ben's Teddy Bear	2
			Ben's Treasure Hunt	2
			Big Kick, The	2
			Father Bear Goes Fishing	2
			Hedgehog is Hungry	2
			Lazy Pig, The	2
			Lizard Loses His Tail	2
			Merry Go Round, The	2
			Photo Book, The	2
			Pussy and the Birds	2
			Sally and the Daisy	2
			Sausages	2
			Tiger, Tiger	2
			Tom is Brave	2
			Wake Up, Dad!	2
		Red Set B	Baby owls, The	2
			Birthday cake for Ben, A	2
			Bumper cars, The	2
			Flower girl, The	2
			Hide and seek	2
			Home for little Teddy, A	2
			Little snowman, The	2
			Where is Hannah?	2
Reading 360	Ginn	Level 1	Ben	2
			Here	2
			Home	2

SERIES	PUBLISHER	SET (OR AUTHOR)	TITLE	BAND
Reading 360	Ginn	Magic Circle Level 3	Look with Mai Ling	2
			Stop! Look!	2
Reading 360 New	Ginn	Little Bks L 1 Set 1	Butterfly	2
			Egg, The	2
			Frog Spell	2
			Is This My Home?	2
			Where is It?	2
			Where is My Bone?	2
		Little Bks L 1 Set 2	Baking	2
			Fire!	2
			Lost	2
			On My Bike	2
			Parade The	2
		Little Bks L 1 Set 3	Day Puppy Got Lost, The	2
			Hard Day's Shopping, A	2
			King's Sock, The	2
			Pirate Treasure	2
			School Fair, The	2
			Where Is The Monster?	2
		Little Bks L 2 Set 1	Up We Go	2
		Little Bks L 4 Set 2	Boy With The Shell, The	2
Reading 360 Upstarts	Ginn	Introductory	Clever Cat, The	2
			Debbie and the Mouse	2
		Level 1	Goat is Eating Debbie, The	2
		Level 1 Extension	Cat and Mouse	2
Reading World	Longman	Level 1 Pack A	Fred's Mess	2
			Goodnight	2
			Picnic, The	2
			Trumpet, The	2
		Level 1 Pack B	Ghost, Ghost are you Scared?	2
			Go Away Stanley	2
			Have you seen Stanley?	2
			Joggers, The	2
			Jumper, The	2
		Level 1 More Books	Wasp, The	2
		Level 2 Pack A	Nobody	2
Ready to Read	Nelson	Early Set A	Our Teacher, Miss Pool	2
			Smile, The	2
		Early Set B	Down at the River	2
			Shush!	2
			Smile! said Dad	2
		Emergent Set A	Going to the Beach	2
		Emergent Set B	Fun with Mo and Toots	2
			Make it spin	2
		Emergent Set B	Stop that Noise!	2
		Emergent Set C	Hello, Dad!	2
			We Dance	2
		Emergent Set D	Fantail, Fantail	2
			Old Tuatara	2
			Open It!	2
			Pedal Power	2
			Sam's Mask	2
Story Chest	Kingscourt	Get-ready Set A	Painting	2
			Storm, The	2
		Get-ready Set AA	Escalator, The	2
			New Pants	2
			Snowman	2
			Waiting	2

SERIES	PUBLISHER	SET (OR AUTHOR)	TITLE	BAND
Story Chest	Kingscourt	Get-ready Set B	Bicycle, The	2
			Big Hill, The	2
			Feet	2
			Houses	2
			Monster Sandwich, A	2
			Mouse	2
			On a Chair	2
		Get-ready Set BB	Bridge, The	2
			Fishing	2
			Green Grass	2
			Rat's Funny Story	2
		Get-ready Set C	Hello	2
			I am frightened	2
			Little brother	2
			One, one is the sun	2
			Silly old possum	2
			What's for lunch?	2
		Get-ready Set CC	Dan Gets Dressed	2
			Jump, Jump, Kangaroo	2
			Look Out, Dan!	2
			My Picture	2
			Nest, The	2
			What Can Jigarees do?	2
		Get-ready Set DD	Boogie-Woogie Man, The	2
			Gifts, The	2
			Happy Birthday, Frog	2
			Ice-Cream Stick	2
		Ready-set-go Set A	Chocolate Cake, The	2
			Come with Me	2
			I Want an Ice-Cream	2
			Round and Round	2
			Splosh	2
			To New York	2
			Where are they Going?	2
		Ready-set-go Set AA	Bears' Picnic, The	2
			Chicken for Dinner	2
			Little Meanie's Lunch	2
			Skating	2
			Umbrella	2
			Valentine's day	2
			Who Can See the Camel?	2
		Ready-set-go Set B	Bee, The	2
			Copy-Cat	2
			Flying	2
			Little Pig	2
			Lost	2
			My Home	2
			Plop!	2
		Ready-set-go Set BB	Doctor Boondoggle	2
			Ducks	2
			How to make Can Stilts	2
			I love Chickens	2
			Roberto's Smile	2
		Ready-set-go Set C	Horace	2
			Look for Me	2
			Sleeping Out	2
			What a Mess!	2
		Ready-set-go Set D	Haunted House, The	2

SERIES	PUBLISHER	SET (OR AUTHOR)	TITLE	BAND
Story Chest	Kingscourt	Ready-set-go Set D	Stop!	2
Storyworlds	Heinemann	Stage 2 Animal World	Bingo and the bone	2
			Bingo wants to play	2
			Yum! Yum!	2
		Stage 2 Fantasy World	Monty and the ghost train	2
			Monty at McBurgers	2
			Monty at the party	2
			Monty at the seaside	2
		Stage 2 Once Upon a Time	Bears and the Honey, The	2
			Fox and the Rabbit, The	2
			Fox and the Stork, The	2
			Old Woman and the Hen, The	2
		Stage 2 Our World	Clever Joe	2
			Dinner Time	2
			Helpers	2
			Naughty Joe	2
		Stage 3 Animal World	Frisky and the cat	2
			Frisky and the ducks	2
			Frisky plays a trick	2
			Frisky wants to sleep	2
		Stage 3 Fantasy World	Mr Marvel and the cake	2
			Mr Marvel and the car	2
			Mr Marvel and the lemonade	2
			Mr Marvel and the washing	2
		Stage 3 Once Upon a Time	Boy who cried Wolf, The	2
			Hare and the Tortoise, The	2
			Selfish Dog, The	2
			Three Billy Goats, The	2
		Stage 3 Our World	Empty Lunchbox, The	2
			Lost coat, The	2
			Robots, The	2
			See-saw, The	2
Sunrise	Heinemann		Aeroplane, The	2
			Farm, The	2
			Great Enormous Hamburger, The	2
			I Write	2
			My Friend	2
			My Home	2
			Our Grandad	2
			Rounders	2
			Space Ark, The	2
			Where's Tim?	2
			Bubbles	2
			Merry-go-round, The	2
Sunshine	Heinemann	Level 1 Non-fiction	Building things	2
			Reading is everywhere	2
			Together	2
			Wheels	2
		Level 1 Set B	Our Granny	2
			Snap!	2
			What is a huggles?	2
		Level 1 Set C	Big and little	2
			Buzzing flies	2
			I am a bookworm	2
			I love my family	2
			My home	2
			Shoo!	2
		Level 1 Set C	Uncle Buncle's house	2

SERIES	PUBLISHER	SET (OR AUTHOR)	TITLE	BAND
Sunshine	Heinemann	Level 1 Set C	When Itchy Witchy sneezes	2
		Level 1 Set D	Hug is warm, A	2
			I can jump	2
			Icecream	2
			Our street	2
			Race, The	2
			Shark in a Sack	2
			Up in a tree	2
		Level 1 Set E	Good for you	2
			Mr Grump	2
			Spider, Spider	2
			Wake up, Mum!	2
			What would you like?	2
Sunshine New	Heinemann	Level 1 Set A	I Can Do Anything!	2
		Level 1 Set B	Astronaut, The	2
			Our Car	2
			Weather Chart, The	2
		Level 1 Set C	I Can Read Anything	2
			No You Can't!	2
			Time for Sleep	2
		Level 1 Set D	Cracker Jack, The	2
			Geoffrey the Dinosaur	2
			Pyjama Party, The	2
			There is a Planet	2
			To Work	2
		Level 1 Set E	Going to the Vet	2
			I have a Home	2
			I'm Brave	2
			Look Out!	2
		Level 1 Set F	Just Like Me!	2
Sunshine Spirals	Heinemann	Set 1	Birthday Party, A	2
			Dragon, The	2
			Where is My Hat?	2
			Who Ate the Bananas?	2
		Set 2	Apple, The	2
			At The Zoo	2
			Elephant Walk	2
			Journey, A	2
			My Bike Can Fly	2
			Night	2
		Set 3	Speed Boat, The	2
Sunshine Spirals Starters	Heinemann	Set C	Tim's Paintings	2
Wonder World	Badger	Set 1	Big and Green	2
			Circus, The	2
			Giant -Size Hamburger, A	2
			One Bird Sat on the Fence	2
			Teeth	2
			Zoo, The	2
		Set 2	Animal Tracks	2
			Divers, The	2
			Fruit Salad	2
			Look Here!	2
			New Shoes	2
			Porcupine, A	2
		Set 3	Beautiful Flowers	2
			Eyes	2
			Making Music	2
			Processed Food	2

SERIES	PUBLISHER	SET (OR AUTHOR)	TITLE	BAND
Wonder World	Badger	Set 3	This Mouth	2
			Where Are the Seeds?	2
		Set 4	Lizard on a Stick	2
			Stop!	2
Individual Titles	Methuen	Bruna, Dick	When I'm Big	2
	Lothian	Campbell, Rod	Henry's Busy Day	2
	Philomel Books	Carle, Eric	What's for Lunch?	2
	Nelson	Cartwright, Pauline	I Wish	2
	Nelson	Cartwright, Pauline	Sand	2
	Walker	Casey, Patricia	Quack, Quack	2
	Picture Puffin	Hutchins, Pat	1 Hunter	2
	Walker	Jonas, Ann	Now We Can Go	2
	Collins Pict Lions	Kerr, Judith	Mog and Me	2
	Walker	King, Phyllis	Hungry Cat, The	2
	Picture Puffin	Martin, Bill	Brown Bear, Brown Bear, What Do You See?	2
	Viking/Kestrel	Peppe, Rodney	Humpty Dumpty	2
	Gollancz	Tafuri, Nancy	Ball Bounced, The	2
	Red Fox	Watanabe, Shigeo	Hello How Are You?	2

Working within Level 1: Learning Focus

- Follow print with eyes only, finger-pointing only at points of difficulty.
- Take more note of punctuation to support the use of grammar and oral language rhythms.
- Cross-check all sources of information more quickly while reading.
- Note familiar words and letter clusters and use these to get to unknown words eg. look ➔ took.
- Search for information in print to predict, confirm or attempt new words while reading.
- Notice relationships between one text and another.
- Predict in more detail.

TEXT CHARACTERISTICS

— some repetition of phrase patterns, ideas and vocabulary

— more variation of sentence structure

— story lines include more episodes following a time sequence

— some literary conventions along with familiar oral language structures

— stories may involve imaginary happenings in framework of familiar experiences

— non-fiction texts still use personal experience and children's language patterns

— illustrations still support the text quite closely

Benchmark Texts

Biff's Aeroplane	Oxford Reading Tree/OUP
The Red Rose	Storychest/Kingscourt
What's the Time, Mr. Wolf?	Colin Hawkins/Little Mammoth
The Park, the Park	Reading 360/Ginn
Eggs for Breakfast	PM Non-Fiction/Nelson
The Sun and the Wind	Storyworlds/Heinemann

SERIES	PUBLISHER	SET (OR AUTHOR)	TITLE	BAND
All Aboard	Ginn	Stage 2 Booster Bks	Sam's Bike	3
			Tilak and the Digger	3
		Stage 2 Sam & Rosie	Guinea Pig For Rosie, A	3
		Stage 2 Set A Patt & Rh	Grandma's Cat	3
			Greedy Nelly	3
			Little Monster	3
		Stage 2 Set B Patt & Rh	Mr Snow	3
			Play with Me	3
			Spacegirl Sue	3
			Ten Jolly Jumpers	3
		Stage 3 Sam & Rosie	Greedy Guinea Pig, The	3
			Home Time	3
			Lizzie and the Car Wash	3
		Stage 3 Set A Patt & Rh	Accident, The	3
			Giant Sandwich, The	3
			I Fell out of Bed	3
			Something in the Fridge	3
		Stage 3 Set B Patt & Rh	Counting Chickens	3
			Town Mouse and Country Mouse	3
All Aboard Non Fiction	Ginn	Stage 2	Birds	3
			Cats	3
			Dinosaurs	3
Beginner Books	Collins	Eastman, P.D.	Go, Dog, Go!	3
Book Project Fiction 1	Longman	Band 1 Read Aloud	Late Again, Mai Ling?	3
		Band 1 Read On	Ben Biggins' box	3
			Come Into the Garden!	3
			Fetch the Stick, Webster!	3
			Freddy's Teddy	3
			Teddy Goes Swimming	3
			Wake Up, Webster!	3
			Webster's Week	3
			Where's Mai Ling?	3
			Who's There?	3
		Band 1 Read On Specials	Get Up, Webster!	3
			Stop it, Webster!	3
			Teddy in the garden	3
			What Webster wants!	3
		Band 2 Read On	Jumping Beans	3
			Lisa's Letter	3
Bright and Early Books	Collins	Berenstain, Stan & Jan	Bears on Wheels	3
			Inside, Outside, Upside Down	3
		Le Seig, Theo	Eye Book, The	3
Cambridge Reading	CUP	Begin to Read Stage B	All Fall Down!	3
			Four Scary Monsters	3
Discovery World	Heinemann	Stage C	Materials	3
			Using Tools	3
		Stage D	Time for a Party	3
Foundations for Reading	Folens	Level 4 Emergent	Baby Elephant Gets Lost	3
			Bay Run	3
			Ben's Banana	3
			Boss	3
			Going Out	3
			Lunch at the Pond	3
			Mr Bumbleticker's Birthday	3
			My Clothes	3
			My Friend	3
			My Old Cat	3
			Rattlesnake Looks for Food, The	3

SERIES	PUBLISHER	SET (OR AUTHOR)	TITLE	BAND
Foundations for Reading	Folens	Level 5 Emergent	All By Myself	3
			Busy Mosquito, The	3
			Dog Show, The	3
			Gardening	3
			I Am Cold	3
			I Am Hot	3
			Jimmy's Birthday Balloon	3
			Looking after Grandpa	3
			Lost Glove, The	3
			Naughty Patch	3
			Sleepy Bear	3
			Too Little	3
		Level 6 Early	Baby Elephant's Sneeze	3
			Big Sneeze, The	3
			Close Your Eyes	3
			Day Shopping, A	3
			Guess What?	3
			Making Things	3
			Mr Crawford	3
			Mum's New Car	3
			Where Can Teddy Go?	3
			Where is the Milk?	3
		Level 7 Early	Farms	3
			Fast Food	3
			Getting Ready for School	3
			I Know That Tune!	3
			Jimmy	3
			Moving In	3
			Our Cat	3
			Playing with Dad	3
			Visit to the Library, A	3
		Level 8 Early	Astronauts, The	3
			Green Plants	3
			Learning New Things	3
			Lizard	3
			My Birthday Surprise	3
			My Old Cat and the Computer	3
			Roller Blades	3
			Storm, The	3
			Three Muddy Monkeys	3
			Trip to the Video Store, A	3
			Washing	3
			What Is It?	3
		Level 9 Early	Pancakes	3
			Watching TV	3
Journeys in Reading	Schofield & Sims	Level 1	Fingers	3
			Signs	3
			So Do I	3
Link Up	Collins		Going to School	3
			Look Around	3
			My Day	3
			Park Street	3
Literacy Links Plus	Kingscourt	Early A	At Night	3
			Bruno's Birthday	3
			Screech!	3
			Trucks	3
		Early B	Roll Over	3
			Sleeping	3

SERIES	PUBLISHER	SET (OR AUTHOR)	TITLE	BAND
Literacy Links Plus	Kingscourt	Emergent B	Dad's Garden	3
			Don't Leave Anything Behind	3
			Hungry Horse	3
			I Can Do It Myself	3
		Emergent C	Ben the Bold	3
			Camping	3
			Train Ride, The	3
			When I was Sick	3
		Emergent D	Boogly, The	3
			Circus Clown, The	3
			Go Back to Sleep	3
			Grandpa Snored	3
			Green Footprints	3
			Hands	3
			Henry the Helicopter	3
			Pets	3
			Shadows	3
			Storm, The	3
			Timmy	3
			Visitors	3
			Wedding, The	3
One, Two, Three & Away	Collins	Blue Platform 11-16	Benjamin, the Witch and the Donkey	3
			Jennifer and the Little Dog	3
			Little Brown Mouse and the Apples, The	3
			Percy Green and Mrs Blue-hat	3
		Blue Platform 1-6	Dog and the Ball, The	3
		Blue Platform 7-10	Billy Blue-hat and the Frog	3
			Sita and the Little Old Woman	3
		Introductory A-D	Old Man, The	3
		Introductory E-H	Jennifer Yellow-hat went out in the Dark	3
			Jennifer Yellow-hat went out in the Sunshine	3
			Roger and Rip	3
			Roger and the Pond	3
		Introductory I-L	Roger and the Little Mouse	3
			Sita and Ramu	3
		Introductory M-P	Little Brown Mouse went out in the Dark	3
			Mrs Blue-hat and the Little Brown Mouse	3
		Introductory Q-V	Crash! The Car hit a Tree	3
			Mrs Blue-hat and the Little Black Cat	3
			Mrs Rig and the Little Black Cat	3
			Percy Green and Mr Red-hat's Car	3
		Main Books 1-2B	Village with Three Corners, The	3
		Pre-reader 9a-12a	Donkey went to School, The	3
		Pre-reader 9b-12b	Roger at the Fair	3
			Stop! Cried Alex	3
Open Door	Nelson	Green Fun Books	Dragon in a Dustbin, A	3
			Giraffe in a Train, A	3
		Yellow Fun Books	Flying Sausages	3
			Pig in Pyjamas, A	3
Oxford Reading Tree	OUP	Stage 2 More Stories A	Baby-sitter, The	3
			Floppy's Bath	3
			Kipper's Balloon	3
			Kipper's Birthday	3
			Spots	3
			Water Fight, The	3
		Stage 2 More Stories B	Biff's Aeroplane	3
			Chase, The	3
			Foggy Day, The	3

SERIES	PUBLISHER	SET (OR AUTHOR)	TITLE	BAND
Oxford Reading Tree	OUP	Stage 2 Storybooks	Go-kart, The	3
			New Trainers	3
			What a bad dog!	3
		Stage 3 More Stories A	At The Seaside	3
			Jumble Sale, The	3
			Kipper the Clown	3
			Snowman, The	3
			Strawberry Jam	3
		Stage 3 More Stories B	At The Pool	3
			Book Week	3
			Bull's eye	3
		Stage 3 Sparrows	Jan and the Anorak	3
			Jan and the Chocolate	3
			Joe and the Bike	3
			Midge in Hospital	3
			Roy and the Budgie	3
		Stage 3 Storybooks	By the Stream	3
			Dolphin Pool, The	3
			On the Sand	3
			Rope Swing, The	3
		Stage 4 More Sparrows	Adam Goes Shopping	3
			Adam's Car	3
			Mosque School	3
			Yasmin's Dress	3
		Stage 4 More Stories A	Poor Old Mum!	3
		Stage 4 More Stories B	Everyone got Wet	3
			Flying Elephant, The	3
			Swap!	3
		Stage 4 More Stories B	Wet Paint	3
		Stage 4 Playscripts	Balloon, The	3
			House for sale	3
			New House, The	3
			Nobody got Wet	3
			Secret Room, The	3
			Storm, The	3
Oxford RT Branch Library	OUP	Lydia Bks Stage 3A	Lydia and the letters	3
		Wildsmith Bks St 1A	What a Tale!	3
		Wildsmith Bks St 2A	Dog Called Mischief, A	3
Pathways	Collins	Stage 0 Set D	Carnival Mask	3
			Fun Run	3
			Molly, the Guide Dog	3
			Our Dog	3
		Stage 1 Set A	Don"t Cry, Little Bear	3
		Stage 1 Set B	David	3
			Grumbly Giant	3
			Making a Chapati	3
		Stage 1 Set C	My Day	3
		Stage 1 Set D	Tomato Sauce	3
		Stage 2 Set A	Luke's First Day	3
			On The Run	3
			Sally's Day	3
		Stage 2 Set B	My Hat	3
			My New Bike	3
			Waste	3
		Stage 2 Set E	My Perfect Pet	3
PM Non-fiction	Nelson	Red Level	Eggs for Breakfast	3
			Look Up, Look Down	3
			Red and Blue and Yellow	3

SERIES	PUBLISHER	SET (OR AUTHOR)	TITLE	BAND
PM Non-fiction	Nelson	Red Level	Roof and a Door, A	3
			Tall Things	3
			Two Eyes, Two Ears	3
PM Storybooks	Nelson	Yellow Set A	Baby Bear Goes Fishing	3
			Ben's Dad	3
			Blackberries	3
			Brave Father Mouse	3
			Fire! Fire!	3
			Friend for Little White Rabbit, A	3
			Hermit Crab	3
			Hungry Kitten, The	3
			Little Bulldozer	3
			Lucky Goes to Dog School	3
			Mumps	3
			New Baby, The	3
			Sally's Beans	3
			Seagull is Clever	3
			Where are the Sun Hats?	3
		Yellow Set B	Baby Hippo	3
			Choosing a puppy	3
			Football at the park	3
			Jolly Roger, the pirate	3
			Lucky day for Little Dinosaur, A	3
			Sally and the sparrows	3
			Snowy gets a wash	3
			Tiny and the big wave	3
Reading 360	Ginn	Level 2	Ben and Lad	3
			Can We Help?	3
			Can You?	3
			I Can Hide	3
		Level 3	Park, The	3
		Magic Circle Level 2	Hide	3
			Park, The Park, The	3
			Ride! Ride! Ride!	3
		Magic Circle Level 3	Cat	3
			Duck in the Park, Duck in the Dark	3
			Where is Zip?	3
		Magic Circle Level 5	Box, Fox, Ox & Peacock	3
Reading 360 New	Ginn	Level 2	Ben and the Duck	3
			Can We Help?	3
			Can You?	3
			I Can Hide	3
			Liz and Digger	3
		Little Bks L 2 Set 1	Can We Play?	3
			Can you See Me?	3
			Come and Play With Me	3
			Hide and Seek	3
			Look Like Me	3
		Little Bks L 2 Set 2	At Night	3
			Bee, The	3
			Come for a Swim	3
			Swim in the Park, A	3
			Where is Jill?	3
		Little Bks L 3 Set 2	Good Book, A	3
		Little Bks L 4 Set 2	Crash Landing	3
Reading 360 Upstarts	Ginn	Introductory	Fun on a Broomstick	3
			Look at my Spots	3
			Lucy the Tiger	3

SERIES	PUBLISHER	SET (OR AUTHOR)	TITLE	BAND
Reading 360 Upstarts	Ginn	Level 1	Paul and the Robber	3
			Rabbit said Miaow, The	3
		Level 1	Shoes had Spots, The	3
			There's a Monster	3
		Level 1 Extension	Balloons, The	3
			Bobby Bear and the Rabbit	3
			Jan and Dan	3
			Jane and the Monster	3
			Jenny and the Dragon	3
			King's Box, The	3
			Monster in the Box, The	3
			Peg and the Fair	3
			Queen and the Cabbage, The	3
			Where is Fred Dragon?	3
		Level 2 Extension	I Like Spaceships	3
Reading World	Longman	Level 1 Pack A	Fred Makes a Shelf	3
			Pancakes	3
			Teatime	3
		Level 1 Pack B	Over and Under and Up and Around	3
		Level 1 More Books	Baby Grumble	3
			Camping	3
			Fred In Space	3
			Sadie Spider Moves In	3
			Skateboard, The	3
			What's For Tea?	3
			Where's My Hairy Bear?	3
			Who Sneezed?	3
			Yum Yum Gum	3
		Level 2 Pack A	Christmas	3
			Grumble, The	3
			What If a Bear Comes?	3
		Level 2: More Books	Cat tricks	3
			Fishing	3
Ready to Read	Nelson	Early Set A	Chinese New Year	3
			Greedy Cat is Hungry	3
			Happy Birthday, Estela!	3
			My Bike	3
			Nick's Glasses	3
		Early Set B	Praying Mantis, The	3
			Rain, Rain	3
			Ready, Steady, Jump!	3
			Water Boatman, The	3
			Where is Miss Pool?	3
		Early Set C	City Scenes	3
			Lonely Bull, The	3
			Make a Lei	3
			Paper Patchwork	3
			Penguin's Chicks	3
		Early Set D	Hogboggit, The	3
		Emergent Set C	Where are My Socks?	3
		Emergent Set D	Wind, The	3
Story Chest	Kingscourt	Get-ready Set DD	How to Make a Hot Dog	3
			Microscope	3
			Sunflower Seeds	3
		Large Read-tog Set 1	Mrs Wishy Washy	3
			Sing a Song	3
			Smarty pants	3
			Dan the Flying Man	3

SERIES	PUBLISHER	SET (OR AUTHOR)	TITLE	BAND
Story Chest	Kingscourt	Large Read-tog Set 2	Jigaree, The	3
			Meanies	3
			Monsters' Party, The	3
			Red Rose, The	3
		Ready-set-go Set AA	Little Hearts	3
		Ready-set-go Set BB	Barn Dance	3
			Ebenezer and the Sneeze	3
			My Brown Cow	3
		Ready-set-go Set C	Night Train, The	3
			Pumpkin, The	3
			Rum-Tum-Tum	3
			Too Big for Me	3
		Ready-set-go Set CC	Lift, The	3
			My Mum and Dad	3
			Pet Shop	3
			Roy G. Biv	3
			Where is Skunk?	3
		Ready-set-go Set D	Danger	3
			Fizz and Splutter	3
			No, No	3
			Oh, jump in a sack	3
			Two little dogs	3
		Ready-set-go Set DD	Gulp!	3
			Hungry Giant's Lunch, The	3
		Small Read-together	In a Dark Dark Wood	3
			Three Little Ducks	3
Storyworlds	Heinemann	Stage 4 Animal World	Max and the apples	3
			Max and the cat	3
			Max and the drum	3
			Max wants to fly	3
		Stage 4 Fantasy World	Pirate Pete and the monster	3
			Pirate Pete and the treasure island	3
			Pirate Pete keeps fit	3
			Pirate Pete loses his hat	3
		Stage 4 Once Upon a Time	Ant and the Dove, The	3
			Little Rabbit	3
			Sun and the Wind, The	3
			Town Mouse and the Country Mouse	3
		Stage 4 Our World	Lucy loses Red Ted	3
			Red Ted at the beach	3
			Red Ted goes to school	3
			Sam hides Red Ted	3
Sunshine	Heinemann	Level 1 Non-fiction	Maths is everywhere	3
		Level 1 Set D	Scat! said the cat	3
		Level 1 Set E	I'm bigger than you!	3
			Monkey bridge, The	3
		Level 1 Set F	Along comes Jake	3
			Bread	3
			Goodbye Lucy	3
			Seed, The	3
			Where are you going, Aja Rose?	3
Sunshine New	Heinemann	Level 1 Set E	Gingerbread Man	3
			Hello, Hello, Hello	3
		Level 1 Set F	I Smell Smoke	3
			In the Desert	3
			Scit, Scat Scaredy Cat!	3
			There's No One Like Me!	3
			Yippy-day-yippy-doo!	3

SERIES	PUBLISHER	SET (OR AUTHOR)	TITLE	BAND
Sunshine New	Heinemann	Level 1 Set G	Come to My House	3
			Rosie the Nosey Goat	3
Sunshine Spirals	Heinemann	Set 1	Big Race, The	3
		Set 3	Cow in the Hole, The	3
			Hungry Lion, The	3
			Jack and the Giant	3
			Magic Machine, The	3
			Penguins, The	3
			Pirate, The	3
			Seals, The	3
			Sky Diver, The	3
			Snow Race, The	3
		Set 4	At The Fair	3
			Babysitters, The	3
			Blueberry Pie, The	3
			Dr Sprocket Makes a Rocket	3
			I Like Worms	3
			Moon Story	3
			Sharks	3
			Whale, The	3
Tiddlywinks	Kingscourt	Bargain Book	Tricking Tracy	3
		Stage 1 Large Books	Cat and Mouse	3
			Good Boy Andrew!	3
			Old Oak Tree, The	3
Wonder World	Badger	Set 1	Grandpa Knits Hats	3
			Legs, Legs, Legs	3
			Sally and the Elephant	3
			Snowball Fight!	3
			Surfer, The	3
		Set 2	Cupboard in the Hall	3
			Flight Deck	3
			Move It	3
			My Skin	3
			Tails And Claws	3
		Set 3	Communities	3
			Masks	3
			My Letter	3
			On the Move	3
		Set 4	Face Painting	3
Individual Titles	Picture Puffin	Ahlberg, Janet & Allen	Baby's Catalogue, The	3
	Picture Puffin	Ahlberg, Janet & Allen	Each Peach Pear Plum	3
	Orchard	Beck, Ian	Five Little Ducks	3
	Patrick Hardy	Brown/Hurd	Goodnight Moon Room	3
	Red Fox	Burningham, John	Blanket, The	3
	Red Fox	Burningham, John	School, The	3
	Lothian	Campbell, Rod	Buster's Bedtime	3
	Lothian	Campbell, Rod	Oh Dear	3
	Nelson	Cowley, Joy	My Bad Mood	3
	Walker	Dale, Penny	Bet You Can't!	3
	Walker	Dale, Penny	Wake Up Mr B	3
	Picture Puffin	Garland, Sarah	Going Shopping	3
	Picture Puffin	Garland, Sarah	Going to Playschool	3
	Picture Puffin	Garland, Sarah	Having a Picnic	3
	A & C Black	Gretz, Suzanna	Teddybears 1-10	3
	Little Mammoth	Hawkins, Colin	What's the time Mr Wolf?	3
	Picture Puffin	Hill, Eric	Where's Spot?	3
	Collins Pict Lions	Isadora, Rachel	I Hear	3
	Collins Pict Lions	Isadora, Rachel	I Touch	3

SERIES	PUBLISHER	SET (OR AUTHOR)	TITLE	BAND
Individual Titles	Simon & Schust'r	Kemp, Moira	I'm A Little Teapot	3
	Simon & Schust'r	Kemp, Moira	Round and Round The Garden	3
	Frances Lincoln	Lewis, Tracey	Eye Spy	3
	Picture Puffin	Maris, Ron	I Wish I Could Fly	3
	Picture Puffin	Maris, Ron	Is Anyone Home?	3
	Sainsbury	Mastrogiovanni, O	Animal Babies	3
	Tree House	Nancy, Helen	If I had a Zoo	3
	Tree House	Nancy, Helen	If I were a Pilot	3
	Nelson	O'Brien, John	John The Bookworm	3
	Safeway	Parker, Ant	Ginger	3
	Nelson	Redhead, J S	Mirrors	3
	Nelson	Redhead, J S	Snoopy Bear	3
	MacMillan	Roffey, Maureen	What's the Weather?	3
	Sainsbury	Sharratt, Nick	Green Queen, The	3
	Sainsbury	Sharratt, Nick	I Look Like This	3
	Sainsbury	Sharratt, Nick	Look What I Found!	3
	Nelson	Speer, Albert	At The Dock	3
	Picture Puffin	Turner, Gwenda	Play Book	3
	Red Fox	Watanabe, Shigeo	How Do I Put It On?	3
	Red Fox	Watanabe, Shigeo	I Can Build a House	3
	Penguin	Watanabe, Shigeo	I Can Do It	3
	Frances Lincoln	Weatherill, Steve	Baby Goz	3
	Frances Lincoln	Weatherill, Steve	Count on Goz	3
	Walker	West, Colin	Have You Seen The Crocodile?	3
	Puffin	Zeifert, Harriet	Daddy, Can You Play With Me?	3

Working Within Level 1: Learning Focus

- Move through text attending to meaning, print and sentence structure flexibly.
- Self-correct more rapidly on the run.
- Re-read to enhance phrasing and clarify precise meaning.
- Solve new words using print information along with attention to meaning.
- Use analogy with known vocabulary to solve new words.
- Manage a greater variety of text genre.
- Discuss content of the text in a manner which indicates precise understanding.

TEXT CHARACTERISTICS

- greater variation in sentence patterns and content
- literary language integrated with natural language
- any repeated language patterns are longer or act as refrains
- more lines of text on page, sometimes up to 6 or 8 lines
- stories have more events
- non-fiction texts include some abstract terms and impersonal sentence structures
- pictures support story line rather than convey precise meaning so closely
- more similar-looking words appearing in text

Benchmark Texts

Dear Zoo	Rod Campbell/Penguin
The Lion and the Mouse	Cambridge Reading/CUP
Rosie's Walk	Pat Hutchins/Penguin
The Windy Day	Ginn Science/Ginn
Victor and the Kite	Oxford Reading Tree/OUP
Ali's Story	Reading 360 Upstarts/Heinemann

SERIES	PUBLISHER	SET (OR AUTHOR)	TITLE	BAND
All Aboard	Ginn	Stage 3 Booster Bks	Den, The	4
			Lost at the School Fair	4
			Mo's Photo	4
			Poor Bobby	4
		Stage 3 Sam & Rosie	Book for Jack, A	4
			Butterfly Sale, The	4
			Ghost In The Castle	4
			Scat Cat!	4
			Tilak's Tooth	4
		Stage 3 Set B Patt & Rh	Big Turnip, The	4
			Magic Porrige Pot, The	4
		Stage 4 Set A Patt & Rh	I'm Running Away	4
		Stage 4 Set A Sam & Ros	Hiccups	4
Book Project Fiction 1	Longman	Band 2 Read On	Go away, Harry!	4
			Little Frog and the Dog	4
			Little Frog and the Frog Olympics	4
			Little Frog and the Tadpoles	4
			Look Out, Harry!	4
			Magic Bean	4
			Pudding	4
		Band 3 Read On	Doodlecloud	4
			Doodledragon	4
			Doodlemaze	4
			Keith's Croak	4
			Mary's Meadow	4
		Band 4 Read On	Monster Who loved Telephones, The	4
			Wake Up!	4
			Water, Water	4
Bright and Early Books	Collins	Berenstain, Stan & Jan	Spooky Old Tree, The	4
		Perkins, Al	Ear Book, The	4
Cambridge Reading	CUP	Becoming a R Stage A	Five Little Monkeys	4
			Gingerbread Man, The	4
			Going Fishing	4
			Lion and the Mouse, The	4
			Lucy's Box	4
			Not Yet Nathan!	4
			One Blue Hen	4
			Wayne's Box	4
		Begin to Read Stage B	Afloat in a Boat	4
			My Dog's Party	4
Discovery World	Heinemann	Stage C	My Bean Diary	4
		Stage D	Closer look at Parks, A	4
			Fun Things to Make and Do	4
Foundations for Reading	Folens	Level 4 Emergent	Buildings in My Street	4
		Level 6 Early	Snails	4
		Level 7 Early	Bird Barn, The	4
			Car Accident, The	4
			Dogs	4
		Level 9 Early	After School	4
			Baby at Our House, The	4
			Fun in the Mud	4
			Good Sports	4
			Grandma's Present	4
			Mother Hippopotamus's Dry Skin	4
			New Nest, The	4
			Three Silly Monkeys	4
			Too Late!	4
			What Am I?	4

SERIES	PUBLISHER	SET (OR AUTHOR)	TITLE	BAND
Foundations for Reading	Folens	Level 10 Early	Colours	4
			Come and See!	4
			Fishing	4
			Going to School	4
			Marco Saves Grandpa	4
			Maria Goes to School	4
			Mr Bumbleticker Likes to Cook	4
			Mum Paints the House	4
		Level 11 Early	Baby Elephant's New Bike	4
			Baseball Game, The	4
			Dad's New Path	4
			Insects That Bother Us	4
			Mother Hippopotamus's Hiccups	4
			My Friend Trent	4
			Rain, The	4
Foundations for Reading	Folens	Level 11 Early	Three Silly Monkeys Go Fishing	4
			Women at Work	4
		Level 13 Experienced	Pepper Goes to School	4
		Level 14 Experienced	Invisible Spy, The	4
Ginn Geography Topic Bks	Ginn	Year 1	Jobs in School	4
			People at Work	4
Ginn Science	Ginn		Look!	4
Ginn Science Info Bks	Ginn	Year 1	Babies	4
			Plants to Eat	4
			Weather Forecast, The	4
Journeys in Reading	Schofield & Sims	Level 1	Supper For a Troll	4
Link Up	Collins	Level 2	Shopping	4
Literacy Links Plus	Kingscourt	Early A	Bang	4
			Can I Play Outside?	4
			Christmas Shopping	4
			Countdown	4
			Dad's Bike	4
			Goodnight, Little Brother	4
			Just Like Grandpa	4
			Riddles	4
			Secret Soup	4
			Sleepy Bear	4
			Sneezes	4
			Words Are Everywhere	4
		Early B	Family Photos	4
			If You're Happy	4
			In the Garden	4
			Inside or Outside	4
			Mrs Bold	4
			Patterns	4
			Printing Machine, The	4
			Skin	4
			T J's Tree	4
			What's Around the Corner	4
			Wobbly Tooth, The	4
		Early C	BMX Billy	4
			Buffy's Tricks	4
			Ten Little Caterpillars	4
		Emergent B	Filbert the Fly	4
		Emergent C	Nests	4
		Emergent D	I Saw a Dinosaur	4
			Noises	4
			Noses	4

SERIES	PUBLISHER	SET (OR AUTHOR)	TITLE	BAND
Literacy Links Plus	Kingscourt	Emergent D	Sitting	4
			When I Pretend	4
One, Two, Three & Away	Collins	Blue Platform 7-10	Magic Wood, The	4
		Blue Platform 11-16	Jennifer in Dark Woods	4
			Little Old Man and the Little Brown Mouse	4
		Blue Platform 17-20	Old Man and the Seven Mice, The	4
			Roger has a Ride	4
		Introductory W-Z	Jennifer and the Little Fox	4
			Kite that Blew Away, The	4
			Miranda and the Dragon	4
			Ramu and Sita and the Robber	4
		Main Books 1-2B	Billy Blue-hat and the Duck-pond	4
			Cat and the Feather, The	4
			Old Man and the Wind, The	4
			Roger and the Ghost	4
Oxford Reading Tree	OUP	Stage 2 More Stories B	Floppy the Hero	4
			Kipper's Laces	4
			Wobbly Tooth, The	4
		Stage 2 Storybooks	Dream, The	4
		Stage 3 More Stories A	Kipper's Idea	4
		Stage 3 More Stories B	Barbecue, The	4
			Carnival, The	4
			Cold Day, The	4
		Stage 3 Sparrows	Pip at the Zoo	4
		Stage 3 Storybooks	Cat in the Tree, A	4
		Stage 4 More Sparrows	Lucky the Goat	4
			Yasmin and the Flood	4
		Stage 4 More Stories A	Nobody Got Wet	4
			Weather Vane, The	4
			Wedding, The	4
		Stage 4 More Stories B	Dragon Dance, The	4
			Scarf, The	4
		Stage 4 Sparrows	Joe and the Mouse	4
			Midge and the Eggs	4
			Pip and the Little Monkey	4
			Roy at the Fun Park	4
		Stage 4 Storybooks	Come In!	4
			House for Sale	4
			New House, The	4
			Play, The	4
			Secret Room, The	4
		Stage 5 More Stories A	Monster Mistake, A	4
		Stage 5 Playscripts	Castle Adventure	4
			Dragon Tree, The	4
			Gran	4
			Magic Key, The	4
			Pirate Adventure	4
			Village in the Snow	4
		Stage 5 Storybooks	Magic Key, The	4
Oxford RT Branch Library	OUP	Lydia Bks Stage 3A	Lydia and her cat	4
			Lydia and her garden	4
			Lydia and the ducks	4
			Lydia and the present	4
			Lydia at the shops	4
		Victor Bks Stage 5A	Victor and the kite	4
Pathways	Collins	Stage 1 Set D	Nobody Laughed	4
		Stage 2 Set A	Mrs Barmy	4
		Stage 2 Set B	Animal House	4

SERIES	PUBLISHER	SET (OR AUTHOR)	TITLE	BAND
Pathways	Collins	Stage 2 Set B	Fishy Tale, A	4
		Stage 2 Set C	Grandad's Ears	4
			Let's Dance	4
			Red Bird	4
			Sam's Bus	4
		Stage 2 Set E	Five Little Men	4
PM Non-fiction	Nelson	Yellow Level	My Big Brother	4
			My Dad	4
			My Gran and Grandad	4
			My Little Sister	4
			Our Baby	4
			Our Mum	4
PM Storybooks	Nelson	Blue Set A	Baby Bear's Present	4
			Best Cake, The	4
			Christmas Tree, The	4
			Come on, Tim	4
			Cows in the Garden	4
			Honey for Baby Bear	4
			House in the Tree, The	4
			Jane's Car	4
			Late For Football	4
			Lion and the Rabbit, The	4
			Magpie's Baking Day	4
			Mushrooms For Dinner	4
			Sally's Friends	4
			Tabby In The Tree	4
		Blue Set B	Birthday balloons	4
			Chug the tractor	4
			Duck with the broken wing, The	4
			Little Bulldozer helps again	4
			Lost at the fun park	4
			Teasing Dad	4
			Tiger runs away	4
			Tim's favourite toy	4
		Red Set A	Sally's Red Bucket	4
Read It Yourself	Ladybird	Level 1	Billy Goats Gruff	4
			Elves and the Shoemaker, The	4
			Goldilocks and the Three Bears	4
			Hansel and Gretel	4
			Sly Fox and the Red Hen, The	4
Reading 2000	Longmans	Storytime Yellows	Robbie's First Day at School	4
Reading 360	Ginn	Level 2	Ben and Sparky	4
			Come for a Ride	4
		Level 3	Horses	4
			I Can Read	4
			Tortoise, The	4
		Level 5	Boys and Girls	4
		Magic Circle Level 4	What is it? said the Dog	4
		Magic Circle Level 5	Say It Fast	4
			Tom Turtle	4
Reading 360 New	Ginn	Level 2	Come For a Ride	4
		Level 3	Digger at School	4
			Don't Run Away	4
			Duck is a Duck, A	4
		Little Bks L 3 Set 1	Play a Play	4
		Little Bks L 3 Set 2	Dog House, The	4
		Little Bks L 3 Set 3	Babysitter, The	4
			Dolly's Magic Brolly	4

SERIES	PUBLISHER	SET (OR AUTHOR)	TITLE	BAND
Reading 360 New	Ginn	Little Bks L 3 Set 3	Sparky the Dragon	4
			Tom Looks for a Home	4
			Where is Little Ted?	4
Reading 360 Upstarts	Ginn	Level 2	Clever Beetle, The	4
			Ghost Behind the Cupboard, The	4
			Katie and Debbie go to the Moon	4
			New Bike, The	4
			Rum-Tum-Tum	4
			Runaway Pram, The	4
		Level 2 Extension	Clever Ghost, The	4
			Clever Mouse, The	4
			Don't Eat the Postman	4
			Greedy Parrot, The	4
			Monster in the Cupboard, The	4
			Mum's New Car	4
			No Dogs Allowed	4
			Silly Elephant, The	4
			Surprise, The	4
			Toyshop, The	4
			Unhappy Giant, The	4
Reading World	Longman	Level 1 Pack B	Sadie Spider	4
			Sadie Spider Strikes Again	4
		Level 2 Pack A	Fred's Birthday	4
		Level 2 More Books	Fred's photo album	4
			Grumble goes for a walk, The	4
			Grumble goes jogging, The	4
			Squirrel is lonely	4
			Sunflower named Bert, A	4
Ready to Read	Nelson	Early Set A	Biggest Cake in the World, The	4
		Early Set C	Along Came Greedy Cat	4
			Bumble Bee	4
			Swamp Hen	4
		Early Set D	Blackbird's Nest	4
			Did you say, Fire?	4
			Hay for Ambrosia	4
			Snap! Splash!	4
			T Shirts	4
		Fluent Set A	Big Game, The	4
			Rosa at the Zoo	4
Scholastic Books	Ashton Scholastic	Krauss, Ruth	Is This You?	4
		Mayer, Mercer	Oops	4
Story Chest	Kingscourt	Large Read-tog Set 1	Lazy Mary	4
		Large Read-tog Set 2	To Town	4
			Who Will be my Mother?	4
		Ready-set-go Set CC	Fantastic Cake	4
			How Many Hot Dogs?	4
			Teeth	4
		Ready-set-go Set D	Grumpy Elephant	4
		Ready-set-go Set DD	Best Children in the World, The	4
			Blueberry Muffins	4
			Clown in the Well	4
			Fire and Water	4
			Giggle Box, The	4
			We'd better make a List	4
		Small Read-together	One Cold Wet Night	4
			Poor Old Polly	4
Storyworlds	Heinemann	Stage 5 Animal World	Dipper and the old wreck	4
			Dipper gets stuck	4

SERIES	PUBLISHER	SET (OR AUTHOR)	TITLE	BAND
Storyworlds	Heinemann	Stage 5 Animal World	Dipper in danger	4
			Dipper to the rescue	4
		Stage 5 Fantasy World	Bag of coal, The	4
			Big snowball, The	4
			Creepy Castle, The	4
			Fire in Wild Wood	4
		Stage 5 Once Upon a Time	Straw House, The	4
		Stage 5 Our World	Grandma's surprise	4
			Mango tree, The	4
			Presents	4
			Who did it?	4
Sunshine	Heinemann	Level 1 Non-fiction	Alien at the zoo	4
			Are you a ladybird?	4
			Dinosaurs	4
			Dreams	4
			I wonder	4
			It takes time to grow	4
			New building, The	4
			Tree, The	4
Sunshine	Heinemann	Level 1 Set F	Don't you laugh at me!	4
			Wind blows strong, The	4
		Level 1 Set G	Cooking pot, The	4
Sunshine New	Heinemann	Level 1 Set F	Catherine the Counter	4
			Eat Up!	4
		Level 1 Set G	Horrible Urktar of Or, The	4
		Level 1 Set H	Carrots, Peas and Beans	4
			Cowboy Jake	4
			Green Dragon, The	4
			Night Noises	4
		Level 1 Set I	Get-up Machine, The	4
		Level 1 Set J	Market Day for Mrs Wordy	4
Sunshine Spirals	Heinemann	Set 4	Grandpa's New Car	4
			Magic Tree, The	4
		Set 5	Aunty Maria and the Cat	4
			Flea Market, The	4
			Footprints on the Moon	4
			New Bed, A	4
			Old Truck, The	4
			Popcorn	4
			When the Balloon Went Pop!	4
			Windsurfing	4
		Set 6	Ali's Story	4
			Animal Olympics, The	4
			Crossing The Road	4
			Kangaroo	4
			Lucy's Rooster	4
			Mrs Pye's Pool	4
		Set 7	Locked Out	4
Tiddlywinks	Kingscourt	Stage 1 Large Books	Boggity Bog	4
			Wiggly Worm	4
Wonder World	Badger	Set 1	Behind the Rocks	4
			Every Shape and Size	4
			It's Noisy at Night	4
		Set 2	Dragon!	4
			Earthquake!	4
			Hay Making	4
			Skin, Skin	4
			Milking	4

SERIES	PUBLISHER	SET (OR AUTHOR)	TITLE	BAND
Wonder World	Badger	Set 2	My Computer	4
			Spiders	4
			Where's Sylvester's Bed	4
		Set 3	Bottle Garden, A	4
			Fishing	4
			From the Air	4
			Gravity	4
			Sandwich Person, A	4
		Set 4	Don't Throw It Away	4
Individual Titles	Corgi	Asch, Frank	Just Like Daddy	4
	Collins Pict Lions	Barton, Byron	How Far Will a Rubber Band Stretch?	4
	OUP	Brychta, Alex	Arrow, The	4
	Picture Knights	Butterworth and Inkpen	Jasper's Beanstalk	4
	Picture Puffin	Campbell, Rod	Dear Zoo	4
	Whitman & Co	Corey, Dorothy	Tomorrow You Can	4
	Walker	Eyles, H & Cooke, A	Zoo in our House, A	4
	Picture Puffin	Garland, Sarah	Coming to Tea	4
	Picture Puffin	Ginsberg, Mirra	Across The Stream	4
	Walker	Grindley, Sally	Four Black Puppies	4
	Little Mammoth	Hawkins, Colin & Jacqui	Old Mother Hubbard	4
	Picture Puffin	Hill, Eric	Spot Goes on Holiday	4
	Nelson	Hucklesby, Hope	I've Got a Secret	4
	Walker	Hughes, Shirley	When we went to the Park	4
	Picture Puffin	Hutchins, Pat	Rosie's Walk	4
	Simon & Schust'r	Kraus, Robert	Herman the Helper	4
	Collins Pict Lions	Kraus, Robert	Herman the Helper Lends a Hand	4
	Collins Pict Lions	Kraus, Robert	Oliver Takes a Bow	4
	Picture Puffin	Kraus, Robert	Whose Mouse Are You?	4
	Walker	Lingard, J & Lewis, J	Can You Find Sammy The Hamster?	4
	Walker	Mansell, Dom	My Old Teddy	4
	Picture Puffin	Maris, Ron	Are You There Bear?	4
	Heinemann	Minarik, E.H.	Cat and Dog	4
	Picture Puffin	Mueller, Virginia	Playhouse for Monster, A	4
	Walker	Ormerod, Jan	Silly Goose	4
	Red Fox	Prater, John	On Friday Something Funny Happened	4
	MacMillan	Roffey, Maureen	Home Sweet Home	4
	Orchard Books	Rogers, Emma & Paul	Do You Dare?	4
	Walker	Waddell, Martin	Squeak-a-lot	4
	Nelson	Wagstaff, Alan	Mud	4
	Red Fox	Watanabe, Shigeo	Ready Steady Go	4
	Piccadilly	Wheeler, Cindy	Marmalade's Nap	4
	Picture Puffin	Zeifert, Harriet	Nicky's Noisy Night	4
	Collins Pict Lions	Ziefert, Harriet	Here Comes A Bus	4
	Walker	Zinnemann-Hope, Pam	Find your coat, Ned	4

Working Within Level 1: Learning Focus

- Read fluently with attention to punctuation.
- Solve new words using print detail while attending to meaning and syntax.
- Track visually additional lines of print without difficulty.
- Manage effectively a growing variety of texts.
- Discuss and interpret character and plot more fully.

TEXT CHARACTERISTICS

- varied and longer sentences
- little or no repetition of phrases
- more varied and larger number of characters involved
- events sustained over several pages
- may have larger number of words on page
- less familiar or specialised vocabulary used
- illustrations may provide only moderate support for the text

Benchmark Texts

Not Now, Bernard	David McKee/Red Fox
Things People Do For Fun	Foundations/Folens
The Pizza Princess	All Aboard/Ginn
The Hat Trick	Bangers and Mash/Longman
A Handy Dragon	Tiddlywinks/Kingscourt
Minibeasts	Discovery World/Heinemann

SERIES	PUBLISHER	SET (OR AUTHOR)	TITLE	BAND
All Aboard	Ginn	Stage 4 Set A Patt & Rh	Clumsy Clara	5
			Hello Big Head!	5
			Pizza Princess	5
		Stage 4 Set A Sam & Ros	Bear in the Park	5
			Big Sister Rosie	5
			Stop It Bobby!	5
		Stage 4 Set B Sam & Ros	Blackberry Pudding	5
			It's Not Fair	5
			Naughty Nog	5
			Very Clever Clown, The	5
		Stage 5 Set A Patt & Rh	Shipwreck at Old Jelly's Farm	5
		Stage 5 Set B Patt & Rh	Blue Jackal, The	5
			Finn MacCool	5
			Flying Turtle, The	5
			John Quilt	5
			King's Porridge, The	5
			Stars	5
All Aboard Non Fiction	Ginn	Stage 3	Animal Homes	5
			Eating Plants	5
			Feast, The	5
			Guinea Pigs	5
		Stage 4	At The Park	5
			Hedgehogs	5
			Hiccups and Burps	5
			Making Masks	5
Bangers and Mash	Longman	Books 1-6 Pack A	Eggs	5
			Hat Trick, The	5
		Books 1A-6A	Ant Eggs	5
			Red nose	5
Beginner Books	Collins	Lopshire, Robert	Put Me In the Zoo	5
Book Project Fiction 1	Longman	Band 3 Read On	Boasting Monsters, The	5
			Minnie meets a monkey	5
			Minnie's bike	5
			Minnie's kite	5
			Story without end	5
			Two silly stories	5
		Band 4 Read On	Come On, Wind!	5
			Monster Who Loved Cameras, The	5
Bright and Early Books	Collins	Perkins, Al	Nose Book, The	5
		Seuss, Dr	Foot Book, The	5
Cambridge Reading	CUP	Becoming a R Stage A	Bad Boy Billy!	5
			Dan's Box	5
			Here Comes Everyone	5
			Raven and the Fox, The	5
			Seal (whole text)	5
			This is the Register	5
			Two by Two	5
			What's the Time?	5
		Becoming a R Stage B	All by Myself	5
			Billy's Box	5
			Clever Tortoise, The	5
			Follow My Leader	5
			Going to School	5
			Little Red Hen, The	5
			Moonlit Owl, The	5
			Over in the Meadow	5
			Peas in a Pod	5
			Please Miss!	5

SERIES	PUBLISHER	SET (OR AUTHOR)	TITLE	BAND
Cambridge Reading	CUP	Becoming a R Stage B	Show-and-Tell	5
			Sophie's Box	5
			Tortoise and the Hare, The	5
			Wiggle and Giggle	5
			Yasmin's Box	5
		Becoming a R Stage C	Everyone is Reading	5
			Well Done, Sam!	5
Cook, Ann	Longman	Monster Books	Monster Comes to the City	5
Discovery World	Heinemann	Stage C	Breakfast	5
			Minibeasts	5
Fables from Aesop	Ginn	Books 1-6	Goose that laid the Golden Egg, The	5
		Books 7-12	Man, his Son and the Ass, The	5
		Books 13-18	Fox and the Stork, The	5
			Lion and the Mouse, The	5
Foundations for Reading	Folens	Level 10 Early	Bikes	5
			Broken Plate, The	5
			Tyres	5
			Uncle Carlos's Barbecue	5
		Level 11 Early	Jimmy's Goal	5
			Making Friends	5
			Our Baby	5
		Level 12 Early	At the Pet Shop	5
			Best Guess, The	5
			Get Lost!	5
			Going to the Hairdresser	5
			Is It Time Yet?	5
			Little Monkey Is Stuck	5
			Lucky We Have an Estate Car	5
			Mr Bumbleticker Likes to Fix Machines	5
			Playing Football	5
			Silly Willy and Silly Billy	5
			Things People Do for Fun	5
			Trucks	5
		Level 13 Experienced	Fierce Old Woman Who ... The	5
			Grandpa's Special Present	5
			Herman's Tooth	5
			Hide and Seek	5
			Mr Bumbleticker Goes Shopping	5
			Who's Looking After the Baby?	5
		Level 14 Experienced	Mother Hippopotamus Gets Wet	5
			Nobody Knew My Name	5
			That Dog!	5
			Trip to the Park, The	5
		Level 15 Experienced	Click!	5
			Monarch Butterfly, The	5
Ginn Geography Topic Bks	Ginn	Year 1	Shops	5
Ginn Science	Ginn		Windy Day, The	5
Ginn Science Info Bks	Ginn	Year 1 Second Set	Owls	5
			Seeds	5
Link Up	Collins	Level 2	Along The Street	5
			Just Like Me	5
			Karen At The Zoo	5
		Level 3	Friends	5
			Gran's Birthday	5
			Runaway Van, The	5
			Silly Children	5
		Level 4	Naughty Nick's Book	5
Literacy Links Plus	Kingscourt	Early A	Moonlight	5

SERIES	PUBLISHER	SET (OR AUTHOR)	TITLE	BAND
Literacy Links Plus	Kingscourt	Early A	Sally's Picture	5
		Early B	Grump The	5
			If You Like Strawberries	5
			Lilly-Lolly-Littlelegs	5
			My Monster Friends	5
			Odd Socks	5
			Pete's New Shoes	5
			Wide Mouthed Frog, The	5
			Woolly,Woolly	5
		Early C	Bossy Bettina	5
			Crab at the Bottom of the Sea, The	5
			Dad Didn't Mind at All	5
			Dad's Bathtime	5
			Hungry Chickens, The	5
			In The Park	5
			No Extras	5
			What is Bat?	5
			Whatever Will These Become?	5
			When I'm Older	5
		Early D	Barnaby's New House, The	5
			Daniel	5
			Friend, A	5
			My House	5
			Papa's Spaghetti	5
			Two Little Mice, The	5
		Emergent D	Tails	5
		Fluent D	In the City of Rome	5
		Traditional Tales	Little Red Hen, The	5
One, Two, Three & Away	Collins	Blue Platform 7-10	Witch and the Donkey, The	5
		Blue Platform 17-20	Miranda and the Flying Broomstick	5
			Miranda and the Magic Stones	5
		Green Platform 1-6	Little Old Man and the Little Black Cat, The	5
			Little Old Woman and the G'father Clock	5
			Roger and the School Bus	5
			Sita Climbs the Wall	5
			When the School Door was Shut	5
		Green Platform 7-10	Benjamin and the Little Fox	5
			Caterpillars and Butterflies	5
			Little Old Man and the Magic Stick, The	5
		Main Books 1-2B	Gopal and the Little White Cat	5
		Main Books 3-4b	Donkey, The	5
			Empty House, The	5
			Haystack, The	5
			House in the Corner of the Wood, The	5
			Island in Deep River, The	5
			Two Giants, The	5
		Red Platform 1-6	Mr. Brown's Goat	5
			Old Red Bus, The	5
			Roger Rings the Bell	5
			Tom and the Monster	5
Oxford Reading Tree	OUP	Stage 4 More Stories A	Balloon, The	5
			Camcorder, The	5
		Stage 4 Storybooks	Storm, The	5
		Stage 5 More Stories A	Great Race, The	5
			Underground Adventure	5
			Vanishing Cream	5
			Whatsit, The	5
		Stage 5 More Stories B	Camping Adventure	5

50

SERIES	PUBLISHER	SET (OR AUTHOR)	TITLE	BAND
Oxford Reading Tree	OUP	Stage 5 More Stories B	Mum to the Rescue	5
			New Baby, The	5
			New Classroom, A	5
			Noah's Ark Adventure	5
			Scarecrows	5
		Stage 5 Storybooks	Castle Adventure	5
			Dragon Tree, The	5
			Gran	5
			Pirate Adventure	5
			Village in the Snow	5
		Stage 6 Owls	In the Garden	5
		Stage 6 Playscripts	Land of the Dinosaurs	5
			Robin Hood	5
Oxford RT Branch Library	OUP	Victor Bks Stage 5A	Victor and the computer cat	5
			Victor and the martian	5
			Victor and the sail-kart	5
		Victor Bks Stage 5A	Victor the champion	5
			Victor the hero	5
Pathways	Collins	Stage 1 Set D	Hedgehogs	5
			Scaredy Cat	5
		Stage 2 Set A	Firefighters	5
			Room Full of Light, A	5
		Stage 2 Set B	Golden Screws, The	5
			Monster's Baking Day	5
			Pack It Up, Ben	5
		Stage 2 Set C	Little Miss Muffet	5
		Stage 2 Set D	Our Place	5
		Stage 2 Set E	If I Were A Giant	5
			Joke Book	5
			Wibble Wobble	5
		Stage 2 Set F	Diwali Party	5
			Three Wishes, The	5
		Stage 3 Set A	When I Left My House	5
PM Non-fiction	Nelson	Blue Level	Dentist, The	5
			Doctor, The	5
			Hairdresser, The	5
			Optometrist, The	5
			Our Parents	5
			Teacher, The	5
PM Storybooks	Nelson	Blue Set A	Lion and the Mouse, The	5
			Locked Out	5
		Green Set A	Ben's Tooth	5
			Brave Triceratops	5
			Candlelight	5
			Clever Penguins, The	5
			Cross Country Race	5
			Flood, The	5
			Fox who Foxed, The	5
			Househunting	5
			Island Picnic, The	5
			Little Red Bus, The	5
			Mrs Spider's Beautiful Web	5
			Naughty Ann, The	5
			Pepper's Adventure	5
			Pete Little	5
			Ten Little Garden Snails	5
			Waving Sheep, The	5
PM Storybooks	Nelson	Green Set B	After the flood	5

SERIES	PUBLISHER	SET (OR AUTHOR)	TITLE	BAND
PM Storybooks	Nelson	Green Set B	Babysitter, The	5
			Father Bear's surprise	5
			Flying fish, The	5
			Joey	5
			Rescue, The	5
			Snow on the hill	5
			Try again, Hannah	5
Read it Yourself	Ladybird	Level 1	Enormous Turnip, The	5
		Level 2	Puss in Boots	5
			Red Riding Hood	5
		Level 3	Cinderella	5
			Sleeping Beauty	5
		Level 4	Peter and the Wolf	5
Reading 360	Ginn	Level 3	Picnic For Tortoise, A	5
			Where are you Going?	5
		Level 4	At the Zoo	5
			Book For Kay, A	5
			Helicopters	5
			What a Surprise!	5
		Magic Circle Level 4	Do You See Mouse?	5
			How Can You Hide an Elephant?	5
			In the Zoo	5
			Inside the Red and White Tent	5
Reading 360 New	Ginn	Level 3	Lost and Found	5
		Little Bks L 3 Set 1	Can I Come With You?	5
			Going to the Shops	5
			Guess What Cat Found	5
			No School Today	5
			Reindeer, The	5
		Little Bks L 3 Set 2	Let The Dog Sleep	5
			Little Rabbit, The	5
		Little Bks L 3 Set 3	Noah's Ark	5
		Little Bks L 4 Set 1	Sam and Sue at the Zoo	5
		Little Bks L 4 Set 2	New Boy At School, A	5
		Little Bks L.4 Set 3	Going Away Bag, The	5
			I'm a Good Boy	5
Reading 360 Upstarts	Ginn	Level 3	James and the Dragon	5
			Lucy Calls the Fire Brigade	5
		Level 3 Extension	Apple Tree, The	5
			Fun at the Zoo	5
			Helpful Hannah	5
			Sunil's Bad Dream	5
Reading World	Longman	Level 2 Pack A	Cat and The Witch, The	5
Ready to Read	Nelson	Early Set D	I'm the King of the Mountain	5
			My Special Job	5
		Fluent Set A	Safe Place, The	5
			When Jose Hits That Ball	5
			Wibble, Wobble, Albatross!	5
		Fluent Set B	Little House	5
			Most Terrible Creature in the World, The	5
			Rock in the Road, The	5
			Wind Power	5
Scholastic Books	Ashton Scholastic	Barchas, Sarah	I Was Walking Down the Road	5
		Gelman, Rita	More Spaghetti I Say	5
		Gelman, Rita	Why Can't I Fly?	5
		Kraus, Robert	Happy Egg, The	5
		Krauss, Ruth	Carrot Seed, The	5
		Nodset, Joan	Who Took the Farmer's Hat?	5

SERIES	PUBLISHER	SET (OR AUTHOR)	TITLE	BAND
Story Chest	Kingscourt	Large Read-tog Set 1	Grandpa, Grandpa	5
			Hairy Bear	5
		Large Read-tog Set 1	Hungry Giant, The	5
		Small Read-together	Big Toe, The	5
			Boo Hoo	5
			Obadiah	5
			Woosh	5
		Stage 2	Birthday Cake, The	5
			Help Me	5
		Stage 3	Let Me In	5
			Yum and Yuk	5
Storyworlds	Heinemann	Stage 5 Once Upon a Time	Lake of Stars, The	5
			Ugly Duckling, The	5
			Wolf and the Kids, The	5
		Stage 7 Animal World	Duma and the lion	5
			Kiboko and the water snake	5
			Mamba and the crocodile bird	5
			Twiga and the moon	5
Sunshine	Heinemann	Level 1 Non-fiction	Clouds	5
			Dandelion, The	5
			Hermit crab, The	5
			Noah's Ark	5
			Small world, A	5
			Space	5
			Sunshine Street	5
			Underwater journey	5
			What am I?	5
			What else?	5
			Whose Eggs Are These?	5
Sunshine	Heinemann	Level 1 Set E	Wet Day at School, A	5
		Level 1 Set F	Come for a swim!	5
		Level 1 Set G	Dad's headache	5
			Little car	5
			My boat	5
			Terrible tiger, The	5
		Level 1 Set H	Red socks and yellow socks	5
		Level 1 Set I	Just this once	5
		Level 3	Christmas Dog	5
		Level 4	Fantastic Washing Machine, The	5
			In the Middle of the Night	5
		Level 1 Set H	Nowhere and Nothing	5
Sunshine New	Heinemann	Level 1 Set I	Big Laugh, The	5
			Elephant for the Holidays, An	5
		Level 1 Set J	Mrs Barnett's Birthday	5
Sunshine Spirals	Heinemann	Set 5	Camping	5
			Crocodiles	5
		Set 6	Elephant's Trunk, The	5
			Hole In The Hedge, The	5
			Signs	5
			Weather, The	5
		Set 7	Flying with Tommy	5
			Horse, The	5
			Mrs Grimble's Grapevine	5
		Set 8	Echo, The	5
			Old Green Machine, The	5
Tiddlywinks	Kingscourt	Stage 1 Large Books	Guinea Pig Grass	5
			Handy Dragon, A	5
			Let's Make Music	5

SERIES	PUBLISHER	SET (OR AUTHOR)	TITLE	BAND
Tiddlywinks	Kingscourt	Stage 1 Large Books	Rat a Tat Tat	5
			Turnips for Dinner	5
		Stage 1 Small Books	Amazing Popple Seed, The	5
			Cow up a Tree	5
			Jessie's Flower	5
		Stage 2	That's Really Weird	5
Wonder World	Badger	Set 1	Old Teeth, New Teeth	5
			Rain and the Sun, The	5
			Tails	5
			What Do I See in the Garden?	5
			Wind, The	5
		Set 2	Ants	5
			Big Round Up, The	5
			Hide And Seek	5
			Houses	5
			My Friend Jess	5
			Pollution	5
		Set 3	Fish	5
			Getting Glasses	5
			I Wonder Why?	5
			People Dance	5
			Rubbish	5
			Stamps	5
			What Was This?	5
		Set 4	Bird's Nests	5
			Cats	5
			Cells	5
			Custard	5
			Picnic, The	5
			Potatoes, Potatoes	5
			Tin Can Telephone	5
Individual Titles	Walker	Alborough, Jez	Where's My Teddy?	5
	Walker	Alexander, Martha	Blackboard Bear	5
	Dinosaur	Althea	Can You Moo?	5
	Picture Puffin	Barton, Byron	Buzz Buzz Buzz	5
	Heinemann	Bonsall, Crosby	Day I Had to Play With My Sister, The	5
	Little Mammoth	Bradman, Tony	Look Out! He's Behind You!	5
	Mammoth	Brown, Margaret Wise	Goodnight Moon	5
	Red Fox	Brown, Ruth	Dark, Dark Tale, A	5
	Frances Lincoln	Bryant, Donna	My Rabbit Bobbie	5
	Red Fox	Burningham, John	Baby, The	5
	Red Fox	Burningham, John	Dog, The	5
	Red Fox	Burningham, John	Rabbit, The	5
	Red Fox	Burningham, John	Snow, The	5
	Lothian	Campbell, Rod	Buster's Morning	5
	Lothian	Campbell, Rod	From Gran	5
	Nelson	Cartwright, Pauline	If I were a Witch	5
	Walker	Dale, Penny	Ten in the Bed	5
	Kingfisher	Denton, Kady	Would They Love a Lion?	5
	Orchard Books	Dunbar, Joyce	Four Fierce Kittens	5
	Methuen	Erickson and Roffey	Tidy-Up Story, The	5
	Picture Puffin	Garland, Sarah	Doing the Garden	5
	Collins Pict Lions	Greeley, Valerie	Where's My Share	5
	Picture Puffin	Harper, Anita	It's Not Fair	5
	Picture Puffin	Hawkins, Colin	Pat the Cat	5
	Walker	Hawkins, Colin & Jacqui	Terrible,Terrible Tiger	5
	Picture Puffin	Hill, Eric	Spot's First Walk	5
	Little Mammoth	Hoffman, M/Northway, J	Nancy No Size	5

SERIES	PUBLISHER	SET (OR AUTHOR)	TITLE	BAND
Individual Titles	Picture Puffin	Hutchins, Pat	Titch	5
	Picture Puffin	Hutchins, Pat	You'll Soon Grow into Them, Titch	5
	Picturemac	Inkpen, Mick	If I Had A Pig	5
	Picturemac	Inkpen, Mick	If I Had a Sheep	5
	Heinemann	Johnson, Crockett	Picture for Harold's Room, A	5
	Picture Puffin	Kraus, Robert	Owliver	5
	Faber and Faber	Lillegard, Dee	Sitting in my Box	5
	Heinemann	Ling	But What Did We Get For Grandpa?	5
	Red Fox	Lloyd, Errol	Nandy's Bedtime	5
	Walker	Maris, Ron	Hold Tight Bear!	5
	Walker	Mark, Jan	Feet	5
	Red Fox	McKee, David	Not Now Bernard	5
	Walker	Miller, Virginia	Eat Your Dinner	5
	Methuen	Peppe, Rodney	Henry's Exercises	5
	Red Fox	Prater, John	Along Came Tom	5
	BBC Books	Ralph, Graham	Spider	5
	Picture Puffin	Sage, A & C	Trouble with Babies, The	5
	Picture Puffin	Van-der-Meer, R	Who's Afraid?	5
	Orchard Books	Walsh, Ellen Stoll	Mouse Paint	5
	Red Fox	Watanabe, Shigeo	How Do I Eat It?	5
	Penguin	Watanabe, Shigeo	I'm The King Of The Castle	5

Working Towards Level 2: Learning Focus

- Get started without relying on illustrations.
- Read longer phrases and more complex sentences.
- Attend to a range of punctuation.
- Cross-check information from meaning, syntax and print on the run.
- Search for and use familiar syllables within words to read longer words.
- Infer meaning from the text.

TEXT CHARACTERISTICS

— stories are longer - 250-300 words

— increased proportion of space allocated to print rather than pictures

— illustrations support overall meaning of text

— more literary language used

— sentence structures becoming more complex

Benchmark Texts

The Monster who loved Toothbrushes	Book Project/Longman
The Little Yellow Chicken	Sunshine/Heinemann
Mister Magnolia	Quentin Blake/Collin's Picture Lions
The Kick-a-lot Shoes	Story Chest/Kingscourt
Robert the Rose Horse	Beginner Books/Collins
Walking in Winter	PM Non-fiction/Nelson

SERIES	PUBLISHER	SET (OR AUTHOR)	TITLE	BAND
All Aboard	Ginn	Stage 5 Set A Patt & Rh	Upside Down Harry Brown	6
			Wishing Fishing Tree, The	6
		Stage 5 Set A Sam & Ros	Speedy's Day Out	6
			When Nan Came to Stay	6
			You Can't Scare Me!	6
		Stage 5 Set B Sam & Ros	Bobby and the Alien	6
			Clever Boy, Charlie	6
			Fun Run, The	6
			Have a Go, Sam	6
		Stage 6 Pattern & Rhyme	Big Bad Bill	6
		Stage 6 Sam & Rosie	Great Lorenzo, The	6
			Lord Scarecrow	6
			Plum Magic	6
			Swan Rescue	6
		Stage 7 Sam & Rosie	Sonic Sid	6
All Aboard Non Fiction	Ginn	Stage 3	Butterflies	6
			Workshop, The	6
		Stage 4	Special Clothes	6
		Stage 5	Biggest and Smallest	6
			Racing Pigeons	6
			Slugs	6
Bangers and Mash	Longman	Books 1-6 Pack A	Clock, The	6
			Wiggly worms	6
		Books 1A-6A	Duck in the Box	6
			Mud Cake	6
		Supplementary Books	Bubble Bath	6
			Hatching is Catching	6
			Jumpers	6
			Tea break	6
Beginner Books	Collins	Berenstain, Stan & Jan	Bike Lesson, The	6
		Brown, Marc	Spooky Riddles	6
		Eastman, P.D.	Are You My Mother?	6
		Eastman, P.D.	Big Dog, Little Dog	6
		Heilbroner, Joan	Robert, the Rose Horse	6
		Sadler, Marilyn	It's Not Easy Being a Bunny	6
		Seuss, Dr	Great Day for Up!	6
		Seuss, Dr	Hop on Pop	6
		Seuss, Dr	I Can Read With My Eyes Shut	6
		Seuss, Dr	Green Eggs and Ham	6
		Stone, Rosetta	Because a Little Bug Went Ka-choo!	6
Book Project Fiction 1	Longman	Band 1 Read Aloud	Ben Biggins' House	6
			Let's Go Into The Jungle	6
		Band 2 Read Aloud	Frog in the Throat, A	6
		Band 3 Read Aloud	Minnie and the Champion Snorer	6
		Band 3 Read On	Pocketful of gold	6
		Band 4 Read On	Monster Who Loved Toothbrushes, The	6
Book Project Fiction 2	Longman	Band 1	Day Poppy Said Yes, The	6
Bright and Early Books	Collins	Tether, Graham	Hair Book, The	6
Cambridge Reading	CUP	Becoming a R Stage C	Friend for Kate, A	6
			Gracie's Cat	6
			Imran and the Watch	6
			Nishal's Box	6
			Rhyming Riddles	6
			Tom's Box	6
Cook, Ann	Longman	Monster Books	Monster Cleans His House	6
			Monster Looks for a Friend	6
			Monster Looks for a House	6
			Monster Meets Lady Monster	6

SERIES	PUBLISHER	SET (OR AUTHOR)	TITLE	BAND
Fables from Aesop	Ginn	Books 1-6	Ass in the Lion's Skin, The	6
			Boy Who cried Wolf, The	6
			Fox and the Crow, The	6
			Town Mouse and Country Mouse	6
		Books 7-12	Ducks and the Tortoise, The	6
			Eagle and the Man, The	6
		Books 13-18	Hare and the Tortoise, The	6
			Sick Lion, The	6
Favourite Tales	Ladybird	-	Little Red Hen, The	6
Foundations for Reading	Folens	Level 13 Experienced	Visiting the Vet	6
		Level 14 Experienced	Dad's Surprise	6
			Mr Bumbleticker's Apples	6
			Rap Party, The	6
		Level 15 Experienced	Accident, The	6
			At the Water Hole	6
			Mother Sea Turtle	6
			Show and Tell	6
			Too Many Steps	6
		Level 16 Experienced	Billy Magee's New Car	6
			Elephants	6
			Obstacle Course, The	6
			Paper Birds, The	6
			Party Games	6
			Sea Wall, The	6
		Level 17 Experienced	Whales	6
Ginn Geography Topic Bks	Ginn	Year 2	Water	6
Ginn Science Info Bks	Ginn	Year 1 Second Set	Milk	6
Literacy Links Plus	Kingscourt	Early A	Water Falling	6
		Early B	Grandma's Memories	6
		Early C	Boxes	6
			Brand-new Butterfly, A	6
			Gregor, The Grumblesome Giant	6
			Hippo's Hiccups	6
			Making Caterpillars and Butterflies	6
			Only An Octopus	6
			Philippa and the Dragon	6
			Pizza For Dinner	6
		Early D	Deer and the Crocodile, The	6
			Dinosaur's Cold, The	6
			Fastest Gazelle, The	6
			Frog Princess, The	6
			Half For You, Half For Me	6
			I Have a Question, Grandma	6
			Mice	6
			Queen's Parrot, The	6
			Rice Cakes	6
			Too Much Noise	6
			Why Elephants Have Long Noses	6
			Wind And Sun	6
		Fluent A	Knit, Knit, Knit, Knit	6
One, Two, Three & Away	Collins	Green Platform 1-6	Big Man, the Witch and the Donkey, The	6
		Green Platform 7-10	Cat and the Witch's Supper, The	6
		Main Books 5-8	Billy Bluehat's Day	6
			White Owls, The	6
		Red Platform 1-6	Billy and Percy Green	6
			Jennifer and the Little Black Horse	6
		Red Platform 7-10	Ghost Train, The	6
			Hole in the Wall, The	6

SERIES	PUBLISHER	SET (OR AUTHOR)	TITLE	BAND
One, Two, Three & Away	Collins	Red Platform 7-10	Little Fox, The	6
			Sita and the Robin	6
		Yellow Platform 1-6	Christmas in the Village with Three Corners	6
			Fire!	6
			House Across the Street, The	6
			Roger and the Cats	6
			Sleeping Giant, The	6
Oxford Reading Tree	OUP	Stage 5 More Stories A	It's Not Fair	6
		Stage 6 More Owls	Christmas Adventure	6
			Fright in the Night, A	6
			Go Kart Race, The	6
			Laughing Princess, The	6
			Rotten Apples	6
			Shiny Key, The	6
		Stage 6 Owls	Kipper and the Giant	6
			Land of the Dinosaurs	6
			Robin Hood	6
		Stage 7 Playscripts	Broken Roof, The	6
			Lost in the Jungle	6
			Lost Key, The	6
			Red Planet	6
		Stage 8 Magpies	Kidnappers, The	6
Oxford RT Branch Library	OUP	Two Bears Bks St 7A	Two Bears find a Pet	6
			Two Bears go Fishing	6
Pathways	Collins	Stage 2 Set D	Davina and the Dinosaurs	6
			Let's Have a Dog	6
			Rainy Day	6
		Stage 2 Set F	Use Your Hanky, Hannah	6
			Watch Out	6
		Stage 3 Set A	Miss Blossom	6
			Red Riding Hood	6
		Stage 3 Set B	Grabber	6
			One Puzzled Parrot	6
		Stage 4 Set C	Bee in my Bonnet, A	6
PM Animal Facts	Nelson	Pets	Budgies	6
			Cats	6
			Dogs	6
			Goldfish	6
			Guinea Pigs	6
			Mice	6
PM Non-fiction	Nelson	Green Level	In the Afternoon	6
			In the Morning	6
			Walking in the Autumn	6
			Walking in the Spring	6
			Walking in the Summer	6
			Walking in the Winter	6
PM Storybooks	Nelson	Orange Set A	Biggest Tree, The	6
			Dinosaur Chase	6
			Jack and Chug	6
			Toby and BJ	6
			Toby and the Big Tree	6
			Toy Farm, The	6
		Orange Set B	Jessica in the Dark	6
			Just One Guinea Pig	6
			Mitch to the Rescue	6
			Pterosaur's Long Flight	6
			Sarah and the Barking Dog	6
			Toby and the Big Red Van	6

SERIES	PUBLISHER	SET (OR AUTHOR)	TITLE	BAND
PM Storybooks	Nelson	Orange Set C	Busy Beavers, The	6
			Careful Crocodile, The	6
			Lost in the Forest	6
			Rebecca and the Concert	6
			Roller Blades for Luke	6
			Two Little Goldfish	6
PM Traditional Tales	Nelson	Orange Level	Chicken-Licken	6
			Gingerbread Man, The	6
			Little Red Hen, The	6
			Tale on the Turnip, The	6
			Three Billy Goats Gruff, The	6
			Three Little Pigs, The	6
Read it Yourself	Ladybird	Level 2	Gingerbread Man	6
		Level 3	Dick Whittington	6
			Town Mouse and Country Mouse	6
		Level 4	Rapunzel	6
Reading 2000	Longmans	Storytime Reds	How Does Your Garden Grow?	6
			Pets Need Vets	6
			Rags in Trouble	6
		Storytime Yellows	Anna Comes To Town	6
			Do I Know You?	6
			Dreamy Robbie	6
			Going Shopping	6
			In The Night	6
			Sky People	6
			Tree House, The	6
Reading 360	Ginn	Level 4	Once Upon a Time	6
		Magic Circle Level 5	Nine on a String	6
		Once Upon a Time 1-4	Cinderella	6
			Goldilocks and the Three Bears	6
			Rumpelstiltskin	6
			Three Little Pigs, The	6
Reading 360 New	Ginn	Level 4	Animal Friends	6
		Level 5	Animal Tracks	6
		Little Bks L 3 Set 2	Duck Trouble	6
		Little Bks L 4 Set 1	About Helicopters, About Animals	6
			Get That Fly	6
			Mum's Surprise Ride	6
			Sam and Sue at the Seaside	6
		Little Bks L.5 Set 3	Day at the Seaside, A	6
			Mrs MacDonald And The Mayor's Tea Party	6
			Town Cat, The	6
			What Did Baby Say?	6
Reading 360 Upstarts	Ginn	Level 3	Babies Are Yuk	6
			Fat Cat, The	6
			Naughty Norman	6
			Pippa and the Witch	6
		Level 3 Extension	Circus Tricks	6
			Pancake Day	6
		Level 4 Extension	Best Watchdog in the World, The	6
			Sandy and the Snowball	6
Reading World	Longman	Level 2 Pack A	Chimney, The	6
			Clean Up Your Room	6
		Level 2 Pack B	April Fool	6
			Get Some Bread, Fred	6
			Secret, The	6
			Stanley Goes to School	6
		Level 2 More Books	Litterbug	6

SERIES	PUBLISHER	SET (OR AUTHOR)	TITLE	BAND
Ready to Read	Nelson	Fluent Set A	Pets	6
			Why Cats Wash After Dinner	6
		Fluent Set B	Dragon	6
Scholastic Books	Ashton Scholastic	Galdone, Paul	Henny Penny	6
		McGovern, Ann	Too Much Noise	6
		Nodset, Joan	Go Away Dog	6
		Seuling, Barbara	Teeny Tiny Woman	6
Story Chest	Kingscourt	Large Read-tog Set 1	Yes Ma'am	6
		Stage 2	Kick-a-Lot Shoes, The	6
			Pirates, The	6
			Roly-Poly	6
			Sun smile	6
			Wet Grass	6
		Stage 3	Dragon, The	6
			Hungry Monster	6
			Jack-in-the-Box	6
Storyworlds	Heinemann	Stage 7 Fantasy World	Magic boots, The	6
			Magic coat, The	6
			Magic hat, The	6
			Magic shoes, The	6
		Stage 7 Once Upon a Time	Elves and the Shoemaker The	6
			Frog Prince, The	6
			Pied Piper, The	6
			Tug of War, The	6
		Stage 7 Our World	Bouncer comes to stay	6
			Cricket bat mystery, The	6
			New boy, The	6
			Next door neighbour, The	6
		Stage 8 Animal World	Bear that wouldn't growl, The	6
			Elephant that forgot, The	6
			Shark with no teeth, The	6
			Snake that couldn't hiss, The	6
Sunshine	Heinemann	Level 1 Set G	Noise	6
			Old Grizzly	6
		Level 1 Set H	My sloppy tiger	6
			Poor sore paw, The	6
			Ratty-tatty	6
			Tiny woman's coat, The	6
		Level 1 Set I	Mrs Grindy's shoes	6
			When Dad went to playschool	6
		Level 1 Set J	Boring old bed	6
			Hundred hugs, A	6
			My sloppy tiger goes to school	6
			Space race	6
			Tess and Paddy	6
		Level 2	Giant Pumpkin, The	6
			Soup	6
			Train Ride Story	6
		Level 3	Big Family, The	6
			Person from Planet X, The	6
			Silly Billys	6
		Level 1 Set I	Mum's Birthday	6
Sunshine New	Heinemann	Level 1 Set J	Job For Giant Jim, A	6
		Level 2	My Two Mums	6
			Chocolate-chip Muffins	6
		Level 3	River Rapids Ride, The	6
			Trog	6
		Level 4	New Bike, The	6

SERIES	PUBLISHER	SET (OR AUTHOR)	TITLE	BAND
Sunshine New	Heinemann	Level 6	Did Not! Did So!	6
Sunshine Spirals	Heinemann	Set 7	Bother Those Barnetts!	6
			Mrs Harriet's Hairdo	6
			Museum, The	6
			Pelican, The	6
			There's A Dragon In My Garden	6
			Tim	6
		Set 8	Bag Of Smiles, The	6
			Brutus	6
			I Spy	6
			Mouse Box, The	6
			Six Little Pigeons	6
			Traveller and the Farmer, The	6
Tiddlywinks	Kingscourt	Stage 1 Large Books	King's Pudding, The	6
		Stage 2	Let's Get a Pet	6
			Monster	6
			Terrible Armadillo, The	6
			What I Would Do	6
		Stage 3	Little Brown House, The	6
			Shoe Grabber, The	6
		Stage 7	Bull and the Matador, The	6
Wonder World	Badger	Set 1	Pig That Learned to Jig, The	6
			Slugs and Snails	6
		Set 2	Animals Grow	6
			Grandma's Heart	6
			Storm!	6
		Set 3	Between the Tides	6
			Tramping with Dad	6
			When the Sun Goes Down	6
		Set 4	Dolphins	6
			My Secret Place	6
			Spinning Top	6
			Water	6
Individual Titles	Picture Puffin	Alexander, Martha	We never get to do anything	6
	Picture Puffin	Allen, Pamela	Bertie and the Bear	6
	Collins Pict Lions	Berenstain, Stan	Old Hat New Hat	6
	Collins Pict Lions	Blake, Quentin	Mister Magnolia	6
	Little Mammoth	Bradman, T/Boroughs, J	Not Like That, Like This	6
	Little Mammoth	Bradman, Tony	Wait and See	6
	Frances Lincoln	Bryant, Donna	My Dog Jessie	6
	Red Fox	Burningham, John	Cupboard, The	6
	Red Fox	Burningham, John	Friend, The	6
	Ladybird	Butterworth/Salisbury	Fly in his Eye, A	6
	Lothian	Campbell, Rod	Buster is Lost	6
	Picture Puffin	Carle, Eric	Very Hungry Caterpillar, The	6
	Nelson	Cartwright, Pauline	Prudence Bunting and her Bike	6
	Picture Puffin	Flack, Marjorie	Angus And The Cat	6
	Picture Puffin	Garland, Sarah	Doing the Washing	6
	Picture Puffin	Garland, Sarah	Polly's Puffin	6
	Walker	Ginsberg, Mirra	Where does the Sun go at Night?	6
	Piccadilly	Hawkins, Colin	Jen the Hen	6
	Walker	Hayes, Sarah	This is the Bear	6
	Picture Puffin	Hill, Eric	Spot's Birthday Party	6
	Heinemann	Hoff, Syd	Albert The Albatross	6
	Heinemann	Hoff, Syd	Chester	6
	Heinemann I	Hoff, Syd	Sammy the Seal	6
	Walker	Hughes, Shirley	Bath Water's Hot	6
	Heinemann	Hurd, Edith Thatcher	Come and Have Fun	6

SERIES	PUBLISHER	SET (OR AUTHOR)	TITLE	BAND
Individual Titles	Picture Puffin	Hutchins, Pat	Goodnight Owl	6
	Picture Puffin	Keats, Ezra Jack	Whistle For Willie	6
	Hippo	Keller, Holly	Ten Sleepy Sheep	6
	Viking/Kestrel	Kraus, Robert	Three Friends	6
	Walker	Lloyd, D & Scruton, C	Cat and Dog	6
	Lothian	Mayers, Hawkinson	Just One More Block	6
	Heinemann	McPhail, D	Pig Pig Rides	6
	Mammoth	Minarik, E.H.	Kiss For Little Bear, A	6
	Picture Puffin	Rice, Eve	Goodnight Goodnight	6
	Walker	Riddell, Chris	Ben and The Bear	6
	Picture Corgi	Rosato, A	Teeny Tiny	6
	Picturemac	Rose, Gerald	Ahhh, Said The Stork	6
	Walker	Rosen, Michael	We're Going on a Bear Hunt	6
	Picture Puffin	Ross, Tony	I'm Coming to Get You	6
	Red Fox	Ross, Tony	Oscar Got the Blame	6
	Picture Puffin	Sage, A & C	That's Mine, That's Yours	6
	Collins Pict Lions	Wells, Rosemary	Noisy Nora	6
	Walker	West, Colin	Ten Little Crocodiles	6

Working Towards Level 2: Learning Focus

- Extract meaning from the text while reading with less dependence on illustrations.
- Approach different genres with increasing flexibility.
- Use punctuation and text layout to read with a greater range of expression.
- Sustain reading through longer sentence structures and paragraphs.
- Tackle a higher ratio of more complex words.

TEXT CHARACTERISTICS

— elaborated episodes and events

— extended descriptions

— more use of literary language

— may have full pages of print

— more unusual and challenging vocabulary

— illustrations provide a lower level of support in fictional texts

— non-fiction texts contain longer, more formal sentences

Benchmark Texts

The Man who Didn't Do His Dishes	Scholastic Books/Ashton Scholastic
The Red Planet	Oxford Reading Tree/OUP
Frog and Toad are Friends	Arnold Lobel/Mammoth
The Cat in the Hat	Beginner Books/Collins
Two Shoes, New Shoes	Shirley Hughes/Walker
Bees	Sunshine Spirals/Heinemann

SERIES	PUBLISHER	SET (OR AUTHOR)	TITLE	BAND
All Aboard	Ginn	Stage 5 Set A Patt & Rh	Computer Kate	7
		Stage 5 Set A Sam & Ros	Sam and the Tadpoles	7
		Stage 6 Pattern & Rhyme	Kangaroos	7
			Lion's Roar, The	7
		Stage 7 Sam & Rosie	Bobby's Bad Day	7
			Noises in the Night	7
All Aboard Non Fiction	Ginn	Stage 4	Road Signs	7
		Stage 5	Roller Coaster	7
			Wearing Glasses	7
Bangers and Mash	Longman	Books 1-6 Pack A	Best Duster, The	7
			In a Jam	7
		Books 1A-6A	Lion Pit	7
			Pond Monster	7
		Books 7-12 Pack B	Ding Dong Baby	7
		Books 13-18 Pack C	Hole Story, The	7
Beginner Books	Collins	Eastman, P.D.	Best Nest, The	7
		Eastman, P.D.	Sam and the Firefly	7
		Le Seig, Theo	Ten Apples Up on Top	7
		Palmer, Helen	Fish out of Water, A	7
		Seuss, Dr	Cat in the Hat, The	7
Book Project Fiction 1	Longman	Band 3 Read On	Monster Feast, The	7
		Band 4 Read Aloud	Leonora and the Giddy House	7
		Band 4 Read On	Giddy Funfair	7
			Giddy up and away	7
Book Project Fiction 2	Longman	Band 1	Blue Moo	7
			Gregorie Peck	7
			King Grumpyguts	7
		Band 2	Jilly's Days	7
		Band 3	Nyamia and the Bag of Gold	7
Bright and Early Books	Collins	Berenstain, Stan & Jan	He Bear, She Bear	7
		Frith, Michael	I'll Teach My Dog 100 Words	7
		Le Seig, Theo	Tooth Book, The	7
		Perkins, Al	Hand, Hand, Fingers, Thumb	7
Cambridge Reading	CUP	Becoming a R Stage A	Osprey (whole text)	7
		Becoming a R Stage B	Bridge, The (whole text)	7
			Forest, The (whole text)	7
		Becoming a R Stage C	Animal Wrestlers, The	7
			Atul's Christmas Hamster	7
			Chinese New Year, The	7
			Sleep Tight	7
			Story of Running Water, The	7
Cook, Ann	Longman	Monster Books	Monster and the Magic Umbrella	7
			Monster on the Bus	7
Discovery World	Heinemann	Stage E	Everyday Forces	7
			Maps	7
Fables from Aesop	Ginn	Books 1-6	Boy and the Lion, The	7
		Books 7-12	Ass in the Pond, The	7
			Donkey and the Lapdog, The	7
			Farmer and his Sons, The	7
		Books 13-18	Bear and the Travellers, The	7
			Monkey and the Fisherman, The	7
Foundations for Reading	Folens	Level 15 Experienced	Going to the Bank	7
		Level 16 Experienced	Going to Hospital	7
			Trouble in the Sandpit	7
		Level 17 Experienced	Amazing Maze, The	7
			Fatima's Tonsils	7
			Guide Dog, The	7
			My Sister's Getting Married	7

SERIES	PUBLISHER	SET (OR AUTHOR)	TITLE	BAND
Foundations for Reading	Folens	Level 17 Experienced	Snakes	7
			Waiting for the Rain	7
			Watching the Whales	7
Literacy Links Plus	Kingscourt	Early B	What Tommy Did	7
		Early C	Emma's Problem	7
		Early C	Goodness Gracious!	7
			Just My Luck	7
		Early D	How Fire Came To Earth	7
			How Turtle Raced Beaver	7
			Monkey And Fire	7
			Trees	7
			Vagabond Crabs	7
		Emergent C	Scarecrow, The	7
		Fluent A	Don't Worry	7
			Grandpa's Birthday	7
			Souvenirs	7
		Fluent B	Dogstar	7
			Little Girl and her Beetle, The	7
			Pumpkin House, The	7
		Fluent D	Boy who went to the North Wind, The	7
			Smallest Tree, The	7
			White Horse, The	7
One, Two, Three & Away	Collins	Main Books 5-8	Cat's Dance, The	7
			Stepping-stones, The	7
		Main Books 9-12	Lost Dog, The	7
			Three Robbers, The	7
		Yellow Platform 1-6	Dancing Ann and the Green-gruff-grackle	7
		Yellow Platform 7-10	Fire in the Magic Wood, The	7
			King of the Magic Mountains, The	7
			Witch Who Lived Next Door, The	7
Oxford Reading Tree	OUP	Stage 6 Owls	Outing, The	7
			Treasure Chest	7
		Stage 6 Robins	Dump, The	7
		Stage 6 Woodpeckers	Boy and the Tiger, The	7
		Stage 7 More Owls	Bully, The	7
			Chinese adventure	7
			Hunt for gold, The	7
			Jigsaw puzzle, The	7
			Motorway, The	7
			Roman adventure	7
		Stage 7 Owls	Broken Roof, The	7
			Lost Key, The	7
			Red Planet	7
		Stage 7 Woodpeckers	Kate and the Crocodile	7
		Stage 8 Magpies	Viking Adventure	7
			Litter Queen, The	7
		Stage 9 Magpies	Storm Castle	7
			Superdog	7
Oxford RT Branch Library	OUP	Two Bears Bks St 7A	Two Bears and the Fireworks	7
			Two Bears in the Snow	7
Pathways	Collins	Stage 2 Set C	Look Closer	7
		Stage 2 Set D	Owl's Party	7
			Tadpoles	7
		Stage 2 Set E	Hide And Seek	7
			Weather	7
		Stage 2 Set F	Hop, Hop, Kangaroo	7
			In The Park	7
		Stage 3 Set A	Make a Book Book, The	7

SERIES	PUBLISHER	SET (OR AUTHOR)	TITLE	BAND
Pathways	Collins	Stage 3 Set C	Shoes	7
PM Storybooks	Nelson	Turquoise Set A	Cabin in the Hills, The	7
			Jonathan Buys a Present	7
			Monkey Tricks	7
			Nelson, the Baby Elephant	7
			Toby and the Accident	7
			When the Volcano Erupted	7
		Turquoise Set B	Bird's Eye View	7
			Hailstorm, The	7
			Little Dinosaur Escapes	7
			Number Plates	7
			Rescuing Nelson	7
			Seat Belt Song, The	7
		Turquoise Set C	Ant City	7
			Grandad's Mask	7
			Jordan's Lucky day	7
			Nesting Place, The	7
			Race to Green End, The	7
			Riding to Craggy Rock	7
PM Traditional Tales	Nelson	Turquoise Level	Brave Little Tailor, The	7
			Elves and the Shoemaker, The	7
			Goldilocks and the Three Bears	7
			Little Red Riding Hood	7
			Stone Soup	7
			Ugly Duckling, The	7
Read It Yourself	Ladybird	Level 3	Jack and the Beanstalk	7
Reading 2000	Longmans	Storytime Reds	Giant's Garden, The	7
			River Run	7
			Treasure House, The	7
			Working Dogs	7
		Storytime Yellows	Cinderella	7
			Robbie's Trousers	7
Reading 360	Ginn	Level 5	All For Fun	7
			Home for a Bunny	7
			Old Tales	7
		Magic Circle Level 5	Big Green Bean, The	7
			Glerp, The	7
			Little Elephant Who Liked to Play, The	7
			Tail of the Mouse, The	7
			Wind and the Sun, The	7
		Magic Circle Level 7	Dancing Nadine	7
Reading 360 New	Ginn	Level 5	All For Fun	7
			Dogs and Whistles	7
			Faraway Tales	7
			In the Town	7
			Old Tales	7
		Little Bks L 4 Set 1	Who Took My Money?	7
		Little Bks L 5 Set 3	Magic Boots	7
			Old Dad Cunningham	7
Reading 360 Upstarts	Ginn	Level 4	Aunt Horrible and the Very Good Idea	7
			Emily the Spy	7
			Magic Carrot, The	7
			Not-so-Silly Billy	7
			Toby and the Space Cats	7
		Level 4 Extension	Cheese that Disappeared, The	7
			Dennis and the Dinosaur	7
			Monty the Monster Mouse	7
			Nancy and the Giant Spotted Newt	7

SERIES	PUBLISHER	SET (OR AUTHOR)	TITLE	BAND
Reading World	Longman	Level 2 Pack B	Fred's Snowman	7
			Lonely Stanley	7
Ready to Read	Nelson	Fluent Set A	Uncle Joe	7
		Fluent Set C	Big Bed, The	7
			Big Surprise, The	7
		Fluent Set D	Quilt for Kiri, A	7
Scholastic Books	Ashton Scholastic	Bridwell, Norman	Clifford, The Big Red Dog	7
		Galdone, Paul	Three Bears	7
		Krasilovsky, Phyllis	Man Who Didn't Do His Dishes, The	7
		Schwart, Alvin	There is a Carrot in my Ear	7
Story Chest	Kingscourt	Stage 4	Barrel Of Gold, The	7
			Clever Mr Brown	7
			Just Like Me	7
			Where is My Spider?	7
Storyworlds	Heinemann	Stage 8 Once Upon a Time	Ali, Hassan and the Donkey	7
			Little Red Riding Hood	7
			Three Wishes, The	7
			Tiger and the Jackal, The	7
		Stage 8 Our World	Highland cattle, The	7
			Highland Games, The	7
			Lost in the mist	7
			Rescue at sea	7
Sunshine	Heinemann	Level 1 Set G	One thousand currant buns	7
		Level 1 Set H	Giant's boy, The	7
			Mr Whisper	7
		Level 1 Set I	Boggywooga	7
			Letters for Mr James	7
			Mishi-na	7
			Quack, quack, quack!	7
		Level 1 Set J	Mum's diet	7
		Level 2	Road Robber	7
		Level 4	Dragon with a Cold	7
		Level 5	Cousin Kira	7
			Jojo and the Robot	7
			Library Day	7
			Morning Bath	7
		Level 6	Baby's Breakfast, The	7
			Pop Group, The	7
			Trouble with Heathrow, The	7
Sunshine New	Heinemann	Level 2	Emilio and the River	7
			Medal for Nicky, A	7
			Priscilla and the Dinosaurs	7
			William's Wild Wheelchair	7
		Level 3	I Like Shopping	7
			Supermarket Chase, The	7
			Too Busy for Pets!	7
			What's for Dinner, Dad?	7
		Level 4	Living in the Sky	7
			Marvellous Treasure, The	7
			Mrs Always Goes Shopping	7
			Mum's Getting Married	7
		Level 5	Greatest Binnie in the World, The	7
			Little Old Lady Who Danced on the Moon The	7
			What Shall I Do?	7
		Level 6	Best Dog in the Whole World, The	7
			My Big Family	7
Sunshine Spirals	Heinemann	Set 8	Bees	7
			Vosper's Boat, The	7

SERIES	PUBLISHER	SET (OR AUTHOR)	TITLE	BAND
Tiddlywinks	Kingscourt	Stage 1 Small Books	Kangaroo From Wooloomooloo, The	7
			Ten Loopy Caterpillars	7
			Yukadoos, The	7
		Stage 2	Magician's Lunch, The	7
		Stage 3	Morning Dance	7
			Most Scary Ghost, The	7
		Stage 4	Adventures of a Kite, The	7
			Smile, The	7
Tiddlywinks	Kingscourt	Stage 4	Train that Ran Away, The	7
		Stage 5	Plants of my Aunt, The	7
			Sophie's Singing Mother	7
		Stage 7	Clever Hamburger	7
Wonder World	Badger	Set 1	Buster McCluster	7
			Jack de Pert at the Supermarket	7
			Porridge	7
		Set 2	Bird Beaks	7
		Set 3	Planets, The	7
			Riding	7
		Set 4	How a Volcano is Formed	7
			Stone Works	7
Individual Titles	Little Mammoth	Ahlberg, Allan	Funnybones	7
	Collins	Ahlberg, Allan	Two Wheels Two Heads	7
	Picture Puffin	Ahlberg, Janet & Allen	Starting School	7
	Picture Puffin	Allen, Pamela	Who Sank the Boat?	7
	Picture Puffin	Armitage, Ronda	When Dad did the Washing	7
	Collins	Baker, Alan	Benjamin Bounces Back	7
	Heinemann	Bonsall, Crosby	And I Mean It Stanley	7
	Red Fox	Burningham, John	Would you Rather?	7
	Picture Puffin	Carle, Eric	Very Busy Spider, The	7
	Little Mammoth	Clarke, Gus	Eddi & Teddy	7
	Collins Pict Lions	Cole, Babette	Trouble with Gran, The	7
	Gerrard Publish'g	DeLage, Ida	Pink Pink	7
	Picture Puffin	Emberley, Ed	Drummer Hoff	7
	Picture Puffin	Gretz, Susanna	Bears who went to the Seaside, The	7
	Walker	Hayes, Sarah	Eat Up, Gemma	7
	Heinemann	Heilbroner, Joan	This is the House Where Jack Lives	7
	Hippo	Henderson, Kathy	Annie And The Birds	7
	Picture Puffin	Hill, Eric	Spot's First Christmas	7
	Mammoth	Hoff, Syd	Danny and the Dinosaur	7
	Heinemann	Hoff, Syd	Horse in Harry's Room, The	7
	Mammoth	Hoff, Syd	Stanley	7
	Picture Puffin	Holl, Adelaide	Rain Puddle, The	7
	Walker	Hughes, Shirley	All Shapes And Sizes	7
	Walker	Hughes, Shirley	Noisy	7
	Walker	Hughes, Shirley	Two Shoes, New Shoes	7
	Picture Puffin	Hutchins, Pat	Clocks and More Clocks	7
	Picture Puffin	Hutchins, Pat	Happy Birthday, Sam	7
	Julia MacRae	Hutchins, Pat	Silly Billy	7
	Picture Puffin	Hutchins, Pat	Tom and Sam	7
	Picture Puffin	Johnson, Crockett	Harold and the Purple Crayon	7
	Collins Pict Lions	Kerr, Judith	Mog and the Baby	7
	Picture Puffin	Kraus, Robert	Milton the Early Riser	7
	Collins Pict Lions	Lear, Edward	Owl and the Pussy Cat, The	7
	Walker	Lloyd, David	Duck	7
	Mammoth	Lobel, Arnold	Frog & Toad Are Friends	7
	Heinemann	Lobel, Arnold	Mouse Tales	7
	Heinemann	Lobel, Arnold	Small Pig	7
	Red Fox	Marshall, James	Three by the Sea	7

SERIES	PUBLISHER	SET (OR AUTHOR)	TITLE	BAND
Individual Titles	Picture Puffin	Martin, Bill	Polar Bear, Polar Bear, What Do You Hear	7
	Red Fox	McKee, David	Isobel's Noisy Tummy	7
	Red Fox	McKee, David	Tusk Tusk	7
	Magnet	McPhail, D	Bear's Toothache, The	7
	Walker	Oxenbury, Helen	Gran and Grandpa	7
	Walker	Oxenbury, Helen	Pippo Gets Lost	7
	Viking/Kestrel	Peppe, Rodney	Henry's Sunbathe	7
	Picture Puffin	Pienkowski, Jan	Meg and Mog	7
	Picture Puffin	Pienkowski, Jan	Meg at Sea	7
	Picture Puffin	Pienkowski, Jan	Meg on the Moon	7
	Picture Puffin	Pienkowski, Jan	Meg's Car	7
	Walker	Prater, John	Greatest Show on Earth, The	7
	Picture Puffin	Rose, Gerald	Trouble in the Ark	7
	Red Fox	Samuels, Vyanne	Boxed In	7
	Collins Pict Lions	Sowter	Maisie Middleton	7
	Picture Puffin	Sutton, Eve	My Cat Likes to Hide in Boxes	7
	Avon Camelot	Thaler, Mike	There's a Hippopotomus Under my Bed	7
	Picture Puffin	Vipont, Elfrida	Elephant and The Bad Baby, The	7
	Walker	Waddell, Martin	Let's Go Home, Little Bear	7
	Walker	Waddell, Martin	Once There Were Giants	7
	Walker	Waddell, Martin	Pig in the Pond, The	7
	Picture Puffin	Wells, Rosemary	Timothy Goes to School	7

Working Towards Level 2: Learning Focus

- Look through a variety of texts with growing independence to predict content, layout and story development.

- Read silently or quietly at a more rapid pace, taking note of punctuation and using it to keep track of longer sentences.

- Solve most unfamiliar words on the run.

- Adapt to fiction, non-fiction or poetic language with growing flexibility.

- Take more conscious account of literary effects used by writers.

TEXT CHARACTERISTICS

— sentence structures becoming longer and more complex

— story plot may be more involved and reflect the feelings of the writer

— wider variety of text genre but still illustrated

–- some books with chapters for more sustained reading

— characters are more distinctive and rounded than at earlier levels

— widening vocabulary and range of terminology

— non-fiction texts cover an increasing curriculum range

Benchmark Texts

Andrew's Bath	David McPhail/Penguin
The Wind Blew	Pat Hutchins/Picture Puffin
Giant Soup	Ready to Read/Nelson
The Tree Doctor	Sunshine/Heinemann
A Big Ball of String	Beginner Books/Collins
The Earthworm	Wonderworld/Badger Books

SERIES	PUBLISHER	SET (OR AUTHOR)	TITLE	BAND
All Aboard	Ginn	Stage 6 Pattern & Rhyme	Granny Big Boots	8
		Stage 8 Sam & Rosie	Bobby Glow-Worm	8
			Detective Tilak	8
			Toad Crossing	8
All Aboard Non Fiction	Ginn	Stage 5	Newts	8
Bangers and Mash	Longman	Books 7-12 Pack B	Bee and the Sea, The	8
			Bikes and Broomsticks	8
			Indians and red spots	8
			Toothday and birthday	8
			Wet paint	8
		Supplementary Books	Snatch and Grab	8
Beginner Books	Collins	Berenstain, Stan & Jan	Bears' Christmas, The	8
		Berenstain, Stan & Jan	Bears' Picnic, The	8
		Berenstain, Stan & Jan	Berenstein Bears and Missing Dinosaur Bone	8
		Gurney, Nancy	King, The Mice and the Cheese, The	8
		Holland, Marion	Big Ball of String, A	8
Book Project Fiction 1	Longman	Band 3 Read Aloud	Doodling Daniel	8
		Band 4 Read Aloud	Oriki and the monster who hated balloons	8
		Band 4 Read On	Crazy Cousins	8
			Missing Bear	8
			Surprise, Surprise!	8
Book Project Fiction 2	Longman	Band 2	Good Dog	8
Cambridge Reading	CUP	Becoming a R Stage A	Dinosaur (Whole text)	8
		Becoming a R Stage B	Harbour, The (whole text)	8
		Becoming a R Stage C	Bubbles	8
			Tiger Dreams	8
			Vicky's Box	8
Cook, Ann	Longman	Monster Books	Monster at School	8
			Monster Goes to School	8
			Monster Goes to the Museum	8
			Monster Goes to the Zoo	8
			Monster has a Party	8
Discovery World	Heinemann	Stage C	Day in the Life of a Victorian Child, A	8
			Eyes	8
			Minibeast Encyclopaedia	8
		Stage D	Amazing Eggs	8
			Change	8
			Looking at Light	8
			What's Underneath	8
Favourite Tales	Ladybird	-	Princess and the Pea, The	8
Literacy Links Plus	Kingscourt	Early D	Gallo and Zorro	8
		Fluent A	Awumpalema	8
			Cat Concert	8
			He Who Listens	8
			Tommy's Treasure	8
			Turtle Flies South	8
		Fluent B	Hare and the Tortoise, The	8
			Lonely Giant, The	8
			Mrs Pepperpot's Pet	8
			Oh, Columbus!	8
			Skeleton on the Bus, The	8
			T-shirt Triplets, The	8
		Fluent C	Look Out for Your Tail	8
			Trojan Horse, The	8
			Why the Sea is Salty	8
			Yellow Overalls	8
		Fluent D	Cabbage Princess, The	8
			Crosby Crocodile's Surprise	8

SERIES	PUBLISHER	SET (OR AUTHOR)	TITLE	BAND
Literacy Links Plus	Kingscourt	Fluent D	Misha Disappears	8
			Rapunzel	8
			Tony and the Butterfly	8
Oxford Reading Tree	OUP	Stage 10 Robins	Holiday, The	8
			Secret Plans, The	8
		Stage 6 More Robins	Max makes breakfast	8
		Stage 7 Owls	Lost in the Jungle	8
		Stage 7 Robins	Old Vase, The	8
		Stage 8 Magpies	Day in London, A	8
			Flying Carpet, The	8
			Rainbow Adventure, The	8
			Victorian Adventure	8
		Stage 8 Robins	Kate and the Sheep	8
		Stage 9 Magpies	Green Island	8
			Survival Adventure	8
		Stage 9 Robins	Proper Bike, A	8
Oxford RT Branch Library	OUP	Two Bears Bks St 7A	Two Bears at the Party	8
			Two Bears at the Seaside	8
Pathways	Collins	Stage 2 Set D	Hatseller and the Monkeys, The	8
		Stage 3 Set A	Letters From Lucy	8
		Stage 3 Set B	My Secret Pet	8
			Owl	8
		Stage 3 Set C	All Aboard	8
			Ginger, Where Are You?	8
			You Can't Park an Elephant	8
		Stage 3 Set D	Bronwen The Brave	8
PM Animal Facts	Nelson	Animals in the Wild	Brown Bears	8
			Elephants	8
			Hippos	8
			Kangaroos	8
			Lions and Tigers	8
			Monkeys and Apes	8
Read It Yourself	Ladybird	Level 2	Snow White and the Seven Dwarfs	8
		Level 4	Pied Piper of Hamelin, The	8
			Wizard of Oz	8
Reading 360	Ginn	Magic Circle Level 5	Angel The Pig	8
		Magic Circle Level 7	Yesterday I lost a Sneaker	8
Reading 360 Upstarts	Ginn	Level 4	Molly And The Giant	8
Reading World	Longman	Level 2 Pack B	Garden Rain	8
			Who Asked the Ants?	8
		Level 2 More Books	Milk Oh!	8
		Level 3	Don't Be Silly, Simon	8
			Lily and the Vacuum Cleaner	8
			Oh, Stanley!	8
			Poor Rabbit	8
			Toad Road	8
Ready to Read	Nelson	Fluent Set B	Paru Has a Bath	8
		Fluent Set C	Crocodile Lake	8
			Fishing Off the Wharf	8
			Football Fever	8
			Giant soup	8
			Good Knee for a Cat, A	8
			Magpie's Tail, The	8
Scholastic Books	Ashton Scholastic	Lobel, Arnold	Uncle Elephant	8
		Slobodkina, Esphyr	Caps For Sale	8
		Weisner, David	Jack and the Beanstalk (1)	8
Story Chest	Kingscourt	Stage 5	Captain Bumble	8
			Cat on the Roof	8

SERIES	PUBLISHER	SET (OR AUTHOR)	TITLE	BAND
Story Chest	Kingscourt	Stage 5	Day in Town, A	8
			Sunflower that Went Flop, The	8
			Well I Never	8
Storyworlds	Heinemann	Stage 8 Fantasy World	Kim and the computer giant	8
			Kim and the computer mouse	8
			Kim and the missing paint pot	8
			Kim and the Shape Dragon	8
Sunshine	Heinemann	Level 1 Set J	Ha-ha powder, The	8
			Secret of Spooky House, The	8
		Level 4	Wedding, The	8
		Level 6	Man Who Enjoyed Grumbling, The	8
		Level 7	Feeling Funny	8
			Tree Doctor, The	8
Sunshine New	Heinemann	Level 3	Moana's Island	8
		Level 5	Cobwebs, Elephants and Stars	8
			Old Bones	8
			Pile in Pete's Room, The	8
		Level 6	Biggest Pool of All, The	8
		Level 7	Paul Bunyan	8
			Stormalong's Great Sea Adventure	8
Tiddlywinks	Kingscourt	Stage 2	Wild Woolly Child, The	8
		Stage 3	Mr Wumple's Travels	8
			Walk with Grandpa, A	8
		Stage 4	Arguments	8
			Frown, The	8
			Mouse Monster	8
			Mr Beep	8
		Stage 5	As Luck Would Have It	8
			Earthquake, The	8
			Robber Pig and The Ginger Bee, The	8
			Robber Pig and The Green Eggs, The	8
		Stage 6	Mouse Wedding, The	8
			Sarah, The Bear and the Kangaroo	8
		Stage 7	Great Pumpkin Battle, The	8
Wonder World	Badger	Set 1	Food Trappers	8
			Shadows	8
			Where is my Caterpillar?	8
		Set 3	Earthworm, The	8
		Set 4	Crabs	8
			Mountain Gorillas	8
			Sharks	8
			Tails Can Tell	8
			What's Inside?	8
			Writer's Work, A	8
Individual Titles	Collins Pict Lions	Allen, Pamela	Mr Archimedes' Bath	8
	Corgi	Asch, Frank	Happy Birthday Mum	8
	Picture Puffin	Blake, Quentin	Patrick	8
	Heinemann	Bonsall, Crosby	Piggle	8
	Picture Puffin	Brandenberg, Franz	I Don't Feel Well	8
	Red Fox	Burningham, John	Come Away from the Water, Shirley	8
	Picture Puffin	Burningham, John	Mr Gumpy's Motor Car	8
	Picture Puffin	Burningham, John	Mr Gumpy's Outing	8
	Picture Corgi	Counsel, June	But Martin!	8
	Penguin/Kestrel	Denton, John	Colour Factory, The	8
	Picture Puffin	Dodd, Lynley	Hairy Maclary	8
	Picture Puffin	Dodd, Lynley	Slinky Malinky	8
	Picture Puffin	Flack, Marjorie	Angus And Wagtail Bess	8
	Seabury Press	Galdone, Paul	Little Tuppen	8

SERIES	PUBLISHER	SET (OR AUTHOR)	TITLE	BAND
Individual Titles	Picture Puffin	Gorden, Margaret	Wilberforce Goes on a Picnic	8
	Picture Puffin	Gorden, Margaret	Wilberforce Goes Shopping	8
	Picture Puffin	Hughes, Shirley	Lucy And Tom Go To School	8
	Heinemann	Hurd, Edith Thatcher	Johnny Lion's Rubber Boots	8
	Picture Puffin	Hutchins, Pat	Don't Forget the Bacon	8
	Picture Puffin	Hutchins, Pat	Surprise Party, The	8
	Picture Puffin	Hutchins, Pat	Wind Blew, The	8
	Picture Puffin	Kent, Jack	Fat Cat, The	8
	Gerrard Publish'g	Lexau, Joan	That's Just Fine and Who-o-o Did It	8
	Mammoth	Lobel, Arnold	Frog & Toad Together	8
	Red Fox	McKee, David	Two Can Toucan	8
	Red Fox	McKee, David	Two Monsters	8
	Puffin Playtime	McPhail, David	Andrew's Bath	8
	Merrill	Mille	Blossom Bird Goes South	8
	Heinemann	Minarik, E.H.	Father Bear Comes Home	8
	OUP	Paul, Korky	Winnie the Witch	8
	Methuen	Peppe, Rodney	Henry	8
	Picture Puffin	Pienkowski, Jan	Meg's Eggs	8
	Picture Puffin	Pienkowski, Jan	Mog at the Zoo	8
	Picture Puffin	Pienkowski, Jan	Mog's Mumps	8
	Picture Puffin	Potter, Beatrix	Tale Of Peter Rabbit, The	8
	Collins Pict Lions	Sendak, Maurice	Where the Wild Things Are	8
	Walker	Smee, Nicola	Finish the Story, Dad	8
	Methuen	Ungerer, Toni	Three Robbers, The	8
	Collins	Zacharias, Thomas	But Where is the Green Parrot?	8

Working Towards Level 2: Learning Focus

- Look through a variety of texts with growing independence to predict content, layout and story development.

- Read silently or quietly at a more rapid pace, taking note of punctuation and using it to keep track of longer sentences.

- Solve most unfamiliar words on the run.

- Adapt to fiction, non-fiction or poetic language with growing flexibility.

- Take more conscious account of literary effects used by writers.

TEXT CHARACTERISTICS

Somewhat more challenging than in BAND 2C

— sentence structures becoming longer and more complex

— story plot may be more involved and reflect the feelings of the writer

— wider variety of text genre but still illustrated

— some books with chapters for more sustained reading

— characters are more distinctive and rounded than at earlier levels

— widening vocabulary and range of terminology

— non-fiction texts cover an increasing curriculum range

Benchmark Texts

Rosie's Babies	Martin Waddell/Walker
Scots Pine	Cambridge Reading/CUP
Umbrellas	New Sunshine/Heinemann
The Bracelet	Reading World/Longman
Lavender the Library Cat	Tiddlywinks/Kingscourt

SERIES	PUBLISHER	SET (OR AUTHOR)	TITLE	BAND
All Aboard	Ginn	Stage 7 Pattern & Rhyme	Fussy Freda	9
			Ghost Next Door, The	9
			Little Eight John	9
		Stage 8 Sam & Rosie	Mountain Rescue	9
Book Project Fiction 1	Longman	Band 4 Read On	Anansi at the Pool	9
			Bhalloo the Greedy Bear	9
			Turtle and the Crane, The	9
Book Project Fiction 2	Longman	Band 1	Shadow Dance, The	9
			Webster and the Treacle Toffee	9
		Band 2	Clever Dog, Webster	9
			Lelang and Julie save the day	9
			Lelang's new friend	9
			Trouble for Lelang and Julie	9
		Band 3	Joshua's Junk	9
Cambridge Reading	CUP	Becoming a R Stage C	Scots Pine, The (whole text)	9
Discovery World	Heinemann	Stage E	Animal Movement	9
			How to Choose a Pet	9
			Insect Body Parts	9
			Pre-historic Record Breakers	9
		Stage F	My Holiday Diary	9
			Science Dictionary	9
Literacy Links Plus	Kingscourt	Fluent A	Scare-kid	9
		Fluent B	Bull in a China Shop, A	9
			Oogly Gum Chasing Gum, The	9
		Fluent C	Spider	9
			Vicky the High Jumper	9
		Fluent D	Three Magicians, The	9
One, Two, Three & Away	Collins	Main Books 9-12	Boat on Deep River, A	9
			House in Dark Woods, The	9
		Yellow Platform 7-10	Horse that Flew in the Moonlight, The	9
Oxford Reading Tree	OUP	Stage 7 More Robins	Long journey, The	9
			Mum's new car	9
		Stage 7 Robins	William and the Dog	9
		Stage 8 More Robins	Surprise, The	9
			William's mistake	9
		Stage 8 Robins	Emergency, The	9
		Stage 9 Magpies	Quest, The	9
		Stage 9 More Robins	Hamid does his best	9
			Treasure hunt, The	9
			William and the Pied Piper	9
		Stage 9 Robins	Photograph, The	9
			Village Show, The	9
Pathways	Collins	Stage 3 Set D	I Want a Party!	9
			Soil	9
PM Animal Facts	Nelson	Farm Animals	Cattle	9
			Chickens	9
			Goats	9
			Horses	9
			Pigs	9
			Sheep	9
Reading World	Longman	Level 3	Bracelet, The	9
			Jimmy James	9
			Rosie's New Pet	9
			Witch Tricks	9
Ready to Read	Nelson	Fluent Set B	How Do You Measure a Dinosaur?	9
			Poppy, The	9
		Fluent Set D	How to Weigh an Elephant	9
			I Can See the Leaves	9

SERIES	PUBLISHER	SET (OR AUTHOR)	TITLE	BAND
Ready to Read	Nelson	Fluent Set D	Maui and the Sun	9
			Rats, Bats, and Black Puddings	9
			So You Want to Move a Building?	9
			Why There Are Shooting Stars	9
			Words	9
Storyworlds	Heinemann	Stage 9 Fantasy World	Adventure at sea	9
			Journey into the earth, The	9
			Magic carpet, The	9
			Voyage into space	9
		Stage 9 Our World	Big Barry Baker and the bullies	9
			Big Barry Baker in big trouble	9
			Big Barry Baker on the stage	9
			Big Barry Baker's parcel	9
Sunshine	Heinemann	Level 7	Garden Party	9
			Muppy's Ball	9
Sunshine New	Heinemann	Level 2 Non-fiction	Crabs	9
			Umbrellas	9
		Level 6	Camping with Our Dad	9
			Grandma's Elephants	9
Tiddlywinks	Kingscourt	Stage 4	Silly Old Story, A	9
		Stage 5	Beautiful Pig	9
			Not so Quiet Evening, A	9
		Stage 6	Cake, The	9
			Catten, The	9
			Lavender the Library Cat	9
			Squeak in the Gate	9
			Tinny Tiny Tinker	9
Wonderworld	Badger	Set 2	Fly Away Home	9
			Houses	9
		Set 3	Flour	9
			I Spy a Fly	9
		Set 4	Acid Rain	9
Individual Titles	Walker	Waddell, Martin	Rosie's Babies	9

Working Towards Level 3: Learning Objectives

- Read silently most of the time.
- Sustain interest in longer text, returning to it easily after a break.
- Use text more fully as a reference and as a model.
- Search for and find information in texts more flexibly.
- Notice the spelling of unfamiliar words and relate to known words.
- Show increased awareness of vocabulary and precise meaning.
- Express reasoned opinions about what is read.
- Offer and discuss interpretations of text.

TEXT CHARACTERISTICS

- widening range of genre and writing style
- storyline or theme may be sustained over a longer period of time with chapters or sub-sections of text
- sentence structures may be longer with more subordinate phrases or clauses
- characters may be more fully developed
- more than one point of view expressed within the text
- information or action may be implied rather than explicit
- texts may contain more metaphorical or technical language
- non-fiction texts placed in a broader context and include more detailed information

Benchmark Texts

Pizza	Brian Moses/Wayland
Lucy Meets a Dragon	Literacy Links Plus/Kingscourt
Jamaica and Brianna	Juanita Havill/Mammoth
Dogger	Shirley Hughes/Collins Picture Lions
Discovery	Oxford Reading Tree/OUP

SERIES	PUBLISHER	SET (OR AUTHOR)	TITLE	BAND
All Aboard	Ginn	Stage 7 Sam & Rosie	Magic Smell, The	10
Book Project Fiction 1	Longman	Band 4 Read On	Giddy Space	10
Book Project Fiction 2	Longman	Band 1	Billy Fishbone	10
		Band 3	Bumbles, The	10
			Crazy Crocs	10
			Horrible Baby	10
		Band 4	BJ Dog	10
			Henry Seamouse	10
			Rachel and the Difference Thief	10
			Rachel versus Bonecrusher the Mighty	10
			Seagull Sweaters	10
Cambridge Reading	CUP	Becoming a R Stage C	Animal Senses (whole text)	10
Discovery World	Heinemann	Stage F	Keeping Tadpoles Alive	10
Literacy Links Plus	Kingscourt	Fluent A	Morning Star	10
			Tongues	10
		Fluent B	Lucy Meets a Dragon	10
			Tom's Handplant	10
		Fluent C	Bringing the Sea Back Home	10
			Three Sillies, The	10
		Fluent D	Charlie	10
			Grandad	10
			I'm a Chef	10
Oxford Reading Tree	OUP	Stage 10 More Robins	Discovery	10
			Ghost tricks	10
Pathways	Collins	Stage 3 Set B	Hattie Hates Hats	10
			Rain Arrow, The	10
		Stage 3 Set C	Then And Now	10
		Stage 3 Set D	Monkeys	10
		Stage 4 Set C	Just a Touch of Magic	10
Storyworlds	Heinemann	Stage 9 Animal World	Canal boat cat	10
			Cherry blossom cat	10
			City cat	10
			Cobra cat	10
		Stage 9 Once Upon a Time	Hansel and Gretel	10
			Little Girl and the Bear, The	10
			Two Giants, The	10
			Jack and the Beanstalk	10
Sunshine New	Heinemann	Level 4 Non-fiction	Bird Behaviour: Living Together	10
			Boats Afloat	10
		Level 5 Non-fiction	Birds of the City	10
			Story of You, The	10
Tiddlywinks	Kingscourt	Stage 4	Long Grass of Tumbledown Road, The	10
Wonderworld	Badger	Set 3	Eggs, Eggs, Eggs	10
			Ships	10
		Set 4	Clothes	10
			Potter in Fiji, A	10
			Whales	10
Individual Titles	Nelson	Cartwright, Pauline	In My Imagination	10
	Picture Puffin	Gretz, Suzanna	Bears Who Stayed Indoors, The	10
	Mammoth	Havill, Juanita	Jamaica and Brianna	10
	Frances Lincoln	Hoffman, Mary	Amazing Grace	10
	Collins Pict Lions	Hughes, Shirley	Dogger	10
	Wayland	Moses, Brian	Pizza	10
	Red Fox	Selway, Martina	Wish You Were Here	10
	Tamarind	Wilkins, Verna	Dave and the Tooth Fairy	10

Listing of Titles in Alphabetical Order

TITLE	SERIES	PUBLISHER	SET (OR AUTHOR)	BAND
1 Hunter		Picture Puffin	Hutchins, Pat	2
About Helicopters, About Animals	Reading 360 New	Ginn	Little Bks L 4 Set 1	6
Accident, The	All Aboard	Ginn	Stage 3 Set A Patt & Rh	3
Accident, The	Foundations for Reading	Folens	Level 15 Experienced	6
Acid Rain	Wonder World	Badger	Set 4	9
Across The Stream		Picture Puffin	Ginsberg, Mirra	4
Adam Goes Shopping	Oxford Reading Tree	OUP	Stage 4 More Sparrows	3
Adam's Car	Oxford Reading Tree	OUP	Stage 4 More Sparrows	3
Adventure at sea	Storyworlds	Heinemann	Stage 9 Fantasy World	9
Adventures of a Kite, The	Tiddlywinks	Kingscourt	Stage 4	7
Aeroplane, The	Sunrise	Heinemann		2
Afloat in a Boat	Cambridge Reading	CUP	Begin to Read Stage B	4
After School	Foundations for Reading	Folens	Level 9 Early	4
After the flood	PM Storybooks	Nelson	Green Set B	5
Ahhh, Said The Stork		Picturemac	Rose, Gerald	6
Albert The Albatross		Heinemann	Hoff, Syd	6
Alex at the Fair	One, Two, Three & Away	Collins	Pre-reader 9a-12a	2
Ali, Hassan and the Donkey	Storyworlds	Heinemann	Stage 8 Once Upon a Time	7
Alien at the zoo	Sunshine	Heinemann	Level 1 Non-fiction	4
Ali's Story	Sunshine Spirals	Heinemann	Set 6	4
All Aboard	Pathways	Collins	Stage 3 Set C	8
All by Myself	Cambridge Reading	CUP	Becoming a R Stage B	5
All By Myself	Foundations for Reading	Folens	Level 5 Emergent	3
All Fall Down	Oxford RT Branch Library	OUP	Wildsmith Bks St 2A	2
All Fall Down!	Cambridge Reading	CUP	Begin to Read Stage B	3
All For Fun	Reading 360	Ginn	Level 5	7
All For Fun	Reading 360 New	Ginn	Level 5	7
All Join In	Literacy Links Plus	Kingscourt	Emergent D	2
All Kinds of Things	Ready to Read	Nelson	Emergent Set A	1
All Shapes And Sizes		Walker	Hughes, Shirley	7
Along Came Greedy Cat	Ready to Read	Nelson	Early Set C	4
Along Came Tom		Red Fox	Prater, John	5
Along comes Jake	Sunshine	Heinemann	Level 1 Set F	3
Along The Street	Link Up	Collins	Level 2	5
Amazing Eggs	Discovery World	Heinemann	Stage D	8
Amazing Grace		Frances Lincoln	Hoffman, Mary	10
Amazing Maze, The	Foundations for Reading	Folens	Level 17 Experienced	7
Amazing Popple Seed, The	Tiddlywinks	Kingscourt	Stage 1 Small Books	5
Amazing Race, The	Sunshine Spirals Starters	Heinemann	Set C	1
Anansi at the Pool	Book Project Fiction 1	Longman	Band 4 Read On	9
And I Mean It Stanley		Heinemann	Bonsall, Crosby	7
Andrew's Bath		Puffin Playtime	McPhail, David	8
Angel The Pig	Reading 360	Ginn	Magic Circle Level 5	8
Angus And The Cat		Picture Puffin	Flack, Marjorie	6
Angus And Wagtail Bess		Picture Puffin	Flack, Marjorie	8
Animal Babies		Sainsbury	Mastrogiovanni, O	3
Animal Friends	Reading 360 New	Ginn	Level 4	6
Animal Homes	All Aboard Non Fiction	Ginn	Stage 3	5
Animal Homes	Pathways	Collins	Stage 1 Set B	2
Animal House	Pathways	Collins	Stage 2 Set B	4
Animal Legs	Discovery World	Heinemann	Stage B	1
Animal Movement	Discovery World	Heinemann	Stage E	9
Animal Olympics, The	Sunshine Spirals	Heinemann	Set 6	4
Animal Senses (whole text)	Cambridge Reading	CUP	Becoming a R Stage C	10
Animal Tracks	Reading 360 New	Ginn	Level 5	6
Animal Tracks	Wonder World	Badger	Set 2	2
Animal Wrestlers, The	Cambridge Reading	CUP	Becoming a R Stage C	7
Animals Grow	Wonder World	Badger	Set 2	6

TITLE	SERIES	PUBLISHER	SET (OR AUTHOR)	BAND
Anna Comes To Town	Reading 2000	Longmans	Storytime Yellows	6
Annie And The Birds		Hippo	Henderson, Kathy	7
Ant and the Dove, The	Storyworlds	Heinemann	Stage 4 Once Upon a Time	3
Ant City	PM Storybooks	Nelson	Turquoise Set C	7
Ant Eggs	Bangers and Mash	Longman	Books 1A-6A	5
Ants	Wonder World	Badger	Set 2	5
Ants Love Picnics Too	Literacy Links Plus	Kingscourt	Emergent B	2
Apple Bird, The	Oxford RT Branch Library	OUP	Wildsmith Bks St 1A	1
Apple On The Bed	Pathways	Collins	Stage 0 Set D	1
Apple Tree, The	Reading 360 Upstarts	Ginn	Level 3 Extension	5
Apple, The	Sunshine Spirals	Heinemann	Set 2	2
April Fool	Reading World	Longman	Level 2 Pack B	6
Are you a ladybird?	Sunshine	Heinemann	Level 1 Non-fiction	4
Are You My Mother?	Beginner Books	Collins	Eastman, P.D.	6
Are You There, Bear?		Picture Puffin	Maris, Ron	4
Arguments	Tiddlywinks	Kingscourt	Stage 4	8
Arrow, The		OUP	Brychta, Alex	4
As Luck Would Have It	Tiddlywinks	Kingscourt	Stage 5	8
Ass in the Lion's Skin, The	Fables from Aesop	Ginn	Books 1-6	6
Ass in the Pond, The	Fables from Aesop	Ginn	Books 7-12	7
Astronaut, The	Sunshine New	Heinemann	Level 1 Set B	2
Astronauts, The	Foundations for Reading	Folens	Level 8 Early	3
At Night	Literacy Links Plus	Kingscourt	Early A	3
At Night	Reading 360 New	Ginn	Little Bks L 2 Set 2	3
At School	Sunrise	Heinemann		1
At The Dock		Nelson	Speer, Albert	3
At The Fair	Sunshine Spirals	Heinemann	Set 4	3
At The Library	PM Storybook Starters	Nelson	Set 2	1
At the Park	All Aboard Non Fiction	Ginn	Stage 4	5
At the Park	Oxford Reading Tree	OUP	Stage 2 Wrens	2
At the Pet Shop	Foundations for Reading	Folens	Level 12 Early	5
At the Pool	Foundations for Reading	Folens	Level 4 Emergent	2
At the Pool	Oxford Reading Tree	OUP	Stage 3 More Stories B	3
At The Seaside	Oxford Reading Tree	OUP	Stage 3 More Stories A	3
At the Water Hole	Foundations for Reading	Folens	Level 15 Experienced	6
At the Zoo	PM Storybook Starters	Nelson	Set 1	1
At the Zoo	Reading 360	Ginn	Level 4	5
At the Zoo	Sunshine Spirals	Heinemann	Set 2	2
Atul's Christmas Hamster	Cambridge Reading	CUP	Becoming a R Stage C	7
Aunt Horrible and the Very Good Idea	Reading 360 Upstarts	Ginn	Level 4	7
Aunty Maria and the Cat	Sunshine Spirals	Heinemann	Set 5	4
Awumpalema	Literacy Links Plus	Kingscourt	Fluent A	8

B				
Babies	Ginn Science Info Bks	Ginn	Year 1	4
Babies Are Yuk	Reading 360 Upstarts	Ginn	Level 3	6
Baby at Our House, The	Foundations for Reading	Folens	Level 9 Early	4
Baby Bear Goes Fishing	PM Storybooks	Nelson	Yellow Set A	3
Baby Bear's Present	PM Storybooks	Nelson	Blue Set A	4
Baby Elephant Gets Lost	Foundations for Reading	Folens	Level 4 Emergent	3
Baby Elephant's New Bike	Foundations for Reading	Folens	Level 11 Early	4
Baby Elephant's Sneeze	Foundations for Reading	Folens	Level 6 Early	3
Baby Gets Dressed	Sunshine	Heinemann	Level 1 Set A	1
Baby Goz		Frances Lincoln	Weatherill, Steve	3
Baby Grumble	Reading World	Longman	Level 1: More Books	3
Baby Hippo	PM Storybooks	Nelson	Yellow Set B	3
Baby in the Trolley	Foundations for Reading	Folens	Level 3 Emergent	2
Baby Lamb's First Drink	PM Storybooks	Nelson	Red Set A	2
Baby owls, The	PM Storybooks	Nelson	Red Set B	2

TITLE	SERIES	PUBLISHER	SET (OR AUTHOR)	BAND
Baby, The		Red Fox	Burningham, John	5
Baby's Breakfast, The	Sunshine	Heinemann	Level 6	7
Baby's Catalogue, The		Picture Puffin	Ahlberg, Janet & Allen	3
Babysitter, The	PM Storybooks	Nelson	Green Set B	5
Babysitter, The	Reading 360 New	Ginn	Little Bks L 3 Set 3	4
Baby-sitter, The	Oxford Reading Tree	OUP	Stage 2 More Stories A	3
Babysitters, The	Sunshine Spirals	Heinemann	Set 4	3
Bad Boy Billy!	Cambridge Reading	CUP	Becoming a R Stage A	5
Bag of coal, The	Storyworlds	Heinemann	Stage 5 Fantasy World	4
Bag Of Smiles, The	Sunshine Spirals	Heinemann	Set 8	6
Baking	Reading 360 New	Ginn	Little Bks L 1 Set 2	2
Ball Bounced, The		Gollancz	Tafuri, Nancy	2
Ball Games	PM Storybook Starters	Nelson	Set 2	1
Balloon, The	All Aboard	Ginn	Easy Start Sam & Rosie	1
Balloon, The	Oxford Reading Tree	OUP	Stage 4 More Stories A	5
Balloon, The	Oxford Reading Tree	OUP	Stage 4 Playscripts	3
Balloons, The	Reading 360 Upstarts	Ginn	Level 1 Extension	3
Balloons, The	Sunshine Spirals	Heinemann	Set 1	1
Band, The	Oxford Reading Tree	OUP	Stage 3 More Wrens	2
Bang	Literacy Links Plus	Kingscourt	Early A	4
Barbecue, The	Oxford Reading Tree	OUP	Stage 3 More Stories B	4
Barbecue, The	Sunrise	Heinemann		1
Barn Dance	Story Chest	Kingscourt	Ready-set-go Set BB	3
Barnaby's New House, The	Literacy Links Plus	Kingscourt	Early D	5
Barrel Of Gold, The	Story Chest	Kingscourt	Stage 4	7
Baseball Game, The	Foundations for Reading	Folens	Level 11 Early	4
Basketball	Wonder World	Badger	Set 1	1
Bat in a Hat	All Aboard	Ginn	Easy Start Patt & Rhyme	1
Bath Water's Hot		Walker	Hughes, Shirley	6
Bath, The	Sunshine Spirals Starters	Heinemann	Set C	1
Bathtime	Wonder World	Badger	Set 2	1
Bay Run	Foundations for Reading	Folens	Level 4 Emergent	3
Be Quiet!	Sunshine Spirals Starters	Heinemann	Set C	1
Bear and the Travellers, The	Fables from Aesop	Ginn	Books 13-18	7
Bear in a Hole, A	Open Door	Nelson	Green Fun Books	2
Bear in the Park	All Aboard	Ginn	Stage 4 Set A Sam & Ros	5
Bear that wouldn't growl, The	Storyworlds	Heinemann	Stage 8 Animal World	6
Bears and the Honey, The	Storyworlds	Heinemann	Stage 2 Once Upon a Time	2
Bears' Christmas, The	Beginner Books	Collins	Berenstain, Stan & Jan	8
Bears In The Night	Bright and Early Books	Collins	Berenstain, Stan & Jan	2
Bears on Wheels	Bright and Early Books	Collins	Berenstain, Stan & Jan	3
Bears' Picnic, The	Beginner Books	Collins	Berenstain, Stan & Jan	8
Bears' Picnic, The	Story Chest	Kingscourt	Ready-set-go Set AA	2
Bear's Toothache, The		Magnet	McPhail, D	7
Bears Who Stayed Indoors, The		Picture Puffin	Gretz, Suzanna	10
Bears Who Went to the Seaside, The		Picture Puffin	Gretz, Susanna	7
Beautiful Flowers	Wonder World	Badger	Set 3	2
Beautiful Pig	Tiddlywinks	Kingscourt	Stage 5	9
Because a Little Bug Went Ka-choo!	Beginner Books	Collins	Stone, Rosetta	6
Bee and the Sea, The	Bangers and Mash	Longman	Books 7-12 Pack B	8
Bee in my Bonnet, A	Pathways	Collins	Stage 4 Set C	6
Bee, The	Reading 360 New	Ginn	Little Bks L 2 Set 2	3
Bee, The	Story Chest	Kingscourt	Ready-set-go Set B	2
Beep, Beep, Beep	Foundations for Reading	Folens	Level 3 Emergent	2
Bees	Sunshine Spirals	Heinemann	Set 8	7
Behind the Rocks	Wonder World	Badger	Set 1	4
Ben	Reading 360	Ginn	Level 1	2
Ben and Lad	Reading 360	Ginn	Level 2	3

TITLE	SERIES	PUBLISHER	SET (OR AUTHOR)	BAND
Ben and Sparky	Reading 360	Ginn	Level 2	4
Ben and The Bear		Walker	Riddell, Chris	6
Ben and the Duck	Reading 360 New	Ginn	Level 2	3
Ben Biggins' box	Book Project Fiction 1	Longman	Band 1 Read On	3
Ben Biggins' House	Book Project Fiction 1	Longman	Band 1 Read Aloud	6
Ben Biggins' playtime	Book Project Fiction 1	Longman	Band 1 Read On Specials	2
Ben Biggins' socks	Book Project Fiction 1	Longman	Band 1 Read On Specials	2
Ben Biggins' tummy	Book Project Fiction 1	Longman	Band 1 Read On	2
Ben Biggins' week	Book Project Fiction 1	Longman	Band 1 Read On Specials	2
Ben the Bold	Literacy Links Plus	Kingscourt	Emergent C	3
Benjamin and the Little Fox	One, Two, Three & Away	Collins	Green Platform 7-10	5
Benjamin Bounces Back		Collins	Baker, Alan	7
Benjamin, the Witch and the Donkey	One, Two, Three & Away	Collins	Blue Platform 11-16	3
Ben's Banana	Foundations for Reading	Folens	Level 4 Emergent	3
Ben's Dad	PM Storybooks	Nelson	Yellow Set A	3
Ben's Red Car	PM Storybook Starters	Nelson	Set 2	1
Ben's Teddy Bear	PM Storybooks	Nelson	Red Set A	2
Ben's Tooth	PM Storybooks	Nelson	Green Set A	5
Ben's Treasure Hunt	PM Storybooks	Nelson	Red Set A	2
Berenstein Bears and Missing Dinosaur Bone	Beginner Books	Collins	Berenstain, Stan & Jan	8
Bertie and the Bear		Picture Puffin	Allen, Pamela	6
Best Cake, The	PM Storybooks	Nelson	Blue Set A	4
Best Children in the World, The	Story Chest	Kingscourt	Ready-set-go Set DD	4
Best Dog in the Whole World, The	Sunshine New	Heinemann	Level 6	7
Best Duster, The	Bangers and Mash	Longman	Books 1-6 Pack A	7
Best Guess, The	Foundations for Reading	Folens	Level 12 Early	5
Best Nest, The	Beginner Books	Collins	Eastman, P.D.	7
Best Watchdog in the World, The	Reading 360 Upstarts	Ginn	Level 4 Extension	6
Bet You Can't!		Walker	Dale, Penny	3
Between the Tides	Wonder World	Badger	Set 3	6
Bhalloo the Greedy Bear	Book Project Fiction 1	Longman	Band 4 Read On	9
Bicycle, The	Story Chest	Kingscourt	Get-ready Set B	2
Biff's Aeroplane	Oxford Reading Tree	OUP	Stage 2 More Stories B	3
Big and Green	Wonder World	Badger	Set 1	2
Big and Little	Foundations for Reading	Folens	Level 1 Emergent	1
Big and Little	One, Two, Three & Away	Collins	Pre-reader 5-8	2
Big and little	Sunshine	Heinemann	Level 1 Set C	2
Big Bad Bill	All Aboard	Ginn	Stage 6 Pattern & Rhyme	6
Big Ball of String, A	Beginner Books	Collins	Holland, Marion	8
Big Barry Baker and the bullies	Storyworlds	Heinemann	Stage 9 Our World	9
Big Barry Baker in big trouble	Storyworlds	Heinemann	Stage 9 Our World	9
Big Barry Baker on the stage	Storyworlds	Heinemann	Stage 9 Our World	9
Big Barry Baker's parcel	Storyworlds	Heinemann	Stage 9 Our World	9
Big Bed, The	Ready to Read	Nelson	Fluent Set C	7
Big Dog and the Little White Cat, The	One, Two, Three & Away	Collins	Blue Platform 1-6	2
Big Dog, Little Dog	Beginner Books	Collins	Eastman, P.D.	6
Big Family, The	Sunshine	Heinemann	Level 3	6
Big Game, The	Ready to Read	Nelson	Fluent Set A	4
Big Green Bean, The	Reading 360	Ginn	Magic Circle Level 5	7
Big Hill, The	Story Chest	Kingscourt	Get-ready Set B	2
Big Kick, The	PM Storybooks	Nelson	Red Set A	2
Big Laugh, The	Sunshine New	Heinemann	Level 1 Set I	5
Big Man and the Little Mouse, The	One, Two, Three & Away	Collins	Pre-reader 5b-8b	2
Big Man, the Witch and the Donkey, The	One, Two, Three & Away	Collins	Green Platform 1-6	6
Big Race, The	Sunshine Spirals	Heinemann	Set 1	3
Big Round Up, The	Wonder World	Badger	Set 2	5
Big Sister Rosie	All Aboard	Ginn	Stage 4 Set A Sam & Ros	5
Big Sneeze, The	Foundations for Reading	Folens	Level 6 Early	3

TITLE	SERIES	PUBLISHER	SET (OR AUTHOR)	BAND
Big snowball, The	Storyworlds	Heinemann	Stage 5 Fantasy World	4
Big Surprise, The	Ready to Read	Nelson	Fluent Set C	7
Big Surprise, The	Storyworlds	Heinemann	Stage 2 Animal World	1
Big Things	PM Storybook Starters	Nelson	Set 1	1
Big Toe, The	Story Chest	Kingscourt	Small Read-together	5
Big Turnip, The	All Aboard	Ginn	Stage 3 Set B Patt & Rh	4
Bigger and Biggest	All Aboard Non Fiction	Ginn	Stage 1 Intro	1
Biggest and Smallest	All Aboard Non Fiction	Ginn	Stage 5	6
Biggest Cake in the World, The	Ready to Read	Nelson	Early Set A	4
Biggest Pool of All, The	Sunshine New	Heinemann	Level 6	8
Biggest Tree, The	PM Storybooks	Nelson	Orange Set A	6
Bike Lesson, The	Beginner Books	Collins	Berenstain, Stan & Jan	6
Bike Parade, The	Literacy Links Plus	Kingscourt	Emergent B	2
Bikes	Foundations for Reading	Folens	Level 10 Early	5
Bikes and Broomsticks	Bangers and Mash	Longman	Books 7-12 Pack B	8
Bill had a Bus	Open Door	Nelson	Green Fun Books	2
Billy and Percy Green	One, Two, Three & Away	Collins	Red Platform 1-6	6
Billy Blue-hat	One, Two, Three & Away	Collins	Introductory A-D	2
Billy Blue-hat and the Duck-pond	One, Two, Three & Away	Collins	Main Books 1-2B	4
Billy Blue-hat and the Frog	One, Two, Three & Away	Collins	Blue Platform 7-10	3
Billy Blue-hat and the Red Mask	One, Two, Three & Away	Collins	Pre-reader 9b-12b	2
Billy Blue-hat and the Snowman	One, Two, Three & Away	Collins	Pre-reader 1b-4b	2
Billy Bluehat's Day	One, Two, Three & Away	Collins	Main Books 5-8	6
Billy Fishbone	Book Project Fiction 2	Longman	Band 1	10
Billy Goats Gruff	Read It Yourself	Ladybird	Level 1	4
Billy Magee's New Car	Foundations for Reading	Folens	Level 16 Experienced	6
Billy went to School	One, Two, Three & Away	Collins	Pre-reader 9-12	2
Billy's Box	Cambridge Reading	CUP	Becoming a R Stage B	5
Billy's Picture	One, Two, Three & Away	Collins	Pre-reader 9a-12a	2
Bingo and the bone	Storyworlds	Heinemann	Stage 2 Animal World	2
Bingo wants to play	Storyworlds	Heinemann	Stage 2 Animal World	2
Bird Barn, The	Foundations for Reading	Folens	Level 7 Early	4
Bird Behaviour: Living Together	Sunshine New	Heinemann	Level 4 Non-fiction	10
Birds	All Aboard	Ginn	Easy Start Patt & Rhyme	2
Birds	All Aboard Non Fiction	Ginn	Stage 2	3
Bird's Eye View	PM Storybooks	Nelson	Turquoise Set B	7
Bird's Nests	Wonder World	Badger	Set 4	5
Birds of the City	Sunshine New	Heinemann	Level 5 Non-fiction	10
Birthday balloons	PM Storybooks	Nelson	Blue Set B	4
Birthday cake for Ben, A	PM Storybooks	Nelson	Red Set B	2
Birthday Cake, The	Literacy Links Plus	Kingscourt	Emergent B	2
Birthday Cake, The	Story Chest	Kingscourt	Stage 2	5
Birthday cake, The	Sunshine	Heinemann	Level 1 Set A	1
Birthday Party, A	Sunshine Spirals	Heinemann	Set 1	2
Birthday Party, The	Sunrise	Heinemann		1
Birthdays	Foundations for Reading	Folens	Level 2 Emergent	1
BJ Dog	Book Project Fiction 2	Longman	Band 4	10
Blackberries	PM Storybooks	Nelson	Yellow Set A	3
Blackberry Pudding	All Aboard	Ginn	Stage 4 Set B Sam & Ros	5
Blackbird's Nest	Ready to Read	Nelson	Early Set D	4
Blackboard Bear		Walker	Alexander, Martha	5
Blanket, The		Red Fox	Burningham, John	3
Blossom Bird Goes South		Merrill	Mille	8
Blowing Bubbles	Cambridge Reading	CUP	Begin to Read Stage B	2
Blue	One, Two, Three & Away	Collins	Pre-reader 1-4	1
Blue Day	Literacy Links Plus	Kingscourt	Emergent A	2
Blue Jackal, The	All Aboard	Ginn	Stage 5 Set B Patt & Rh	5
Blue Moo	Book Project Fiction 2	Longman	Band 1	7

TITLE	SERIES	PUBLISHER	SET (OR AUTHOR)	BAND
Blueberry Muffins	Story Chest	Kingscourt	Ready-set-go Set DD	4
Blueberry Pie, The	Sunshine Spirals	Heinemann	Set 4	3
BMX Billy	Literacy Links Plus	Kingscourt	Early C	4
Boasting Monsters, The	Book Project Fiction 1	Longman	Band 3 Read On	5
Boat on Deep River, A	One, Two, Three & Away	Collins	Main Books 9-12	9
Boat, The	Ready to Read	Nelson	Emergent Set A	1
Boats Afloat	Sunshine New	Heinemann	Level 4 Non-fiction	10
Bobby and the Alien	All Aboard	Ginn	Stage 5 Set B Sam & Ros	6
Bobby Bear and the Rabbit	Reading 360 Upstarts	Ginn	Level 1 Extension	3
Bobby Glow-Worm	All Aboard	Ginn	Stage 8 Sam & Rosie	8
Bobby's Bad Day	All Aboard	Ginn	Stage 7 Sam & Rosie	7
Boggity Bog	Tiddlywinks	Kingscourt	Stage 1 Large Books	4
Boggywooga	Sunshine	Heinemann	Level 1 Set I	7
Boo Hoo	Story Chest	Kingscourt	Small Read-together	5
Boogie-Woogie Man, The	Story Chest	Kingscourt	Get-ready Set DD	2
Boogly, The	Literacy Links Plus	Kingscourt	Emergent D	3
Book for Jack, A	All Aboard	Ginn	Stage 3 Sam & Rosie	4
Book For Kay, A	Reading 360	Ginn	Level 4	5
Book Week	Oxford Reading Tree	OUP	Stage 3 More Stories B	3
Books	Sunrise	Heinemann		1
Books	Sunshine Spirals Starters	Heinemann	Set B	1
Boots for Toots	Ready to Read	Nelson	Emergent Set A	1
Boring old bed	Sunshine	Heinemann	Level 1 Set J	6
Boss	Foundations for Reading	Folens	Level 4 Emergent	3
Bossy Bettina	Literacy Links Plus	Kingscourt	Early C	5
Bother Those Barnetts!	Sunshine Spirals	Heinemann	Set 7	6
Bottle Garden, A	Wonder World	Badger	Set 3	4
Bouncer comes to stay	Storyworlds	Heinemann	Stage 7 Our World	6
Box, Fox, Ox & Peacock	Reading 360	Ginn	Magic Circle Level 5	3
Boxed In		Red Fox	Samuels, Vyanne	7
Boxes	Foundations for Reading	Folens	Level 4 Emergent	2
Boxes	Literacy Links Plus	Kingscourt	Early C	6
Boy and the Lion, The	Fables from Aesop	Ginn	Books 1-6	7
Boy and the Tiger, The	Oxford Reading Tree	OUP	Stage 6 Woodpeckers	7
Boy who cried Wolf, The	Fables from Aesop	Ginn	Books 1-6	6
Boy who cried Wolf, The	Storyworlds	Heinemann	Stage 3 Once Upon a Time	2
Boy who went to the North Wind, The	Literacy Links Plus	Kingscourt	Fluent D	7
Boy with the Shell, The	Reading 360 New	Ginn	Little Bks L 4 Set 2	2
Boys and Girls	Reading 360	Ginn	Level 5	4
Bracelet, The	Reading World	Longman	Level 3	9
Brand-new Butterfly, A	Literacy Links Plus	Kingscourt	Early C	6
Brave Father Mouse	PM Storybooks	Nelson	Yellow Set A	3
Brave Little Tailor, The	PM Traditional Tales	Nelson	Turquoise Level	7
Brave Triceratops	PM Storybooks	Nelson	Green Set A	5
Bread	Sunshine	Heinemann	Level 1 Set F	3
Breakfast	Discovery World	Heinemann	Stage C	5
Breakfast	Foundations for Reading	Folens	Level 3 Emergent	2
Brenda's Birthday	Story Chest	Kingscourt	Get-ready Set AA	1
Bridge, The	Story Chest	Kingscourt	Get-ready Set BB	2
Bridge, The (whole text)	Cambridge Reading	CUP	Becoming a R Stage B	7
Bringing the Sea Back Home	Literacy Links Plus	Kingscourt	Fluent C	10
Broken Plate, The	Foundations for Reading	Folens	Level 10 Early	5
Broken Roof, The	Oxford Reading Tree	OUP	Stage 7 Owls	7
Broken Roof, The	Oxford Reading Tree	OUP	Stage 7 Playscripts	6
Bronwen The Brave	Pathways	Collins	Stage 3 Set D	8
Brother & Sister	Pathways	Collins	Stage 1 Set C	2
Brown	One, Two, Three & Away	Collins	Pre-reader 1-4	1
Brown Bear, Brown Bear, What Do You See?		Picture Puffin	Martin, Bill	2

TITLE	SERIES	PUBLISHER	SET (OR AUTHOR)	BAND
Brown Bears	PM Animal Facts	Nelson	Animals in the Wild	8
Bruno's Birthday	Literacy Links Plus	Kingscourt	Early A	3
Brutus	Sunshine Spirals	Heinemann	Set 8	6
Bubble Bath	Bangers and Mash	Longman	Supplementary Books	6
Bubbles	All Aboard	Ginn	Easy Start Sam & Rosie	1
Bubbles	Cambridge Reading	CUP	Becoming a R Stage C	8
Bubbles	Sunrise	Heinemann		2
Budgies	PM Animal Facts	Nelson	Pets	6
Buffy	Literacy Links Plus	Kingscourt	Emergent A	2
Buffy's Tricks	Literacy Links Plus	Kingscourt	Early C	4
Bug in a Mug	All Aboard	Ginn	Stage 1 Intro Patt & Rh	2
Building things	Sunshine	Heinemann	Level 1 Non-fiction	2
Building With Blocks	Sunrise	Heinemann		1
Buildings in My Street	Foundations for Reading	Folens	Level 4 Emergent	4
Bull and the Matador, The	Tiddlywinks	Kingscourt	Stage 7	6
Bull in a China Shop, A	Literacy Links Plus	Kingscourt	Fluent B	9
Bull's eye	Oxford Reading Tree	OUP	Stage 3 More Stories B	3
Bully, The	Oxford Reading Tree	OUP	Stage 7 More Owls	7
Bumbershoot, The	Reading 360	Ginn	Magic Circle Level 1	1
Bumble Bee	Ready to Read	Nelson	Early Set C	4
Bumbles, The	Book Project Fiction 2	Longman	Band 3	10
Bumper cars, The	PM Storybooks	Nelson	Red Set B	2
Buster is Lost		Lothian	Campbell, Rod	6
Buster McCluster	Wonder World	Badger	Set 1	7
Buster's Bedtime		Lothian	Campbell, Rod	3
Buster's Morning		Lothian	Campbell, Rod	5
Busy Beavers, The	PM Storybooks	Nelson	Orange Set C	6
Busy Bird	Ready to Read	Nelson	Emergent Set A	1
Busy Mosquito, The	Foundations for Reading	Folens	Level 5 Emergent	3
But Martin!		Picture Corgi	Counsel, June	8
But What Did We Get For Grandpa?		Heinemann	Ling	5
But Where is the Green Parrot?		Collins	Zacharias, Thomas	8
Butterflies	All Aboard Non Fiction	Ginn	Stage 3	6
Butterfly	Reading 360 New	Ginn	Little Bks L 1 Set 1	2
Butterfly Sale, The	All Aboard	Ginn	Stage 3 Sam & Rosie	4
Buzz Buzz Buzz		Picture Puffin	Barton, Byron	5
Buzzing flies	Sunshine	Heinemann	Level 1 Set C	2
By the Stream	Oxford Reading Tree	OUP	Stage 3 Storybooks	3
C				
Cabbage Princess, The	Literacy Links Plus	Kingscourt	Fluent D	8
Cabin in the Hills, The	PM Storybooks	Nelson	Turquoise Set A	7
Cake, The	Tiddlywinks	Kingscourt	Stage 6	9
Camcorder, The	Oxford Reading Tree	OUP	Stage 4 More Stories A	5
Camping	Foundations for Reading	Folens	Level 2 Emergent	1
Camping	Literacy Links Plus	Kingscourt	Emergent C	3
Camping	Reading World	Longman	Level 1: More Books	3
Camping	Sunshine Spirals	Heinemann	Set 5	5
Camping Adventure	Oxford Reading Tree	OUP	Stage 5 More Stories B	5
Camping with Our Dad	Sunshine New	Heinemann	Level 6	9
Can I Come With You?	Reading 360 New	Ginn	Little Bks L 3 Set 1	5
Can I Play Outside?	Literacy Links Plus	Kingscourt	Early A	4
Can I Play?	Book Project	Longman	Beginner Band 1	2
Can We Help?	Reading 360	Ginn	Level 2	3
Can We Help?	Reading 360 New	Ginn	Level 2	3
Can We Play?	Reading 360 New	Ginn	Little Bks L 2 Set 1	3
Can You Do This?	Book Project	Longman	Beginner Band 1	1
Can You Find Sammy The Hamster?		Walker	Lingard, J & Lewis, J	4
Can You Fly?	Foundations for Reading	Folens	Level 2 Emergent	1

TITLE	SERIES	PUBLISHER	SET (OR AUTHOR)	BAND
Can You Moo?		Dinosaur	Althea	5
Can you See Me?	Reading 360 New	Ginn	Little Bks L 2 Set 1	3
Can You See The Eggs?	PM Storybook Starters	Nelson	Set 2	1
Can You?	Reading 360	Ginn	Level 2	3
Can You?	Reading 360 New	Ginn	Level 2	3
Canal boat cat	Storyworlds	Heinemann	Stage 9 Animal World	10
Candlelight	PM Storybooks	Nelson	Green Set A	5
Caps For Sale	Scholastic Books	Ashton Scholastic	Slobodkina, Esphyr	8
Captain Bumble	Story Chest	Kingscourt	Stage 5	8
Car Accident, The	Foundations for Reading	Folens	Level 7 Early	4
Careful Crocodile, The	PM Storybooks	Nelson	Orange Set C	6
Carnival Mask	Pathways	Collins	Stage 0 Set D	3
Carnival, The	Oxford Reading Tree	OUP	Stage 3 More Stories B	4
Carrot Seed, The	Scholastic Books	Ashton Scholastic	Krauss, Ruth	5
Carrots, Peas and Beans	Sunshine New	Heinemann	Level 1 Set H	4
Castle Adventure	Oxford Reading Tree	OUP	Stage 5 Playscripts	4
Castle Adventure	Oxford Reading Tree	OUP	Stage 5 Storybooks	5
Cat	Reading 360	Ginn	Magic Circle Level 3	3
Cat and a Fiddle, A	Open Door	Nelson	Yellow Fun Books	2
Cat and Dog		Walker	Lloyd, D & Scruton, C	6
Cat and Dog		Heinemann	Minarik, E.H.	4
Cat and Mouse	PM Storybook Starters	Nelson	Set 2	1
Cat and Mouse	Reading 360 Upstarts	Ginn	Level 1 Extension	2
Cat and Mouse	Tiddlywinks	Kingscourt	Stage 1 Large Books	3
Cat and the Feather, The	One, Two, Three & Away	Collins	Main Books 1-2B	4
Cat and the Mouse, the Dog and the Frog	One, Two, Three & Away	Collins	Pre-reader 9-12	2
Cat and The Witch, The	Reading World	Longman	Level 2 Pack A	5
Cat and the Witch's Supper, The	One, Two, Three & Away	Collins	Green Platform 7-10	6
Cat Concert	Literacy Links Plus	Kingscourt	Fluent A	8
Cat in the Hat, The	Beginner Books	Collins	Seuss, Dr	7
Cat in the Tree, A	Oxford Reading Tree	OUP	Stage 3 Storybooks	4
Cat on the Mat	Oxford RT Branch Library	OUP	Wildsmith Bks St 2A	1
Cat on the Roof	Story Chest	Kingscourt	Stage 5	8
Cat tricks	Reading World	Longman	Level 2: More Books	3
Cat, The	Sunshine Spirals Starters	Heinemann	Set D	1
Caterpillars and Butterflies	One, Two, Three & Away	Collins	Green Platform 7-10	5
Catherine the Counter	Sunshine New	Heinemann	Level 1 Set F	4
Cats	All Aboard Non Fiction	Ginn	Stage 2	3
Cats	PM Animal Facts	Nelson	Pets	6
Cats	Wonder World	Badger	Set 4	5
Cat's Dance, The	One, Two, Three & Away	Collins	Main Books 5-8	7
Catten, The	Tiddlywinks	Kingscourt	Stage 6	9
Cattle	PM Animal Facts	Nelson	Farm Animals	9
Cells	Wonder World	Badger	Set 4	5
Chairs	All Aboard Non Fiction	Ginn	Stage 1	2
Change	Discovery World	Heinemann	Stage D	8
Charlie	Literacy Links Plus	Kingscourt	Fluent D	10
Chase, The	Oxford Reading Tree	OUP	Stage 2 More Stories B	3
Cheese that Disappeared, The	Reading 360 Upstarts	Ginn	Level 4 Extension	7
Cherry blossom cat	Storyworlds	Heinemann	Stage 9 Animal World	10
Chester		Heinemann	Hoff, Syd	6
Chew, Chew, Chew	Literacy Links Plus	Kingscourt	Emergent C	2
Chicken for Dinner	Story Chest	Kingscourt	Ready-set-go Set AA	2
Chicken-Licken	PM Traditional Tales	Nelson	Orange Level	6
Chickens	PM Animal Facts	Nelson	Farm Animals	9
Chick's Walk	Story Chest	Kingscourt	Get-ready Set BB	1
Children	Link Up	Collins	Starter Books	1
Chimney, The	Reading World	Longman	Level 2 Pack A	6

TITLE	SERIES	PUBLISHER	SET (OR AUTHOR)	BAND
Chinese adventure	Oxford Reading Tree	OUP	Stage 7 More Owls	7
Chinese New Year	Ready to Read	Nelson	Early Set A	3
Chinese New Year, The	Cambridge Reading	CUP	Becoming a R Stage C	7
Chocolate Cake, The	Story Chest	Kingscourt	Ready-set-go Set A	2
Chocolate-chip Muffins	Sunshine New	Heinemann	Level 2	6
Choosing a puppy	PM Storybooks	Nelson	Yellow Set B	3
Choosing Cards	Discovery World	Heinemann	Stage A	1
Christmas	Reading World	Longman	Level 2 Pack A	3
Christmas	Sunshine Spirals Starters	Heinemann	Set A	1
Christmas Adventure	Oxford Reading Tree	OUP	Stage 6 More Owls	6
Christmas Dog	Sunshine	Heinemann	Level 3	5
Christmas in the Village with Three Corners	One, Two, Three & Away	Collins	Yellow Platform 1-6	6
Christmas Shopping	Literacy Links Plus	Kingscourt	Early A	4
Christmas Tree, The	PM Storybooks	Nelson	Blue Set A	4
Chug the tractor	PM Storybooks	Nelson	Blue Set B	4
Cinderella	Read it Yourself	Ladybird	Level 3	5
Cinderella	Reading 2000	Longmans	Storytime Yellows	7
Cinderella	Reading 360	Ginn	Once Upon a Time 1-4	6
Circus Clown, The	Literacy Links Plus	Kingscourt	Emergent D	3
Circus Tricks	Reading 360 Upstarts	Ginn	Level 3 Extension	6
Circus, The	Literacy Links Plus	Kingscourt	Emergent A	1
Circus, The	Wonder World	Badger	Set 1	2
Circus, The		OUP	Wildsmith, Brian	1
City cat	Storyworlds	Heinemann	Stage 9 Animal World	10
City Scenes	Ready to Read	Nelson	Early Set C	3
Clean Up Your Room	Reading World	Longman	Level 2 Pack A	6
Cleaning Teeth	Wonder World	Badger	Set 4	1
Clever Beetle, The	Reading 360 Upstarts	Ginn	Level 2	4
Clever Boy, Charlie	All Aboard	Ginn	Stage 5 Set B Sam & Ros	6
Clever Cat, The	Reading 360 Upstarts	Ginn	Introductory	2
Clever Clowns	All Aboard Non Fiction	Ginn	Stage 1 Intro	1
Clever Dog, Webster	Book Project Fiction 2	Longman	Band 2	9
Clever Ghost, The	Reading 360 Upstarts	Ginn	Level 2 Extension	4
Clever Hamburger	Tiddlywinks	Kingscourt	Stage 7	7
Clever Joe	Storyworlds	Heinemann	Stage 2 Our World	2
Clever Mouse, The	Reading 360 Upstarts	Ginn	Level 2 Extension	4
Clever Mr Brown	Story Chest	Kingscourt	Stage 4	7
Clever Penguins, The	PM Storybooks	Nelson	Green Set A	5
Clever Tortoise, The	Cambridge Reading	CUP	Becoming a R Stage B	5
Click!	Foundations for Reading	Folens	Level 15 Experienced	5
Clifford, The Big Red Dog	Scholastic Books	Ashton Scholastic	Bridwell, Norman	7
Climbing	Literacy Links Plus	Kingscourt	Emergent C	1
Climbing	PM Storybook Starters	Nelson	Set 1	1
Clock, The	Bangers and Mash	Longman	Books 1-6 Pack A	6
Clocks and More Clocks		Picture Puffin	Hutchins, Pat	7
Close Your Eyes	Foundations for Reading	Folens	Level 6 Early	3
Closer look at Parks, A	Discovery World	Heinemann	Stage D	4
Clothes	Wonder World	Badger	Set 4	10
Clouds	All Aboard	Ginn	Stage 2 Set A Patt & Rh	2
Clouds	Sunshine	Heinemann	Level 1 Non-fiction	5
Clown and Elephant	Story Chest	Kingscourt	Get-ready Set C	1
Clown in the Well	Story Chest	Kingscourt	Ready-set-go Set DD	4
Clown, The	Sunshine Spirals Starters	Heinemann	Set A	1
Clumsy Clara	All Aboard	Ginn	Stage 4 Set A Patt & Rh	5
Cobra cat	Storyworlds	Heinemann	Stage 9 Animal World	10
Cobwebs, Elephants and Stars	Sunshine New	Heinemann	Level 5	8
Cold Day, The	Oxford Reading Tree	OUP	Stage 3 More Stories B	4
Colour Factory, The		Penguin/Kestrel	Denton, John	8

TITLE	SERIES	PUBLISHER	SET (OR AUTHOR)	BAND
Colours	Foundations for Reading	Folens	Level 10 Early	4
Colours		Picture Puffin	Pienkowski, Jan	1
Come and Have Fun		Heinemann	Hurd, Edith Thatcher	6
Come and Play With Me	Reading 360 New	Ginn	Little Bks L 2 Set 1	3
Come and See!	Foundations for Reading	Folens	Level 10 Early	4
Come Away from the Water, Shirley		Red Fox	Burningham, John	8
Come Back, Teddy!	Book Project Fiction 1	Longman	Band 1 Read On	2
Come for a Ride	Reading 360	Ginn	Level 2	4
Come For a Ride	Reading 360 New	Ginn	Level 2	4
Come for a Swim	Reading 360 New	Ginn	Little Bks L 2 Set 2	3
Come for a swim!	Sunshine	Heinemann	Level 1 Set F	5
Come In!	Book Project	Longman	Beginner Band 1	1
Come In!	Oxford Reading Tree	OUP	Stage 4 Storybooks	4
Come Into the Garden!	Book Project Fiction 1	Longman	Band 1 Read On	3
Come On	Sunrise	Heinemann		1
Come on, Tim	PM Storybooks	Nelson	Blue Set A	4
Come On, Wind!	Book Project Fiction 1	Longman	Band 4 Read On	5
Come to My House	Sunshine New	Heinemann	Level 1 Set G	3
Come with Me	Story Chest	Kingscourt	Ready-set-go Set A	2
Coming to Tea		Picture Puffin	Garland, Sarah	4
Communities	Wonder World	Badger	Set 3	3
Computer Kate	All Aboard	Ginn	Stage 5 Set A Patt & Rh	7
Cooking pot, The	Sunshine	Heinemann	Level 1 Set G	4
Copy-Cat	Story Chest	Kingscourt	Ready-set-go Set B	2
Count on Goz		Frances Lincoln	Weatherill, Steve	3
Countdown	Literacy Links Plus	Kingscourt	Early A	4
Counting Chickens	All Aboard	Ginn	Stage 3 Set B Patt & Rh	3
Cousin Kira	Sunshine	Heinemann	Level 5	7
Cow in the Hole, The	Sunshine Spirals	Heinemann	Set 3	3
Cow up a Tree	Tiddlywinks	Kingscourt	Stage 1 Small Books	5
Cowboy Jake	Sunshine New	Heinemann	Level 1 Set H	4
Cows in the Garden	PM Storybooks	Nelson	Blue Set A	4
Crab at the Bottom of the Sea, The	Literacy Links Plus	Kingscourt	Early C	5
Crabs	Sunshine New	Heinemann	Level 2 Non-fiction	9
Crabs	Wonder World	Badger	Set 4	8
Cracker Jack, The	Sunshine New	Heinemann	Level 1 Set D	2
Crash Landing	Reading 360 New	Ginn	Little Bks L 4 Set 2	3
Crash! The Car hit a Tree	One, Two, Three & Away	Collins	Introductory Q-V	3
Crazy Cousins	Book Project Fiction 1	Longman	Band 4 Read On	8
Crazy Crocs	Book Project Fiction 2	Longman	Band 3	10
Creepy Castle, The	Storyworlds	Heinemann	Stage 5 Fantasy World	4
Creepy Crawly	Oxford Reading Tree	OUP	Stage 3 Wrens	2
Cricket bat mystery, The	Storyworlds	Heinemann	Stage 7 Our World	6
Crocodile Lake	Ready to Read	Nelson	Fluent Set C	8
Crocodiles	Sunshine Spirals	Heinemann	Set 5	5
Crosby Crocodile's Disguise	Literacy Links Plus	Kingscourt	Fluent D	8
Cross Country Race	PM Storybooks	Nelson	Green Set A	5
Crossing The Road	Sunshine Spirals	Heinemann	Set 6	4
Cupboard in the Hall	Wonder World	Badger	Set 2	3
Cupboard, The		Red Fox	Burningham, John	6
Custard	Wonder World	Badger	Set 4	5
D				
Dad	Book Project Fiction 1	Longman	Band 2 Read On	2
Dad	PM Storybook Starters	Nelson	Set 1	1
Dad Didn't Mind at All	Literacy Links Plus	Kingscourt	Early C	5
Daddy, Can You Play With Me?		Puffin	Zeifert, Harriet	3
Dad's Bathtime	Literacy Links Plus	Kingscourt	Early C	5
Dad's Bike	Literacy Links Plus	Kingscourt	Early A	4

TITLE	SERIES	PUBLISHER	SET (OR AUTHOR)	BAND
Dad's Garden	Literacy Links Plus	Kingscourt	Emergent B	3
Dad's headache	Sunshine	Heinemann	Level 1 Set G	5
Dad's New Path	Foundations for Reading	Folens	Level 11 Early	4
Dad's Surprise	Foundations for Reading	Folens	Level 14 Experienced	6
Dan Gets Dressed	Story Chest	Kingscourt	Get-ready Set CC	2
Dan the Flying Man	Story Chest	Kingscourt	Large Read-tog Set 2	3
Dancing Ann and the Green-gruff-grackle	One, Two, Three & Away	Collins	Yellow Platform 1-6	7
Dancing Nadine	Reading 360	Ginn	Magic Circle Level 7	7
Dancing Shoes	Literacy Links Plus	Kingscourt	Emergent A	2
Dandelion, The	Sunshine	Heinemann	Level 1 Non-fiction	5
Danger	Story Chest	Kingscourt	Ready-set-go Set D	3
Daniel	Literacy Links Plus	Kingscourt	Early D	5
Danny and the Dinosaur		Mammoth	Hoff, Syd	7
Dan's Box	Cambridge Reading	CUP	Becoming a R Stage A	5
Dark, Dark Tale, A		Red Fox	Brown, Ruth	5
Dave and the Tooth Fairy		Tamarind	Wilkins, Verna	10
David	Pathways	Collins	Stage 1 Set B	3
Davina and the Dinosaurs	Pathways	Collins	Stage 2 Set D	6
Day and Night Animals	Discovery World	Heinemann	Stage A	1
Day at the Seaside, A	Reading 360 New	Ginn	Little Bks L.5 Set 3	6
Day I Had to Play With My Sister, The		Heinemann	Bonsall, Crosby	5
Day in London, A	Oxford Reading Tree	OUP	Stage 8 Magpies	8
Day in the Life of a Victorian Child, A	Discovery World	Heinemann	Stage C	8
Day in Town, A	Story Chest	Kingscourt	Stage 5	8
Day Poppy Said Yes, The	Book Project Fiction 1	Longman	Band 1	6
Day Poppy Went Out	Book Project Fiction 2	Longman	Band 2	7
Day Puppy Got Lost, The	Reading 360 New	Ginn	Little Bks L 1 Set 3	2
Day Shopping, A	Foundations for Reading	Folens	Level 6 Early	3
Dear Santa	Literacy Links Plus	Kingscourt	Emergent C	2
Dear Zoo		Picture Puffin	Campbell, Rod	4
Debbie and the Mouse	Reading 360 Upstarts	Ginn	Introductory	2
Deema's Dragon	Pathways	Collins	Stage 0 Set B	2
Deer and the Crocodile, The	Literacy Links Plus	Kingscourt	Early D	6
Den, The	All Aboard	Ginn	Stage 3 Booster Bks	4
Dennis and the Dinosaur	Reading 360 Upstarts	Ginn	Level 4 Extension	7
Dentist, The	PM Non-fiction	Nelson	Blue Level	5
Detective Tilak	All Aboard	Ginn	Stage 8 Sam & Rosie	8
Dick Whittington	Read it Yourself	Ladybird	Level 3	6
Did Not! Did So!	Sunshine New	Heinemann	Level 6	6
Did you say, Fire?	Ready to Read	Nelson	Early Set D	4
Digger at School	Reading 360 New	Ginn	Level 3	4
Ding Dong Baby	Bangers and Mash	Longman	Books 7-12 Pack B	7
Dinner Time	Storyworlds	Heinemann	Stage 2 Our World	2
Dinner!	Sunshine	Heinemann	Level 1 Set A	1
Dinnertime	Sunshine Spirals	Heinemann	Set 2	1
Dinosaur (Whole text)	Cambridge Reading	CUP	Becoming a R Stage A	8
Dinosaur Chase	PM Storybooks	Nelson	Orange Set A	6
Dinosaur Jumper, The	All Aboard	Ginn	Stage 2 Sam & Rosie	2
Dinosaur Party	Sunshine Spirals Starters	Heinemann	Set C	1
Dinosaurs	All Aboard Non Fiction	Ginn	Stage 2	3
Dinosaurs	Sunshine	Heinemann	Level 1 Non-fiction	4
Dinosaur's Cold, The	Literacy Links Plus	Kingscourt	Early D	6
Dipper and the old wreck	Storyworlds	Heinemann	Stage 5 Animal World	4
Dipper gets stuck	Storyworlds	Heinemann	Stage 5 Animal World	4
Dipper in danger	Storyworlds	Heinemann	Stage 5 Animal World	4
Dipper to the rescue	Storyworlds	Heinemann	Stage 5 Animal World	4
Dirty Car, The	All Aboard	Ginn	Stage 2 Booster Bks	2
Dirty Dog	Cambridge Reading	CUP	Begin to Read Stage B	2

TITLE	SERIES	PUBLISHER	SET (OR AUTHOR)	BAND
Discovery	Oxford Reading Tree	OUP	Stage 10 More Robins	10
Divers, The	Wonder World	Badger	Set 2	2
Diwali Party	Pathways	Collins	Stage 2 Set F	5
Do I Know You?	Reading 2000	Longmans	Storytime Yellows	6
Do You Dare?		Orchard Books	Rogers, Emma & Paul	4
Do You See Mouse?	Reading 360	Ginn	Magic Circle Level 4	5
Do You Want to be my Friend?		Picture Puffin	Carle, Eric	1
Doctor Boondoggle	Story Chest	Kingscourt	Ready-set-go Set BB	2
Doctor, The	PM Non-fiction	Nelson	Blue Level	5
Dog	Ready to Read	Nelson	Emergent Set C	1
Dog and the Ball, The	One, Two, Three & Away	Collins	Blue Platform 1-6	3
Dog Called Mischief, A	Oxford RT Branch Library	OUP	Wildsmith Bks St 2A	3
Dog House, The	Reading 360 New	Ginn	Little Bks L 3 Set 2	4
Dog Show, The	Foundations for Reading	Folens	Level 5 Emergent	3
Dog, The		Red Fox	Burningham, John	5
Dogger		Collins Pict Lions	Hughes, Shirley	10
Dogs	Foundations for Reading	Folens	Level 7 Early	4
Dogs	PM Animal Facts	Nelson	Pets	6
Dogs and Whistles	Reading 360 New	Ginn	Level 5	7
Dogstar	Literacy Links Plus	Kingscourt	Fluent B	7
Doing the Garden		Picture Puffin	Garland, Sarah	5
Doing the Washing		Picture Puffin	Garland, Sarah	6
Dolly Dot	All Aboard	Ginn	Stage 1 Intro Patt & Rh	2
Dolly's Magic Brolly	Reading 360 New	Ginn	Little Bks L 3 Set 3	4
Dolphin Pool, The	Oxford Reading Tree	OUP	Stage 3 Storybooks	3
Dolphins	Wonder World	Badger	Set 4	6
Donkey and the Lapdog, The	Fables from Aesop	Ginn	Books 7-12	7
Donkey went to School, The	One, Two, Three & Away	Collins	Pre-reader 9a-12a	3
Donkey went to Town, The	One, Two, Three & Away	Collins	Introductory M-P	2
Donkey, The	One, Two, Three & Away	Collins	Main Books 3-4b	5
Don't Be Silly, Simon	Reading World	Longman	Level 3	8
Don''t Cry, Little Bear	Pathways	Collins	Stage 1 Set A	3
Don't Eat the Postman	Reading 360 Upstarts	Ginn	Level 2 Extension	4
Don't Forget the Bacon		Picture Puffin	Hutchins, Pat	8
Don't Leave Anything Behind	Literacy Links Plus	Kingscourt	Emergent B	3
Don't Run Away	Reading 360 New	Ginn	Level 3	4
Don't Throw It Away	Wonder World	Badger	Set 4	4
Don't Wake the Baby	Literacy Links Plus	Kingscourt	Emergent B	1
Don't Worry	Literacy Links Plus	Kingscourt	Fluent A	7
Don't you laugh at me!	Sunshine	Heinemann	Level 1 Set F	4
Doodlecloud	Book Project Fiction 1	Longman	Band 3 Read On	4
Doodledragon	Book Project Fiction 1	Longman	Band 3 Read On	4
Doodlemaze	Book Project Fiction 1	Longman	Band 3 Read On	4
Doodling Daniel	Book Project Fiction 1	Longman	Band 3 Read Aloud	8
Down at the River	Ready to Read	Nelson	Early Set B	2
Down to town	Sunshine	Heinemann	Level 1 Set A	1
Dr Sprocket Makes a Rocket	Sunshine Spirals	Heinemann	Set 4	3
Dragon	Ready to Read	Nelson	Fluent Set B	6
Dragon at the Pool	Pathways	Collins	Stage 0 Set C	2
Dragon Dance, The	Oxford Reading Tree	OUP	Stage 4 More Stories B	4
Dragon in a Dustbin, A	Open Door	Nelson	Green Fun Books	3
Dragon Tree, The	Oxford Reading Tree	OUP	Stage 5 Playscripts	4
Dragon Tree, The	Oxford Reading Tree	OUP	Stage 5 Storybooks	5
Dragon with a Cold	Sunshine	Heinemann	Level 4	7
Dragon!	Wonder World	Badger	Set 2	4
Dragon, The	Story Chest	Kingscourt	Stage 3	6
Dragon, The	Sunshine Spirals	Heinemann	Set 1	2
Dream, The	Oxford Reading Tree	OUP	Stage 2 Storybooks	4

TITLE	SERIES	PUBLISHER	SET (OR AUTHOR)	BAND
Dreams	Sunshine	Heinemann	Level 1 Non-fiction	4
Dreamy Robbie	Reading 2000	Longmans	Storytime Yellows	6
Dressing Up	Literacy Links Plus	Kingscourt	Emergent A	2
Dressing Up	PM Storybook Starters	Nelson	Set 1	1
Dressing Up	Sunrise	Heinemann		1
Dressing up	Sunshine Spirals Starters	Heinemann	Set B	1
Drivers	Link Up	Collins	Starter Build-Up	1
Drummer Hoff		Picture Puffin	Emberley, Ed	7
Duck		Walker	Lloyd, David	7
Duck in the Box	Bangers and Mash	Longman	Books 1A-6A	6
Duck in the Park, Duck in the Dark	Reading 360	Ginn	Magic Circle Level 3	3
Duck is a Duck, A	Reading 360 New	Ginn	Level 3	4
Duck Trouble	Reading 360 New	Ginn	Little Bks L 3 Set 2	6
Duck with the broken wing, The	PM Storybooks	Nelson	Blue Set B	4
Ducks	Story Chest	Kingscourt	Ready-set-go Set BB	2
Ducks and the Tortoise, The	Fables from Aesop	Ginn	Books 7-12	6
Duma and the lion	Storyworlds	Heinemann	Stage 7 Animal World	5
Dump, The	Oxford Reading Tree	OUP	Stage 6 Robins	7
E				
Each Peach Pear Plum		Picture Puffin	Ahlberg, Janet & Allen	3
Eagle and the Man, The	Fables from Aesop	Ginn	Books 7-12	6
Ear Book, The	Bright and Early Books	Collins	Perkins, Al	4
Earthquake!	Wonder World	Badger	Set 2	4
Earthquake, The	Tiddlywinks	Kingscourt	Stage 5	8
Earthworm, The	Wonder World	Badger	Set 3	8
Eat Up!	Sunshine New	Heinemann	Level 1 Set F	4
Eat Up, Gemma		Walker	Hayes, Sarah	7
Eat Your Dinner		Walker	Miller, Virginia	5
Eating	Foundations for Reading	Folens	Level 1 Emergent	1
Eating Plants	All Aboard Non Fiction	Ginn	Stage 3	5
Ebenezer and the Sneeze	Story Chest	Kingscourt	Ready-set-go Set BB	3
Echo, The	Sunshine Spirals	Heinemann	Set 8	5
Eddi & Teddy		Little Mammoth	Clarke, Gus	7
Egg, The	Reading 360 New	Ginn	Little Bks L 1 Set 1	2
Eggs	Bangers and Mash	Longman	Books 1-6 Pack A	5
Eggs, Eggs, Eggs	Wonder World	Badger	Set 3	10
Eggs for Breakfast	PM Non-fiction	Nelson	Red Level	3
Eight, Nine, Ten, Eleven, Twelve	One, Two, Three & Away	Collins	Pre-reader 5b-8b	1
Elena Makes Tortillas	Ready to Read	Nelson	Emergent Set D	1
Elephant and The Bad Baby, The		Picture Puffin	Vipont, Elfrida	7
Elephant for the Holidays, An	Sunshine New	Heinemann	Level 1 Set I	5
Elephant that forgot, The	Storyworlds	Heinemann	Stage 8 Animal World	6
Elephant Walk	Sunshine Spirals	Heinemann	Set 2	2
Elephants	Foundations for Reading	Folens	Level 16 Experienced	6
Elephants	PM Animal Facts	Nelson	Animals in the Wild	8
Elephants Going to Bed	Open Door	Nelson	Blue Fun Books	2
Elephant's Trunk, The	Sunshine Spirals	Heinemann	Set 6	5
Elves and the Shoemaker The	Storyworlds	Heinemann	Stage 7 Once Upon a Time	6
Elves and the Shoemaker, The	PM Traditional Tales	Nelson	Turquoise Level	7
Elves and the Shoemaker, The	Read it Yourself	Ladybird	Level 1	4
Emergency, The	Oxford Reading Tree	OUP	Stage 8 Robins	9
Emilio and the River	Sunshine New	Heinemann	Level 2	7
Emily the Spy	Reading 360 Upstarts	Ginn	Level 4	7
Emma's Problem	Literacy Links Plus	Kingscourt	Early C	7
Empty House, The	One, Two, Three & Away	Collins	Main Books 3-4b	5
Empty Lunchbox, The	Storyworlds	Heinemann	Stage 3 Our World	2
Enormous Turnip, The	Read it Yourself	Ladybird	Level 1	5
Entering the Ark	Cambridge Reading	CUP	Begin to Read Stage A	1

TITLE	SERIES	PUBLISHER	SET (OR AUTHOR)	BAND
Escalator, The	Story Chest	Kingscourt	Get-ready Set AA	2
Every Shape and Size	Wonder World	Badger	Set 1	4
Everyday Forces	Discovery World	Heinemann	Stage E	7
Everyone got Wet	Oxford Reading Tree	OUP	Stage 4 More Stories B	3
Everyone is Reading	Cambridge Reading	CUP	Becoming a R Stage C	5
Eye Book, The	Bright and Early Books	Collins	Le Seig, Theo	3
Eye Spy		Frances Lincoln	Lewis, Tracey	3
Eyes	Discovery World	Heinemann	Stage C	8
Eyes	Wonder World	Badger	Set 3	2
F				
Face Painting	Wonder World	Badger	Set 4	3
Face Sandwich, The	Sunshine New	Heinemann	Level 1 Set A	1
Faces	Sunrise	Heinemann		1
Family Photos	Literacy Links Plus	Kingscourt	Early B	4
Fancy Dress	Oxford Reading Tree	OUP	Stage 2 Wrens	1
Fantail, Fantail	Ready to Read	Nelson	Emergent Set D	2
Fantastic Cake	Story Chest	Kingscourt	Ready-set-go Set CC	4
Fantastic Washing Machine, The	Sunshine	Heinemann	Level 4	5
Faraway Tales	Reading 360 New	Ginn	Level 5	7
Farm		Picture Puffin	Pienkowski, Jan	1
Farm Concert, The	Story Chest	Kingscourt	Large Read-tog Set 2	1
Farm In Spring, The	PM Storybook Starters	Nelson	Set 2	1
Farm, The	Literacy Links Plus	Kingscourt	Emergent A	1
Farm, The	Sunrise	Heinemann		2
Farm, The	Sunshine Spirals Starters	Heinemann	Set A	1
Farmer and his Sons, The	Fables from Aesop	Ginn	Books 7-12	7
Farms	Foundations for Reading	Folens	Level 7 Early	3
Fast Asleep	All Aboard	Ginn	Easy Start Patt & Rhyme	2
Fast Food	Foundations for Reading	Folens	Level 7 Early	3
Fast Machines	Foundations for Reading	Folens	Level 4 Emergent	2
Fastest Gazelle, The	Literacy Links Plus	Kingscourt	Early D	6
Fat Cat, The	Reading 360 Upstarts	Ginn	Level 3	6
Fat Cat, The		Picture Puffin	Kent, Jack	8
Father Bear Comes Home		Heinemann	Minarik, E.H.	8
Father Bear Goes Fishing	PM Storybooks	Nelson	Red Set A	2
Father Bear's surprise	PM Storybooks	Nelson	Green Set B	5
Fatima's Tonsils	Foundations for Reading	Folens	Level 17 Experienced	7
Feast, The	All Aboard Non Fiction	Ginn	Stage 3	5
Feeling Funny	Sunshine	Heinemann	Level 7	8
Feelings	All Aboard Non Fiction	Ginn	Stage 1 Intro	1
Feet	Story Chest	Kingscourt	Get-ready Set B	2
Feet		Walker	Mark, Jan	5
Fetch the Stick, Webster!	Book Project Fiction 1	Longman	Band 1 Read On	3
Fierce Old Woman Who ... The	Foundations for Reading	Folens	Level 13 Experienced	5
Filbert the Fly	Literacy Links Plus	Kingscourt	Emergent B	4
Find your coat, Ned		Walker	Zinnemann-Hope, Pam	4
Fingers	Journeys in Reading	Schofield & Sims	Level 1	3
Finish the Story, Dad		Walker	Smee, Nicola	8
Finn MacCool	All Aboard	Ginn	Stage 5 Set B Patt & Rh	5
Fire and Water	Story Chest	Kingscourt	Ready-set-go Set DD	4
Fire in the Magic Wood, The	One, Two, Three & Away	Collins	Yellow Platform 7-10	7
Fire in Wild Wood	Storyworlds	Heinemann	Stage 5 Fantasy World	4
Fire!	One, Two, Three & Away	Collins	Yellow Platform 1-6	6
Fire!	Reading 360 New	Ginn	Little Bks L 1 Set 2	2
Fire! Fire!	PM Storybooks	Nelson	Yellow Set A	3
Firefighters	Pathways	Collins	Stage 2 Set A	5
Fish	Wonder World	Badger	Set 3	5
Fish out of Water, A	Beginner Books	Collins	Palmer, Helen	7

TITLE	SERIES	PUBLISHER	SET (OR AUTHOR)	BAND
Fishing	Foundations for Reading	Folens	Level 10 Early	4
Fishing	PM Storybook Starters	Nelson	Set 2	1
Fishing	Reading World	Longman	Level 2: More Books	3
Fishing	Story Chest	Kingscourt	Get-ready Set BB	2
Fishing	Wonder World	Badger	Set 3	4
Fishing Off the Wharf	Ready to Read	Nelson	Fluent Set C	8
Fishy Numbers	Cambridge Reading	CUP	Begin to Read Stage A	2
Fishy Tale, A	Pathways	Collins	Stage 2 Set B	4
Fitness	Foundations for Reading	Folens	Level 2 Emergent	1
Five Green Monsters	Cambridge Reading	CUP	Begin to Read Stage B	2
Five Little Ducks		Orchard	Beck, Ian	3
Five Little Men	Pathways	Collins	Stage 2 Set E	4
Five Little Monkeys	Cambridge Reading	CUP	Becoming a R Stage A	4
Fizz and Splutter	Story Chest	Kingscourt	Ready-set-go Set D	3
Flea Market, The	Sunshine Spirals	Heinemann	Set 5	4
Flight Deck	Wonder World	Badger	Set 2	3
Flood, The	PM Storybooks	Nelson	Green Set A	5
Floppy Floppy	Oxford Reading Tree	OUP	Stage 1 First Words	1
Floppy the Hero	Oxford Reading Tree	OUP	Stage 2 More Stories B	4
Floppy's Bath	Oxford Reading Tree	OUP	Stage 2 More Stories A	3
Flour	Wonder World	Badger	Set 3	9
Flower girl, The	PM Storybooks	Nelson	Red Set B	2
Flower Pots and Forget-me-nots	All Aboard	Ginn	Stage 1 Intro Patt & Rh	2
Fly Away Home	Wonder World	Badger	Set 2	9
Fly in his Eye, A		Ladybird	Butterworth/Salisbury	6
Flying	Story Chest	Kingscourt	Ready-set-go Set B	2
Flying Carpet, The	Oxford Reading Tree	OUP	Stage 8 Magpies	8
Flying Elephant, The	Oxford Reading Tree	OUP	Stage 4 More Stories B	3
Flying fish, The	PM Storybooks	Nelson	Green Set B	5
Flying Sausages	Open Door	Nelson	Yellow Fun Books	3
Flying Turtle, The	All Aboard	Ginn	Stage 5 Set B Patt & Rh	5
Flying with Tommy	Sunshine Spirals	Heinemann	Set 7	5
Foggy Day, The	Oxford Reading Tree	OUP	Stage 2 More Stories B	3
Follow My Leader	Cambridge Reading	CUP	Becoming a R Stage B	5
Food		Picture Puffin	Pienkowski, Jan	1
Food Trappers	Wonder World	Badger	Set 2	8
Foot Book, The	Bright and Early Books	Collins	Seuss, Dr	5
Football at the park	PM Storybooks	Nelson	Yellow Set B	3
Football Fever	Ready to Read	Nelson	Fluent Set C	8
Footprints on the Moon	Sunshine Spirals	Heinemann	Set 5	4
Forest, The (whole text)	Cambridge Reading	CUP	Becoming a R Stage B	7
Four Black Puppies		Walker	Grindley, Sally	4
Four Fierce Kittens		Orchard Books	Dunbar, Joyce	5
Four Ice Creams	PM Storybook Starters	Nelson	Set 2	1
Four Scary Monsters	Cambridge Reading	CUP	Begin to Read Stage B	3
Four, Five, Six	One, Two, Three & Away	Collins	Pre-reader 5b-8b	1
Fox and the Crow, The	Fables from Aesop	Ginn	Books 1-6	6
Fox and the Rabbit, The	Storyworlds	Heinemann	Stage 2 Once Upon a Time	2
Fox and the Stork, The	Fables from Aesop	Ginn	Books 13-18	5
Fox and the Stork, The	Storyworlds	Heinemann	Stage 2 Once Upon a Time	2
Fox who Foxed, The	PM Storybooks	Nelson	Green Set A	5
Fred In Space	Reading World	Longman	Level 1: More Books	3
Fred Makes a Shelf	Reading World	Longman	Level 1 Pack A	3
Freddy's Teddy	Book Project Fiction 1	Longman	Band 1 Read On	3
Fred's Birthday	Reading World	Longman	Level 2 Pack A	4
Fred's Mess	Reading World	Longman	Level 1 Pack A	2
Fred's photo album	Reading World	Longman	Level 2: More Books	4
Fred's Snowman	Reading World	Longman	Level 2 Pack B	7

TITLE	SERIES	PUBLISHER	SET (OR AUTHOR)	BAND
Friend for Kate, A	Cambridge Reading	CUP	Becoming a R Stage C	6
Friend for Little White Rabbit, A	PM Storybooks	Nelson	Yellow Set A	3
Friend, A	Literacy Links Plus	Kingscourt	Early D	5
Friend, The		Red Fox	Burningham, John	6
Friends	All Aboard	Ginn	Easy Start Sam & Rosie	1
Friends	Link Up	Collins	Level 3	5
Fright in the Night, A	Oxford Reading Tree	OUP	Stage 6 More Owls	6
Frisky and the cat	Storyworlds	Heinemann	Stage 3 Animal World	2
Frisky and the ducks	Storyworlds	Heinemann	Stage 3 Animal World	2
Frisky plays a trick	Storyworlds	Heinemann	Stage 3 Animal World	2
Frisky wants to sleep	Storyworlds	Heinemann	Stage 3 Animal World	2
Frog & Toad Are Friends		Mammoth	Lobel, Arnold	7
Frog & Toad Together		Mammoth	Lobel, Arnold	8
Frog and the Fly, The	Oxford RT Branch Library	OUP	Wildsmith Bks St 2A	2
Frog in the Throat, A	Book Project Fiction 1	Longman	Band 2 Read Aloud	6
Frog Prince, The	Storyworlds	Heinemann	Stage 7 Once Upon a Time	6
Frog Princess, The	Literacy Links Plus	Kingscourt	Early D	6
Frog Spell	Reading 360 New	Ginn	Little Bks L 1 Set 1	2
From Gran		Lothian	Campbell, Rod	5
From the Air	Wonder World	Badger	Set 3	4
Frown, The	Tiddlywinks	Kingscourt	Stage 4	8
Fruit Salad	Literacy Links Plus	Kingscourt	Emergent A	1
Fruit Salad	Wonder World	Badger	Set 2	2
Fun at the Beach	Oxford Reading Tree	OUP	Stage 1 First Words	1
Fun at the Zoo	Reading 360 Upstarts	Ginn	Level 3 Extension	5
Fun in the Mud	Foundations for Reading	Folens	Level 9 Early	4
Fun on a Broomstick	Reading 360 Upstarts	Ginn	Introductory	3
Fun Run	Pathways	Collins	Stage 0 Set D	3
Fun Run, The	All Aboard	Ginn	Stage 5 Set B Sam & Ros	6
Fun Things to Make and Do	Discovery World	Heinemann	Stage D	4
Fun with Mo and Toots	Ready to Read	Nelson	Emergent Set B	2
Funnybones		Little Mammoth	Ahlberg, Allan	7
Fussy Freda	All Aboard	Ginn	Stage 7 Pattern & Rhyme	9
G				
Gallo and Zorro	Literacy Links Plus	Kingscourt	Early D	8
Garden friends	Book Project Fiction 1	Longman	Band 1 Read On Specials	2
Garden Party	Sunshine	Heinemann	Level 7	9
Garden Rain	Reading World	Longman	Level 2 Pack B	8
Garden, A	Foundations for Reading	Folens	Level 1 Emergent	1
Gardening	Foundations for Reading	Folens	Level 5 Emergent	3
Geoffrey the Dinosaur	Sunshine New	Heinemann	Level 1 Set D	2
Get Lost!	Foundations for Reading	Folens	Level 12 Early	5
Get Some Bread, Fred	Reading World	Longman	Level 2 Pack B	6
Get That Fly	Reading 360 New	Ginn	Little Bks L 4 Set 1	6
Get Up, Webster!	Book Project Fiction 1	Longman	Band 1 Read On Specials	3
Getting Dressed	Sunrise	Heinemann		1
Getting Fit	Wonder World	Badger	Set 1	1
Getting Glasses	Wonder World	Badger	Set 3	5
Getting Ready for School	Foundations for Reading	Folens	Level 7 Early	3
Getting Ready for the Ball	Literacy Links Plus	Kingscourt	Emergent A	2
Getting There	Wonder World	Badger	Set 1	1
Get-up Machine, The	Sunshine New	Heinemann	Level 1 Set I	4
Ghost Behind the Cupboard, The	Reading 360 Upstarts	Ginn	Level 2	4
Ghost In The Castle	All Aboard	Ginn	Stage 3 Sam & Rosie	4
Ghost Next Door, The	All Aboard	Ginn	Stage 7 Pattern & Rhyme	9
Ghost Train	Pathways	Collins	Stage 1 Set C	1
Ghost Train, The	All Aboard	Ginn	Stage 2 Sam & Rosie	2
Ghost Train, The	One, Two, Three & Away	Collins	Red Platform 7-10	6

TITLE	SERIES	PUBLISHER	SET (OR AUTHOR)	BAND
Ghost tricks	Oxford Reading Tree	OUP	Stage 10 More Robins	10
Ghost, Ghost are you Scared?	Reading World	Longman	Level 1 Pack B	2
Ghost, The	Story Chest	Kingscourt	Get-ready Set A	1
Giant Pumpkin, The	Sunshine	Heinemann	Level 2	6
Giant Sandwich, The	All Aboard	Ginn	Stage 3 Set A Patt & Rh	3
Giant -Size Hamburger, A	Wonder World	Badger	Set 1	2
Giant soup	Ready to Read	Nelson	Fluent Set C	8
Giant's boy, The	Sunshine	Heinemann	Level 1 Set H	7
Giant's Breakfast, The	Literacy Links Plus	Kingscourt	Emergent C	2
Giant's Day Out, The	Sunshine Spirals Starters	Heinemann	Set D	1
Giant's Garden, The	Reading 2000	Longmans	Storytime Reds	7
Giddy Funfair	Book Project Fiction 1	Longman	Band 4 Read On	7
Giddy Space	Book Project Fiction 1	Longman	Band 4 Read On	10
Giddy up and away	Book Project Fiction 1	Longman	Band 4 Read On	7
Gifts, The	Story Chest	Kingscourt	Get-ready Set DD	2
Giggle Box, The	Story Chest	Kingscourt	Ready-set-go Set DD	4
Ginger		Safeway	Parker, Ant	3
Ginger, Where Are You?	Pathways	Collins	Stage 3 Set C	8
Gingerbread Man	Read it Yourself	Ladybird	Level 2	6
Gingerbread Man	Sunshine New	Heinemann	Level 1 Set E	3
Gingerbread Man, The	Cambridge Reading	CUP	Becoming a R Stage A	4
Gingerbread Man, The	PM Traditional Tales	Nelson	Orange Level	6
Giraffe in a Train, A	Open Door	Nelson	Green Fun Books	3
Give me a Hug	Sunrise	Heinemann		1
Glerp, The	Reading 360	Ginn	Magic Circle Level 5	7
Go Away Dog	Scholastic Books	Ashton Scholastic	Nodset, Joan	6
Go Away Stanley	Reading World	Longman	Level 1 Pack B	2
Go away, Harry!	Book Project Fiction 1	Longman	Band 2 Read On	4
Go Back to Sleep	Literacy Links Plus	Kingscourt	Emergent D	3
Go Cart, The	PM Storybook Starters	Nelson	Set 1	1
Go Kart Race, The	Oxford Reading Tree	OUP	Stage 6 More Owls	6
Go, Dog, Go!	Beginner Books	Collins	Eastman, P.D.	3
Go, Go, Go	Story Chest	Kingscourt	Get-ready Set A	1
Goal!	Oxford Reading Tree	OUP	Stage 2 More Wrens	2
Goat is Eating Debbie, The	Reading 360 Upstarts	Ginn	Level 1	2
Goats	PM Animal Facts	Nelson	Farm Animals	9
Going Away Bag, The	Reading 360 New	Ginn	Little Bks L.4 Set 3	5
Going Fishing	Cambridge Reading	CUP	Becoming a R Stage A	4
Going in the Car	Sunshine New	Heinemann	Level 1 Set B	1
Going Out	Foundations for Reading	Folens	Level 4 Emergent	3
Going Shopping	Reading 2000	Longmans	Storytime Yellows	6
Going Shopping		Picture Puffin	Garland, Sarah	3
Going to Hospital	Foundations for Reading	Folens	Level 16 Experienced	7
Going to Playschool		Picture Puffin	Garland, Sarah	3
Going to School	Cambridge Reading	CUP	Becoming a R Stage B	5
Going to School	Foundations for Reading	Folens	Level 10 Early	4
Going to School	Link Up	Collins	Level 1	3
Going to School	Story Chest	Kingscourt	Get-ready Set C	1
Going to School	Sunshine Spirals Starters	Heinemann	Set A	1
Going to the Bank	Foundations for Reading	Folens	Level 15 Experienced	7
Going to the Beach	Ready to Read	Nelson	Emergent Set A	2
Going to the Hairdresser	Foundations for Reading	Folens	Level 12 Early	5
Going to the Shops	Reading 360 New	Ginn	Little Bks L 3 Set 1	5
Going to the Vet	Sunshine New	Heinemann	Level 1 Set E	2
Go-kart, The	Oxford Reading Tree	OUP	Stage 2 Storybooks	3
Golden Screws, The	Pathways	Collins	Stage 2 Set B	5
Goldfish	PM Animal Facts	Nelson	Pets	6
Goldilocks and the Three Bears	PM Traditional Tales	Nelson	Turquoise Level	7

TITLE	SERIES	PUBLISHER	SET (OR AUTHOR)	BAND
Goldilocks and the Three Bears	Read it Yourself	Ladybird	Level 1	4
Goldilocks and the Three Bears	Reading 360	Ginn	Once Upon a Time 1-4	6
Good Book, A	Reading 360 New	Ginn	Little Bks L 3 Set 2	3
Good Boy Andrew!	Tiddlywinks	Kingscourt	Stage 1 Large Books	3
Good for you	Sunshine	Heinemann	Level 1 Set E	2
Good Dog	Book Project Fiction 2	Longman	Band 2	8
Good Knee for a Cat, A	Ready to Read	Nelson	Fluent Set C	8
Good Old Mum!	Oxford Reading Tree	OUP	Stage 2 Wrens	2
Good Sports	Foundations for Reading	Folens	Level 9 Early	4
Good Trick, A	Oxford Reading Tree	OUP	Stage 1 First Words	1
Goodbye Lucy	Sunshine	Heinemann	Level 1 Set F	3
Goodness Gracious!	Literacy Links Plus	Kingscourt	Early C	7
Goodnight	Reading World	Longman	Level 1 Pack A	2
Goodnight Goodnight		Picture Puffin	Rice, Eve	6
Goodnight Little Brother	Literacy Links Plus	Kingscourt	Early A	4
Goodnight Moon		Mammoth	Brown, Margaret Wise	5
Goodnight Moon Room		Patrick Hardy	Brown/Hurd	3
Goodnight Owl		Picture Puffin	Hutchins, Pat	6
Goose that laid the Golden Egg, The	Fables from Aesop	Ginn	Books 1-6	5
Gopal and the Little White Cat	One, Two, Three & Away	Collins	Main Books 1-2B	5
Gotcha Box, The	Story Chest	Kingscourt	Get-ready Set BB	1
Grabber	Pathways	Collins	Stage 3 Set B	6
Gracie's Cat	Cambridge Reading	CUP	Becoming a R Stage C	6
Gran	Oxford Reading Tree	OUP	Stage 5 Playscripts	4
Gran	Oxford Reading Tree	OUP	Stage 5 Storybooks	5
Gran and Grandpa		Walker	Oxenbury, Helen	7
Grandad	Literacy Links Plus	Kingscourt	Fluent D	10
Grandad's Balloon	All Aboard	Ginn	Stage 1 Intro Sam & Ro	1
Grandad's Ears	Pathways	Collins	Stage 2 Set C	4
Grandad's Mask	PM Storybooks	Nelson	Turquoise Set C	7
Grandma's Cat	All Aboard	Ginn	Stage 2 Set A Patt & Rh	3
Grandma's Elephants	Sunshine New	Heinemann	Level 6	9
Grandma's Heart	Wonder World	Badger	Set 2	6
Grandma's Letter	Foundations for Reading	Folens	Level 3 Emergent	2
Grandma's Memories	Literacy Links Plus	Kingscourt	Early B	6
Grandma's Present	Foundations for Reading	Folens	Level 9 Early	4
Grandma's surprise	Storyworlds	Heinemann	Stage 5 Our World	4
Grandpa Knits Hats	Wonder World	Badger	Set 1	3
Grandpa Snored	Literacy Links Plus	Kingscourt	Emergent D	3
Grandpa, Grandpa	Story Chest	Kingscourt	Large Read-tog Set 1	5
Grandpa's Birthday	Literacy Links Plus	Kingscourt	Fluent A	7
Grandpa's Chair	Pathways	Collins	Stage 1 Set C	2
Grandpa's New Car	Sunshine Spirals	Heinemann	Set 4	4
Grandpa's Special Present	Foundations for Reading	Folens	Level 13 Experienced	5
Granny Big Boots	All Aboard	Ginn	Stage 6 Pattern & Rhyme	8
Gran's Birthday	Link Up	Collins	Level 3	5
Gravity	Wonder World	Badger	Set 3	4
Great Day for Up!	Beginner Books	Collins	Seuss, Dr	6
Great Enormous Hamburger, The	Sunrise	Heinemann		2
Great Lorenzo, The	All Aboard	Ginn	Stage 6 Sam & Rosie	6
Great Pumpkin Battle, The	Tiddlywinks	Kingscourt	Stage 7	8
Great Race, The	Oxford Reading Tree	OUP	Stage 5 More Stories A	5
Greatest Binnie in the World, The	Sunshine New	Heinemann	Level 5	7
Greatest Show on Earth, The		Walker	Prater, John	7
Greedy Cat is Hungry	Ready to Read	Nelson	Early Set A	3
Greedy Guinea Pig, The	All Aboard	Ginn	Stage 3 Sam & Rosie	3
Greedy Monster	Sunshine Spirals Starters	Heinemann	Set B	1
Greedy Nelly	All Aboard	Ginn	Stage 2 Set A Patt & Rh	3

TITLE	SERIES	PUBLISHER	SET (OR AUTHOR)	BAND
Greedy Parrot, The	Reading 360 Upstarts	Ginn	Level 2 Extension	4
Green	One, Two, Three & Away	Collins	Pre-reader 1a-4a	2
Green Dragon, The	Sunshine New	Heinemann	Level 1 Set H	4
Green Eggs and Ham	Beginner Books	Collins	Seuss. Dr	6
Green Footprints	Literacy Links Plus	Kingscourt	Emergent D	3
Green Grass	Story Chest	Kingscourt	Get-ready Set BB	2
Green Island	Oxford Reading Tree	OUP	Stage 9 Magpies	8
Green Plants	Foundations for Reading	Folens	Level 8 Early	3
Green Queen, The		Sainsbury	Sharratt, Nick	3
Gregor, The Grumblesome Giant	Literacy Links Plus	Kingscourt	Early C	6
Gregorie Peck	Book Project Fiction 2	Longman	Band 1	7
Growing		Victor Gollancz	Pragoff, Fiona	1
Grumble goes for a walk, The	Reading World	Longman	Level 2: More Books	4
Grumble goes jogging, The	Reading World	Longman	Level 2: More Books	4
Grumble, The	Reading World	Longman	Level 2 Pack A	3
Grumbly Giant	Pathways	Collins	Stage 1 Set B	3
Grump The	Literacy Links Plus	Kingscourt	Early B	5
Grumpy Elephant	Story Chest	Kingscourt	Ready-set-go Set D	4
Guess What Cat Found	Reading 360 New	Ginn	Little Bks L 3 Set 1	5
Guess What!	Literacy Links Plus	Kingscourt	Emergent C	2
Guess What?	Foundations for Reading	Folens	Level 6 Early	3
Guess Who I Am!	Cambridge Reading	CUP	Begin to Read Stage B	2
Guide Dog, The	Foundations for Reading	Folens	Level 17 Experienced	7
Guinea Pig For Rosie, A	All Aboard	Ginn	Stage 2 Sam & Rosie	3
Guinea Pig Grass	Tiddlywinks	Kingscourt	Stage 1 Large Books	5
Guinea Pigs	All Aboard Non Fiction	Ginn	Stage 3	5
Guinea Pigs	PM Animal Facts	Nelson	Pets	6
Gulp!	Story Chest	Kingscourt	Ready-set-go Set DD	3
H				
Ha-ha powder, The	Sunshine	Heinemann	Level 1 Set J	8
Hailstorm, The	PM Storybooks	Nelson	Turquoise Set B	7
Hair	Foundations for Reading	Folens	Level 2 Emergent	1
Hair Book, The	Bright and Early Books	Collins	Tether, Graham	6
Hairdresser, The	PM Non-fiction	Nelson	Blue Level	5
Hairy Bear	Story Chest	Kingscourt	Large Read-tog Set 1	5
Hairy Maclary		Picture Puffin	Dodd, Lynley	8
Half For You, Half For Me	Literacy Links Plus	Kingscourt	Early D	6
Halloween	Story Chest	Kingscourt	Get-ready Set CC	1
Hamid does his best	Oxford Reading Tree	OUP	Stage 9 More Robins	9
Hand, Hand, Fingers, Thumb	Bright and Early Books	Collins	Perkins, Al	7
Hands	Literacy Links Plus	Kingscourt	Emergent D	3
Handy Dragon, A	Tiddlywinks	Kingscourt	Stage 1 Large Books	5
Hansel and Gretel	Read it Yourself	Ladybird	Level 1	4
Hansel and Gretel	Storyworlds	Heinemann	Stage 9 Once Upon a Time	10
Happy Birthday Mum		Corgi	Asch, Frank	8
Happy Birthday, Estela!	Ready to Read	Nelson	Early Set A	3
Happy Birthday, Frog	Story Chest	Kingscourt	Get-ready Set DD	2
Happy Birthday, Sam		Picture Puffin	Hutchins, Pat	7
Happy Egg, The	Scholastic Books	Ashton Scholastic	Kraus, Robert	5
Happy Face, Sad Face	Foundations for Reading	Folens	Level 3 Emergent	2
Harbour, The (whole text)	Cambridge Reading	CUP	Becoming a R Stage B	8
Hard Day's Shopping, A	Reading 360 New	Ginn	Little Bks L 1 Set 3	2
Hare and the Tortoise, The	Fables from Aesop	Ginn	Books 13-18	6
Hare and the Tortoise, The	Literacy Links Plus	Kingscourt	Fluent B	8
Hare and the Tortoise, The	Storyworlds	Heinemann	Stage 3 Once Upon a Time	2
Harold and the Purple Crayon		Picture Puffin	Johnson, Crockett	7
Hat Trick, The	Bangers and Mash	Longman	Books 1-6 Pack A	5
Hat Trick, The	Literacy Links Plus	Kingscourt	Emergent B	2

104

TITLE	SERIES	PUBLISHER	SET (OR AUTHOR)	BAND
Hatching is Catching	Bangers and Mash	Longman	Supplementary Books	6
Hats	All Aboard Non Fiction	Ginn	Stage 1	2
Hatseller and the Monkeys, The	Pathways	Collins	Stage 2 Set D	8
Hattie Hates Hats	Pathways	Collins	Stage 3 Set B	10
Haunted House, The	Story Chest	Kingscourt	Ready-set-go Set D	2
Have a Go, Sam	All Aboard	Ginn	Stage 5 Set B Sam & Ros	6
Have You Seen My Duckling?		Picture Puffin	Ginsberg, Mirra	1
Have you seen Stanley?	Reading World	Longman	Level 1 Pack B	2
Have You Seen The Crocodile?		Walker	West, Colin	3
Have You Seen?	Literacy Links Plus	Kingscourt	Emergent C	2
Having a Picnic		Picture Puffin	Garland, Sarah	3
Hay for Ambrosia	Ready to Read	Nelson	Early Set D	4
Hay Making	Wonder World	Badger	Set 2	4
Haystack, The	One, Two, Three & Away	Collins	Main Books 3-4b	5
He Bear, She Bear	Bright and Early Books	Collins	Berenstain, Stan & Jan	7
He Who Listens	Literacy Links Plus	Kingscourt	Fluent A	8
Headache, The	Oxford Reading Tree	OUP	Stage 2 Wrens	1
Hedgehog is Hungry	PM Storybooks	Nelson	Red Set A	2
Hedgehogs	All Aboard Non Fiction	Ginn	Stage 4	5
Hedgehogs	Pathways	Collins	Stage 1 Set D	5
Helicopters	Reading 360	Ginn	Level 4	5
Hello	Story Chest	Kingscourt	Get-ready Set C	2
Hello Big Head!	All Aboard	Ginn	Stage 4 Set A Patt & Rh	5
Hello How Are You?		Red Fox	Watanabe, Shigeo	2
Hello, Dad!	Ready to Read	Nelson	Emergent Set C	2
Hello, Goodbye	Literacy Links Plus	Kingscourt	Emergent B	2
Hello, Hello, Hello	Sunshine New	Heinemann	Level 1 Set E	3
Help	Open Door	Nelson	Red Fun Books	1
Help	Reading 360	Ginn	Level 1	1
Help Me	Story Chest	Kingscourt	Stage 2	5
Helpers	Storyworlds	Heinemann	Stage 2 Our World	2
Helpful Hannah	Reading 360 Upstarts	Ginn	Level 3 Extension	5
Helping Dad	Sunshine New	Heinemann	Level 1 Set B	1
Henny Penny	Scholastic Books	Ashton Scholastic	Galdone, Paul	6
Henry		Methuen	Peppe, Rodney	8
Henry Seamouse	Book Project Fiction 2	Longman	Band 4	10
Henry the Helicopter	Literacy Links Plus	Kingscourt	Emergent D	3
Henry's Busy Day		Lothian	Campbell, Rod	2
Henry's Exercises		Methuen	Peppe, Rodney	5
Henry's Sunbathe		Viking/Kestrel	Peppe, Rodney	7
Here	Reading 360	Ginn	Level 1	2
Here Comes A Bus		Collins Pict Lions	Ziefert, Harriet	4
Here Comes Everyone	Cambridge Reading	CUP	Becoming a R Stage A	5
Here's What I Made	Literacy Links Plus	Kingscourt	Emergent B	2
Herman the Helper		Simon & Schust'r	Kraus, Robert	4
Herman the Helper Lends a Hand		Collins Pict Lions	Kraus, Robert	4
Herman's Tooth	Foundations for Reading	Folens	Level 13 Experienced	5
Hermit Crab	PM Storybooks	Nelson	Yellow Set A	3
Hermit Crab, The	Sunshine	Heinemann	Level 1 Non-fiction	5
Hey Diddle Diddle	Cambridge Reading	CUP	Begin to Read Stage A	2
Hey Presto!	Oxford Reading Tree	OUP	Stage 3 Wrens	2
Hiccups	All Aboard	Ginn	Stage 4 Set A Sam & Ros	4
Hiccups and Burps	All Aboard Non Fiction	Ginn	Stage 4	5
Hickory, Dickory, Dock	Cambridge Reading	CUP	Begin to Read Stage A	2
Hide	Reading 360	Ginn	Magic Circle Level 2	3
Hide and Seek	All Aboard	Ginn	Easy Start Sam & Rosie	1
Hide and Seek	Foundations for Reading	Folens	Level 13 Experienced	5
Hide and Seek	Pathways	Collins	Stage 2 Set E	7

TITLE	SERIES	PUBLISHER	SET (OR AUTHOR)	BAND
Hide and seek	PM Storybooks	Nelson	Red Set B	2
Hide and Seek	Reading 360 New	Ginn	Little Bks L 2 Set 1	3
Hide and Seek	Wonder World	Badger	Set 2	5
Hiding	Foundations for Reading	Folens	Level 5 Emergent	2
Highland cattle, The	Storyworlds	Heinemann	Stage 8 Our World	7
Highland Games, The	Storyworlds	Heinemann	Stage 8 Our World	7
Hill Street	Link Up	Collins	Starter Build-Up	2
Hippos	PM Animal Facts	Nelson	Animals in the Wild	8
Hippo's Hiccups	Literacy Links Plus	Kingscourt	Early C	6
Hogboggit, The	Ready to Read	Nelson	Early Set D	3
Hold Tight Bear!		Walker	Maris, Ron	5
Hole In The Hedge, The	Sunshine Spirals	Heinemann	Set 6	5
Hole in the Wall, The	One, Two, Three & Away	Collins	Red Platform 7-10	6
Hole Story, The	Bangers and Mash	Longman	Books 13-18 Pack C	7
Holiday, The	Oxford Reading Tree	OUP	Stage 10 Robins	8
Holidays	Sunshine Spirals Starters	Heinemann	Set B	1
Home	Reading 360	Ginn	Level 1	2
Home for a Bunny	Reading 360	Ginn	Level 5	7
Home for little Teddy, A	PM Storybooks	Nelson	Red Set B	2
Home Sweet Home		MacMillan	Roffey, Maureen	4
Home Time	All Aboard	Ginn	Stage 3 Sam & Rosie	3
Homes		Picture Puffin	Pienkowski, Jan	1
Homes	Discovery World	Heinemann	Stage B	2
Honey for Baby Bear	PM Storybooks	Nelson	Blue Set A	4
Honeybee	All Aboard Non Fiction	Ginn	Stage 1	2
Hop on Pop	Beginner Books	Collins	Seuss, Dr	6
Hop, Hop, Kangaroo	Pathways	Collins	Stage 2 Set F	7
Horace	Story Chest	Kingscourt	Ready-set-go Set C	2
Horrible Baby	Book Project Fiction 2	Longman	Band 3	10
Horrible Urktar of Or, The	Sunshine New	Heinemann	Level 1 Set G	4
Horse in Harry's Room, The		Heinemann	Hoff, Syd	7
Horse that Flew in the Moonlight, The	One, Two, Three & Away	Collins	Yellow Platform 7-10	9
Horse, The	Sunshine Spirals	Heinemann	Set 7	5
Horses	PM Animal Facts	Nelson	Farm Animals	9
Horses	Reading 360	Ginn	Level 3	4
Hot Dog		Collins Pict Lions	Powling, Chris	1
Hot Potato and Cold Potato	Foundations for Reading	Folens	Level 2 Emergent	1
House Across the Street, The	One, Two, Three & Away	Collins	Yellow Platform 1-6	6
House for sale	Oxford Reading Tree	OUP	Stage 4 Playscripts	3
House for sale	Oxford Reading Tree	OUP	Stage 4 Storybooks	4
House in Dark Woods, The	One, Two, Three & Away	Collins	Main Books 9-12	9
House in the Corner of the Wood, The	One, Two, Three & Away	Collins	Main Books 3-4b	5
House in the Tree, The	PM Storybooks	Nelson	Blue Set A	4
House, A	PM Storybook Starters	Nelson	Set 1	1
Househunting	PM Storybooks	Nelson	Green Set A	5
Houses	One, Two, Three & Away	Collins	Pre-reader 5-8	2
Houses	Story Chest	Kingscourt	Get-ready Set B	2
Houses	Wonder World	Badger	Set 2	9
How a Volcano is Formed	Wonder World	Badger	Set 4	7
How Can You Hide an Elephant?	Reading 360	Ginn	Magic Circle Level 4	5
How Do I Eat It?		Red Fox	Watanabe, Shigeo	5
How Do I Put It On?		Red Fox	Watanabe, Shigeo	3
How Do You Measure a Dinosaur?	Ready to Read	Nelson	Fluent Set B	9
How Does Your Garden Grow?	Reading 2000	Longmans	Storytime Reds	6
How Far Will a Rubber Band Stretch?		Collins Pict Lions	Barton, Byron	4
How Fire Came To Earth	Literacy Links Plus	Kingscourt	Early D	7
How Many Candles?	Pathways	Collins	Stage 0 Set B	1
How Many Hot Dogs?	Story Chest	Kingscourt	Ready-set-go Set CC	4

TITLE	SERIES	PUBLISHER	SET (OR AUTHOR)	BAND
How to Choose a Pet	Discovery World	Heinemann	Stage E	9
How to Make a Hot Dog	Story Chest	Kingscourt	Get-ready Set DD	3
How to make Can Stilts	Story Chest	Kingscourt	Ready-set-go Set BB	2
How to Weigh an Elephant	Ready to Read	Nelson	Fluent Set D	9
How Turtle Raced Beaver	Literacy Links Plus	Kingscourt	Early D	7
Hug is warm, A	Sunshine	Heinemann	Level 1 Set D	2
Huggles' breakfast	Sunshine	Heinemann	Level 1 Set A	1
Huggles can juggle	Sunshine	Heinemann	Level 1 Set A	1
Huggles goes away	Sunshine	Heinemann	Level 1 Set A	1
Humpty Dumpty	Cambridge Reading	CUP	Begin to Read Stage A	2
Humpty Dumpty		Viking/Kestrel	Peppe, Rodney	2
Hundred hugs, A	Sunshine	Heinemann	Level 1 Set J	6
Hungry Bear	Sunshine Spirals Starters	Heinemann	Set B	1
Hungry Cat, The		Walker	King, Phyllis	2
Hungry Chickens, The	Literacy Links Plus	Kingscourt	Early C	5
Hungry Giant, The	Story Chest	Kingscourt	Large Read-tog Set 1	5
Hungry Giant's Lunch, The	Story Chest	Kingscourt	Ready-set-go Set DD	3
Hungry Horse	Literacy Links Plus	Kingscourt	Emergent B	3
Hungry Kitten, The	PM Storybooks	Nelson	Yellow Set A	3
Hungry Lion, The	Sunshine Spirals	Heinemann	Set 3	3
Hungry Monster	Story Chest	Kingscourt	Stage 3	6
Hunt for gold, The	Oxford Reading Tree	OUP	Stage 7 More Owls	7
Hunting in the Marshes	Cambridge Reading	CUP	Begin to Read Stage A	1

I				

TITLE	SERIES	PUBLISHER	SET (OR AUTHOR)	BAND
I am a bookworm	Sunshine	Heinemann	Level 1 Set C	2
I am Cold	Foundations for Reading	Folens	Level 5 Emergent	3
I am frightened	Story Chest	Kingscourt	Get-ready Set C	2
I am Hot	Foundations for Reading	Folens	Level 5 Emergent	3
I am Red	Book Project	Longman	Beginner Band 1	1
I am...	Sunrise	Heinemann		1
I Can	Pathways	Collins	Stage O Set B	2
I Can Build a House		Red Fox	Watanabe, Shigeo	3
I Can Climb	Sunshine Spirals	Heinemann	Set 2	1
I Can Do Anything!	Sunshine New	Heinemann	Level 1 Set A	2
I Can Do It		Penguin	Watanabe, Shigeo	3
I Can Do It Myself	Literacy Links Plus	Kingscourt	Emergent B	3
I can fly	Sunshine	Heinemann	Level 1 Set A	1
I Can Hide	Reading 360	Ginn	Level 2	3
I Can Hide	Reading 360 New	Ginn	Level 2	3
I can jump	Sunshine	Heinemann	Level 1 Set D	2
I Can Make You Red	Book Project	Longman	Beginner Band 1	2
I Can Read	Ready to Read	Nelson	Emergent Set A	1
I Can Read	Reading 360	Ginn	Level 3	4
I Can Read Anything	Sunshine New	Heinemann	Level 1 Set C	2
I Can Read With My Eyes Shut	Beginner Books	Collins	Seuss, Dr	6
I Can See the Leaves	Ready to Read	Nelson	Fluent Set D	9
I Don't Feel Well		Picture Puffin	Brandenberg, Franz	8
I Fell out of Bed	All Aboard	Ginn	Stage 3 Set A Patt & Rh	3
I go, go, go	Sunrise	Heinemann		1
I have a Home	Sunshine New	Heinemann	Level 1 Set E	2
I Have a Question, Grandma	Literacy Links Plus	Kingscourt	Early D	6
I Hear		Collins Pict Lions	Isadora, Rachel	3
I Know That Tune!	Foundations for Reading	Folens	Level 7 Early	3
I Like	Literacy Links Plus	Kingscourt	Emergent C	2
I Like Green	Book Project	Longman	Beginner Band 1	1
I Like Shopping	Sunshine New	Heinemann	Level 3	7
I Like Spaceships	Reading 360 Upstarts	Ginn	Level 2 Extension	3
I Like Worms	Sunshine Spirals	Heinemann	Set 4	3

TITLE	SERIES	PUBLISHER	SET (OR AUTHOR)	BAND
I Like...	Sunrise	Heinemann		1
I Look Like This		Sainsbury	Sharratt, Nick	3
I love Chickens	Story Chest	Kingscourt	Ready-set-go Set BB	2
I Love My Family	Foundations for Reading	Folens	Level 1 Emergent	1
I love my family	Sunshine	Heinemann	Level 1 Set C	2
I Paint	Literacy Links Plus	Kingscourt	Emergent B	1
I Saw a Dinosaur	Literacy Links Plus	Kingscourt	Emergent D	4
I see Green!	One, Two, Three & Away	Collins	Pre-reader 5a-8a	2
I Smell Smoke	Sunshine New	Heinemann	Level 1 Set F	3
I Spy	Literacy Links Plus	Kingscourt	Emergent B	2
I Spy	Sunshine Spirals	Heinemann	Set 8	6
I Spy a Fly	Wonder World	Badger	Set 3	9
I Touch		Collins Pict Lions	Isadora, Rachel	3
I Want A Go!	All Aboard	Ginn	Stage 2 Sam & Rosie	2
I Want a Party!	Pathways	Collins	Stage 3 Set D	9
I Want A Red Ball	Book Project	Longman	Beginner Band 1	2
I Want an Ice-Cream	Story Chest	Kingscourt	Ready-set-go Set A	2
I Want To Be	Book Project	Longman	Beginner Band 1	2
I Was Walking Down the Road	Scholastic Books	Ashton Scholastic	Barchas, Sarah	5
I Went to School This Morning	Cambridge Reading	CUP	Begin to Read Stage B	2
I Wish		Nelson	Cartwright, Pauline	2
I Wish I Could Fly		Picture Puffin	Maris, Ron	3
I wonder	Sunshine	Heinemann	Level 1 Non-fiction	4
I Wonder Why?	Foundations for Reading	Folens	Level 5 Emergent	2
I Wonder Why?	Wonder World	Badger	Set 3	5
I Write	Sunrise	Heinemann		2
Icecream	Sunshine	Heinemann	Level 1 Set D	2
Ice-Cream Stick	Story Chest	Kingscourt	Get-ready Set DD	2
If I Had A Pig		Picturemac	Inkpen, Mick	5
If I Had a Sheep		Picturemac	Inkpen, Mick	5
If I had a Zoo		Tree House	Nancy, Helen	3
If I Were A Giant	Pathways	Collins	Stage 2 Set E	5
If I were a Pilot		Tree House	Nancy, Helen	3
If I were a Witch		Nelson	Cartwright, Pauline	5
If You Like Strawberries	Literacy Links Plus	Kingscourt	Early B	5
If You Meet a Dragon	Story Chest	Kingscourt	Get-ready Set A	1
If You're Happy	Literacy Links Plus	Kingscourt	Early B	4
I'll Teach My Dog 100 Words	Bright and Early Books	Collins	Frith, Michael	7
I'm a Chef	Literacy Links Plus	Kingscourt	Fluent D	10
I'm a Good Boy	Reading 360 New	Ginn	Little Bks L.4 Set 3	5
I'm A Little Teapot		Simon & Schust'r	Kemp, Moira	3
I'm bigger than you!	Sunshine	Heinemann	Level 1 Set E	3
I'm Brave	Sunshine New	Heinemann	Level 1 Set E	2
I'm Coming to Get You		Picture Puffin	Ross, Tony	6
I'm Running Away	All Aboard	Ginn	Stage 4 Set A Patt & Rh	4
I'm The King Of The Castle		Penguin	Watanabe, Shigeo	5
I'm the King of the Mountain	Ready to Read	Nelson	Early Set D	5
Imran and the Watch	Cambridge Reading	CUP	Becoming a R Stage C	6
In a Dark Dark Wood	Story Chest	Kingscourt	Small Read-together	3
In a Jam	Bangers and Mash	Longman	Books 1-6 Pack A	7
In My Bed	Literacy Links Plus	Kingscourt	Emergent C	2
In My House		Methuen	Bruna, Dick	1
In My Imagination		Nelson	Cartwright, Pauline	10
In My Room	Literacy Links Plus	Kingscourt	Emergent C	2
In the Afternoon	PM Non-fiction	Nelson	Green Level	6
In the Bathroom	Sunshine Spirals Starters	Heinemann	Set D	1
In the Box	Book Project	Longman	Beginner Band 1	2
In the City of Rome	Literacy Links Plus	Kingscourt	Fluent D	5

TITLE	SERIES	PUBLISHER	SET (OR AUTHOR)	BAND
In the Dark Forest	Ready to Read	Nelson	Emergent Set C	1
In the Desert	Sunshine New	Heinemann	Level 1 Set F	3
In the Garden	Oxford Reading Tree	OUP	Stage 6 Owls	5
In the Garden	Literacy Links Plus	Kingscourt	Early B	4
In the Middle of the Night	Sunshine	Heinemann	Level 4	5
In the Mirror	Story Chest	Kingscourt	Get-ready Set A	1
In the Morning	All Aboard Non Fiction	Ginn	Stage 1 Intro	2
In the Morning	PM Non-fiction	Nelson	Green Level	6
In the Night	Reading 2000	Longmans	Storytime Yellows	6
In the Park	Foundations for Reading	Folens	Level 2 Emergent	1
In the Park	Literacy Links Plus	Kingscourt	Early C	5
In the Park	Pathways	Collins	Stage 2 Set F	7
In the Town	Reading 360 New	Ginn	Level 5	7
In the Toy Shop	Book Project	Longman	Beginner Band 1	2
In the Trolley	PM Storybook Starters	Nelson	Set 1	1
In the Zoo	Reading 360	Ginn	Magic Circle Level 4	5
In Trouble	Sunshine Spirals Starters	Heinemann	Set B	1
In Went Goldilocks	Literacy Links Plus	Kingscourt	Emergent D	2
Incy Wincy Spider	Cambridge Reading	CUP	Begin to Read Stage A	2
Indians and red spots	Bangers and Mash	Longman	Books 7-12 Pack B	8
Insect Body Parts	Discovery World	Heinemann	Stage E	9
Insects That Bother Us	Foundations for Reading	Folens	Level 11 Early	4
Inside or Outside	Literacy Links Plus	Kingscourt	Early B	4
Inside the Red and White Tent	Reading 360	Ginn	Magic Circle Level 4	5
Inside, Outside, Upside Down	Bright and Early Books	Collins	Berenstain, Stan & Jan	3
Invisible Spy, The	Foundations for Reading	Folens	Level 14 Experienced	4
Is Anyone Home?		Picture Puffin	Maris, Ron	3
Is It Time Yet?	Foundations for Reading	Folens	Level 12 Early	5
Is This My Home?	Reading 360 New	Ginn	Little Bks L 1 Set 1	2
Is This You?	Scholastic Books	Ashton Scholastic	Krauss, Ruth	4
Island in Deep River, The	One, Two, Three & Away	Collins	Main Books 3-4b	5
Island Picnic, The	PM Storybooks	Nelson	Green Set A	5
Island, The	Oxford RT Branch Library	OUP	Wildsmith Bks St 2A	2
Isobel's Noisy Tummy		Red Fox	McKee, David	7
It takes time to grow	Sunshine	Heinemann	Level 1 Non-fiction	4
It's My Bread	Ready to Read	Nelson	Emergent Set C	1
It's Noisy at Night	Wonder World	Badger	Set 1	4
It's Not Easy Being a Bunny	Beginner Books	Collins	Sadler, Marilyn	6
It's Not Fair	All Aboard	Ginn	Stage 4 Set B Sam & Ros	5
It's Not Fair	Oxford Reading Tree	OUP	Stage 5 More Stories A	6
It's Not Fair		Picture Puffin	Harper, Anita	5
It's The Weather	Oxford Reading Tree	OUP	Stage 3 Wrens	2
I've Got a Secret		Nelson	Hucklesby, Hope	4
J				
Jabeen and the New Moon	All Aboard	Ginn	Stage 1 Intro Sam & Ro	2
Jack and Chug	PM Storybooks	Nelson	Orange Set A	6
Jack and the Beanstalk	Read It Yourself	Ladybird	Level 3	7
Jack and the Beanstalk	Storyworlds	Heinemann	Stage 9 Once Upon a Time	10
Jack and the Beanstalk (1)	Scholastic Books	Ashton Scholastic	Weisner, David	8
Jack and the Giant	Sunshine Spirals	Heinemann	Set 3	3
Jack de Pert at the Supermarket	Wonder World	Badger	Set 1	7
Jack in the Box	All Aboard	Ginn	Stage 1 Sam & Rosie	2
Jack-in-the-Box	Story Chest	Kingscourt	Stage 3	6
Jamaica and Brianna		Mammoth	Havill, Juanita	10
James and the Dragon	Reading 360 Upstarts	Ginn	Level 3	5
Jan and Dan	Reading 360 Upstarts	Ginn	Level 1 Extension	3
Jan and the Anorak	Oxford Reading Tree	OUP	Stage 3 Sparrows	3
Jan and the Chocolate	Oxford Reading Tree	OUP	Stage 3 Sparrows	3

TITLE	SERIES	PUBLISHER	SET (OR AUTHOR)	BAND
Jane and the Monster	Reading 360 Upstarts	Ginn	Level 1 Extension	3
Jane's Car	PM Storybooks	Nelson	Blue Set A	4
January	Cambridge Reading	CUP	Begin to Read Stage A	1
Jasper's Beanstalk		Picture Knights	Butterworth and Inkpen	4
Jen the Hen		Piccadilly	Hawkins, Colin	6
Jennifer Yellow-hat and the White Cat	One, Two, Three & Away	Collins	Pre-reader 1b-4b	2
Jennifer and the Little Black Horse	One, Two, Three & Away	Collins	Red Platform 1-6	6
Jennifer and the Little Dog	One, Two, Three & Away	Collins	Blue Platform 11-16	3
Jennifer and the Little Fox	One, Two, Three & Away	Collins	Introductory W-Z	4
Jennifer and the Little Yellow Cat	One, Two, Three & Away	Collins	Pre-reader 5a-8a	2
Jennifer in Dark Woods	One, Two, Three & Away	Collins	Blue Platform 11-16	4
Jennifer went to School	One, Two, Three & Away	Collins	Pre-reader 9-12	2
Jennifer Yellow-hat and Mr Brown's Goat	One, Two, Three & Away	Collins	Pre-reader 1b-4b	2
Jennifer Yellow-hat went out in the Dark	One, Two, Three & Away	Collins	Introductory E-H	3
Jennifer Yellow-hat went to Town	One, Two, Three & Away	Collins	Introductory I-L	2
Jenny and the Dragon	Reading 360 Upstarts	Ginn	Level 1 Extension	3
Jessica in the Dark	PM Storybooks	Nelson	Orange Set B	6
Jessie's Flower	Tiddlywinks	Kingscourt	Stage 1 Small Books	5
Jennifer Yellow-hat went out in the Sunshine	One, Two, Three & Away	Collins	Introductory E-H	3
Jigaree, The	Story Chest	Kingscourt	Large Read-tog Set 2	3
Jigsaw puzzle, The	Oxford Reading Tree	OUP	Stage 7 More Owls	7
Jigsaw, The	Sunshine Spirals Starters	Heinemann	Set D	1
Jilly's Days	Book Project Fiction 2	Longman	Band 2	7
Jimmy	Foundations for Reading	Folens	Level 7 Early	3
Jimmy James	Reading World	Longman	Level 3	9
Jimmy's Birthday Balloon	Foundations for Reading	Folens	Level 5 Emergent	3
Jimmy's Goal	Foundations for Reading	Folens	Level 11 Early	5
Job For Giant Jim, A	Sunshine New	Heinemann	Level 1 Set J	6
Jobs in School	Ginn Geography Topic Bks	Ginn	Year 1	4
Joe and the Bike	Oxford Reading Tree	OUP	Stage 3 Sparrows	3
Joe and the Mouse	Oxford Reading Tree	OUP	Stage 4 Sparrows	4
Joey	PM Storybooks	Nelson	Green Set B	5
Joggers, The	Reading World	Longman	Level 1 Pack B	2
John Quilt	All Aboard	Ginn	Stage 5 Set B Patt & Rh	5
John The Bookworm		Nelson	O'Brien, John	3
Johnny and Jennifer Yellow-hat	One, Two, Three & Away	Collins	Introductory A-D	2
Johnny Lion's Rubber Boots		Heinemann	Hurd, Edith Thatcher	8
Jojo and the Robot	Sunshine	Heinemann	Level 5	7
Joke Book	Pathways	Collins	Stage 2 Set E	5
Jolly Roger, the pirate	PM Storybooks	Nelson	Yellow Set B	3
Jonathan Buys a Present	PM Storybooks	Nelson	Turquoise Set A	7
Jordan's Lucky day	PM Storybooks	Nelson	Turquoise Set C	7
Joshua's Junk	Book Project Fiction 2	Longman	Band 3	9
Journey into the earth, The	Storyworlds	Heinemann	Stage 9 Fantasy World	9
Journey, A	Sunshine Spirals	Heinemann	Set 2	2
Journey, The	Oxford Reading Tree	OUP	Stage 2 More Wrens	1
Juggler, The	Pathways	Collins	Stage 0 Set C	1
Juggler, The	Sunshine Spirals	Heinemann	Set 1	1
Jumble Sale, The	Oxford Reading Tree	OUP	Stage 3 More Stories A	3
Jump, Jump, Kangaroo	Story Chest	Kingscourt	Get-ready Set CC	2
Jumper, The	Reading World	Longman	Level 1 Pack B	2
Jumpers	Bangers and Mash	Longman	Supplementary Books	6
Jumpers	Sunshine New	Heinemann	Level 1 Set A	1
Jumping	Cambridge Reading	CUP	Begin to Read Stage A	2
Jumping Beans	Book Project Fiction 1	Longman	Band 2 Read On	3
Just a Touch of Magic	Pathways	Collins	Stage 4 Set C	10
Just Add Water	Discovery World	Heinemann	Stage B	2
Just Like Daddy		Corgi	Asch, Frank	4

TITLE	SERIES	PUBLISHER	SET (OR AUTHOR)	BAND
Just Like Grandpa	Literacy Links Plus	Kingscourt	Early A	4
Just Like Me	Link Up	Collins	Level 2	5
Just Like Me	Story Chest	Kingscourt	Stage 4	7
Just Like Me!	Sunshine New	Heinemann	Level 1 Set F	2
Just Look at You!	Sunrise	Heinemann		1
Just My Luck	Literacy Links Plus	Kingscourt	Early C	7
Just One Guinea Pig	PM Storybooks	Nelson	Orange Set B	6
Just One More Block		Lothian	Mayers, Hawkinson	6
Just this once	Sunshine	Heinemann	Level 1 Set I	5
K				
Kangaroo	Sunshine Spirals	Heinemann	Set 6	4
Kangaroo From Wooloomooloo, The	Tiddlywinks	Kingscourt	Stage 1 Small Books	7
Kangaroos	All Aboard	Ginn	Stage 6 Pattern & Rhyme	7
Kangaroos	PM Animal Facts	Nelson	Animals in the Wild	8
Karen At The Zoo	Link Up	Collins	Level 2	5
Kate and the Crocodile	Oxford Reading Tree	OUP	Stage 7 Woodpeckers	7
Kate and the Sheep	Oxford Reading Tree	OUP	Stage 8 Robins	8
Katie and Debbie go to the Moon	Reading 360 Upstarts	Ginn	Level 2	4
Keeping Tadpoles Alive	Discovery World	Heinemann	Stage F	10
Keith's Croak	Book Project Fiction 1	Longman	Band 3 Read On	4
Ketchup on your Cornflakes		Picture Hippo	Sharratt, Nick	1
Kiboko and the water snake	Storyworlds	Heinemann	Stage 7 Animal World	5
Kick-a-Lot Shoes, The	Story Chest	Kingscourt	Stage 2	6
Kidnappers, The	Oxford Reading Tree	OUP	Stage 8 Magpies	6
Kim and the computer giant	Storyworlds	Heinemann	Stage 8 Fantasy World	8
Kim and the computer mouse	Storyworlds	Heinemann	Stage 8 Fantasy World	8
Kim and the missing paint pot	Storyworlds	Heinemann	Stage 8 Fantasy World	8
Kim and the Shape Dragon	Storyworlds	Heinemann	Stage 8 Fantasy World	8
King Grumpyguts	Book Project Fiction 2	Longman	Band 1	7
King of the Magic Mountains, The	One, Two, Three & Away	Collins	Yellow Platform 7-10	7
King, The Mice and the Cheese, The	Beginner Books	Collins	Gurney, Nancy	8
King's Box, The	Reading 360 Upstarts	Ginn	Level 1 Extension	3
King's Porridge, The	All Aboard	Ginn	Stage 5 Set B Patt & Rh	5
King's Pudding, The	Tiddlywinks	Kingscourt	Stage 1 Large Books	6
King's Sock, The	Reading 360 New	Ginn	Little Bks L 1 Set 3	2
Kipper and the Giant	Oxford Reading Tree	OUP	Stage 6 Owls	6
Kipper the Clown	Oxford Reading Tree	OUP	Stage 3 More Stories A	3
Kipper's Balloon	Oxford Reading Tree	OUP	Stage 2 More Stories A	3
Kipper's Birthday	Oxford Reading Tree	OUP	Stage 2 More Stories A	3
Kipper's Idea	Oxford Reading Tree	OUP	Stage 3 More Stories A	4
Kipper's Laces	Oxford Reading Tree	OUP	Stage 2 More Stories B	4
Kiss For Little Bear, A		Mammoth	Minarik, E.H.	6
Kite that Blew Away, The	One, Two, Three & Away	Collins	Introductory W-Z	4
Kittens	Literacy Links Plus	Kingscourt	Emergent B	2
Knit, Knit, Knit, Knit	Literacy Links Plus	Kingscourt	Fluent A	6
Koalas	Literacy Links Plus	Kingscourt	Emergent B	2
L				
Lad	Reading 360	Ginn	Level 1	1
Lake of Stars, The	Storyworlds	Heinemann	Stage 5 Once Upon a Time	5
Land of the Dinosaurs	Oxford Reading Tree	OUP	Stage 6 Owls	6
Land of the Dinosaurs	Oxford Reading Tree	OUP	Stage 6 Playscripts	5
Late Again, Mai Ling?	Book Project Fiction 1	Longman	Band 1 Read Aloud	3
Late At Night	All Aboard	Ginn	Stage 1 Pattern & Rhyme	2
Late For Football	PM Storybooks	Nelson	Blue Set A	4
Laughing Princess, The	Oxford Reading Tree	OUP	Stage 6 More Owls	6
Lavender the Library Cat	Tiddlywinks	Kingscourt	Stage 6	9
Lazy Mary	Story Chest	Kingscourt	Large Read-tog Set 1	4
Lazy Pig, The	PM Storybooks	Nelson	Red Set A	2

TITLE	SERIES	PUBLISHER	SET (OR AUTHOR)	BAND
Learning New Things	Foundations for Reading	Folens	Level 8 Early	3
Legs	Literacy Links Plus	Kingscourt	Early A	2
Legs, Legs, Legs	Wonder World	Badger	Set 1	3
Lelang and Julie save the day	Book Project Fiction 2	Longman	Band 2	9
Lelang's new friend	Book Project Fiction 2	Longman	Band 2	9
Leonora and the Giddy House	Book Project Fiction 1	Longman	Band 4 Read Aloud	7
Let Me In	Story Chest	Kingscourt	Stage 3	5
Let The Dog Sleep	Reading 360 New	Ginn	Little Bks L 3 Set 2	5
Let's Build a Tower	Literacy Links Plus	Kingscourt	Emergent A	1
Let's Dance	Pathways	Collins	Stage 2 Set C	4
Let's Get a Pet	Tiddlywinks	Kingscourt	Stage 2	6
Let's Go Home, Little Bear		Walker	Waddell, Martin	7
Let's Go Into The Jungle	Book Project Fiction 1	Longman	Band 1 Read Aloud	6
Let's Have a Dog	Pathways	Collins	Stage 2 Set D	6
Let's Make Music	Tiddlywinks	Kingscourt	Stage 1 Large Books	5
Let's Play Monsters	All Aboard	Ginn	Stage 2 Sam & Rosie	2
Letters for Mr James	Sunshine	Heinemann	Level 1 Set I	7
Letters From Lucy	Pathways	Collins	Stage 3 Set A	8
Library Day	Sunshine	Heinemann	Level 5	7
Lift, The	Story Chest	Kingscourt	Ready-set-go Set CC	3
Lights at Night	Ready to Read	Nelson	Emergent Set B	1
Lilly-Lolly-Littlelegs	Literacy Links Plus	Kingscourt	Early B	5
Lily and the Vacuum Cleaner	Reading World	Longman	Level 3	8
Lion and the Mouse, The	Cambridge Reading	CUP	Becoming a R Stage A	4
Lion and the Mouse, The	Fables from Aesop	Ginn	Books 13-18	5
Lion and the Mouse, The	PM Storybooks	Nelson	Blue Set A	5
Lion and the Rabbit, The	PM Storybooks	Nelson	Blue Set A	4
Lion Pit	Bangers and Mash	Longman	Books 1A-6A	7
Lions and Tigers	PM Animal Facts	Nelson	Animals in the Wild	8
Lion's Roar, The	All Aboard	Ginn	Stage 6 Pattern & Rhyme	7
Lisa's Letter	Book Project Fiction 1	Longman	Band 2 Read On	3
Litter Queen, The	Oxford Reading Tree	OUP	Stage 9 Magpies	7
Litterbug	Reading World	Longman	Level 2: More Books	6
Little brother	Story Chest	Kingscourt	Get-ready Set C	2
Little brother	Sunshine	Heinemann	Level 1 Set B	1
Little Brown House, The	Tiddlywinks	Kingscourt	Stage 3	6
Little Brown Mouse and the Apples, The	One, Two, Three & Away	Collins	Blue Platform 11-16	3
Little Brown Mouse went out in the Dark	One, Two, Three & Away	Collins	Introductory M-P	3
Little Bulldozer	PM Storybooks	Nelson	Yellow Set A	3
Little Bulldozer helps again	PM Storybooks	Nelson	Blue Set B	4
Little car	Sunshine	Heinemann	Level 1 Set G	5
Little Dinosaur Escapes	PM Storybooks	Nelson	Turquoise Set B	7
Little Dragon, The	Oxford Reading Tree	OUP	Stage 3 More Wrens	2
Little Eight John	All Aboard	Ginn	Stage 7 Pattern & Rhyme	9
Little Elephant Who Liked to Play, The	Reading 360	Ginn	Magic Circle Level 5	7
Little Fox, The	One, Two, Three & Away	Collins	Red Platform 7-10	6
Little Frog and the Dog	Book Project Fiction 1	Longman	Band 2 Read On	4
Little Frog and the Frog Olympics	Book Project Fiction 1	Longman	Band 2 Read On	4
Little Frog and the Tadpoles	Book Project Fiction 1	Longman	Band 2 Read On	4
Little Girl and her Beetle, The	Literacy Links Plus	Kingscourt	Fluent B	7
Little Girl and the Bear, The	Storyworlds	Heinemann	Stage 9 Once Upon a Time	10
Little Hearts	Story Chest	Kingscourt	Ready-set-go Set AA	3
Little House	Ready to Read	Nelson	Fluent Set B	5
Little Meanie's Lunch	Story Chest	Kingscourt	Ready-set-go Set AA	2
Little Miss Muffet	Pathways	Collins	Stage 2 Set C	5
Little Monkey Is Stuck	Foundations for Reading	Folens	Level 12 Early	5
Little Monster	All Aboard	Ginn	Stage 2 Set A Patt & Rh	3
Little Old Lady Who Danced on the Moon The	Sunshine New	Heinemann	Level 5	7

TITLE	SERIES	PUBLISHER	SET (OR AUTHOR)	BAND
Little Old Man and the Donkey, The	One, Two, Three & Away	Collins	Blue Platform 1-6	2
Little Old Man and the Little Black Cat, The	One, Two, Three & Away	Collins	Green Platform 1-6	5
Little Old Man and the Little Brown Mouse	One, Two, Three & Away	Collins	Blue Platform 11-16	4
Little Old Man and the Magic Stick, The	One, Two, Three & Away	Collins	Green Platform 7-10	5
Little Old Woman and the G'father Clock	One, Two, Three & Away	Collins	Green Platform 1-6	5
Little Old Woman, The	One, Two, Three & Away	Collins	Blue Platform 1-6	2
Little Pig	Story Chest	Kingscourt	Ready-set-go Set B	2
Little Rabbit	Storyworlds	Heinemann	Stage 4 Once Upon a Time	3
Little Rabbit, The	Reading 360 New	Ginn	Little Bks L 3 Set 2	5
Little Red Bus, The	PM Storybooks	Nelson	Green Set A	5
Little Red Hen, The	Cambridge Reading	CUP	Becoming a R Stage B	5
Little Red Hen, The	Favourite Tales	Ladybird		6
Little Red Hen, The	Literacy Links Plus	Kingscourt	Traditional Tales	5
Little Red Hen, The	PM Traditional Tales	Nelson	Orange Level	6
Little Red Riding Hood	PM Traditional Tales	Nelson	Turquoise Level	7
Little Red Riding Hood	Storyworlds	Heinemann	Stage 8 Once Upon a Time	7
Little Seed, A	Sunshine Spirals Starters	Heinemann	Set A	1
Little snowman, The	PM Storybooks	Nelson	Red Set B	2
Little Things	PM Storybook Starters	Nelson	Set 1	1
Little Tuppen		Seabury Press	Galdone, Paul	8
Little Yellow Cat & the Little Brown Mouse	One, Two, Three & Away	Collins	Pre-reader 9-12	2
Living in the Sky	Sunshine New	Heinemann	Level 4	7
Liz and Digger	Reading 360 New	Ginn	Level 2	3
Lizard	Foundations for Reading	Folens	Level 8 Early	3
Lizard Loses His Tail	PM Storybooks	Nelson	Red Set A	2
Lizard on a Stick	Wonder World	Badger	Set 4	2
Lizzie and the Car Wash	All Aboard	Ginn	Stage 3 Sam & Rosie	3
Locked Out	PM Storybooks	Nelson	Blue Set A	5
Locked Out	Sunshine Spirals	Heinemann	Set 7	4
Lollies	All Aboard	Ginn	Easy Start Sam & Rosie	1
Lonely Bull, The	Ready to Read	Nelson	Early Set C	3
Lonely Giant, The	Literacy Links Plus	Kingscourt	Fluent B	8
Lonely Stanley	Reading World	Longman	Level 2 Pack B	7
Long Grass of Tumbledown Road, The	Tiddlywinks	Kingscourt	Stage 4	10
Long journey, The	Oxford Reading Tree	OUP	Stage 7 More Robins	9
Long, long tail, The	Sunshine	Heinemann	Level 1 Set B	1
Longer, Faster and Bigger	Open Door	Nelson	Yellow Fun Books	2
Look	Reading 360	Ginn	Level 1	1
Look	Reading 360	Ginn	Magic Circle Level 3	1
Look Around	Link Up	Collins	Level 1	3
Look At Me	Journeys in Reading	Schofield & Sims	Level 1	2
Look At Me	Open Door	Nelson	Red Fun Books	2
Look at Me	PM Storybook Starters	Nelson	Set 1	1
Look at my Spots	Reading 360 Upstarts	Ginn	Level 1	3
Look Closer	Pathways	Collins	Stage 2 Set C	7
Look for Me	Story Chest	Kingscourt	Ready-set-go Set C	2
Look Here!	Wonder World	Badger	Set 2	2
Look Inside		Lothian	Campbell, Rod	1
Look Like Me	Reading 360 New	Ginn	Little Bks L 2 Set 1	3
Look Out for Your Tail	Literacy Links Plus	Kingscourt	Fluent C	8
Look Out!	Literacy Links Plus	Kingscourt	Emergent B	1
Look Out!	Pathways	Collins	Stage 0 Set C	1
Look Out!	Sunshine New	Heinemann	Level 1 Set E	2
Look Out! He's Behind You!		Little Mammoth	Bradman, Tony	5
Look Out, Dan!	Story Chest	Kingscourt	Get-ready Set CC	2
Look Out, Harry!	Book Project Fiction 1	Longman	Band 2 Read On	4
Look Up, Look Down	PM Non-fiction	Nelson	Red Level	3
Look What I Can Do		Collins Pict Lions	Aruego, Jose	1

TITLE	SERIES	PUBLISHER	SET (OR AUTHOR)	BAND
Look What I Found!		Sainsbury	Sharratt, Nick	3
Look with Mai Ling	Reading 360	Ginn	Magic Circle Level 3	2
Look!	Ginn Science	Ginn		4
Look...	Sunrise	Heinemann		1
Looking after Grandpa	Foundations for Reading	Folens	Level 5 Emergent	3
Looking at Light	Discovery World	Heinemann	Stage D	8
Looking Down	PM Storybook Starters	Nelson	Set 2	1
Looking For Dragons	Cambridge Reading	CUP	Begin to Read Stage A	2
Lord Scarecrow	All Aboard	Ginn	Stage 6 Sam & Rosie	6
Lost	Reading 360 New	Ginn	Little Bks L 1 Set 2	2
Lost	Story Chest	Kingscourt	Ready-set-go Set B	2
Lost	Sunshine Spirals Starters	Heinemann	Set D	1
Lost and Found	Reading 360 New	Ginn	Level 3	5
Lost at the fun park	PM Storybooks	Nelson	Blue Set B	4
Lost at the School Fair	All Aboard	Ginn	Stage 3 Booster Bks	4
Lost coat, The	Storyworlds	Heinemann	Stage 3 Our World	2
Lost Dog, The	One, Two, Three & Away	Collins	Main Books 9-12	7
Lost Glove, The	Foundations for Reading	Folens	Level 5 Emergent	3
Lost in the Forest	PM Storybooks	Nelson	Orange Set C	6
Lost in the Jungle	Oxford Reading Tree	OUP	Stage 7 Owls	8
Lost in the Jungle	Oxford Reading Tree	OUP	Stage 7 Playscripts	6
Lost in the mist	Storyworlds	Heinemann	Stage 8 Our World	7
Lost Key, The	Oxford Reading Tree	OUP	Stage 7 Owls	7
Lost Key, The	Oxford Reading Tree	OUP	Stage 7 Playscripts	6
Lost Puppy, The	Oxford Reading Tree	OUP	Stage 3 More Wrens	2
Lucky day for Little Dinosaur, A	PM Storybooks	Nelson	Yellow Set B	3
Lucky Goes to Dog School	PM Storybooks	Nelson	Yellow Set A	3
Lucky the Goat	Oxford Reading Tree	OUP	Stage 4 More Sparrows	4
Lucky We Have an Estate Car	Foundations for Reading	Folens	Level 12 Early	5
Lucy And Tom Go To School		Picture Puffin	Hughes, Shirley	8
Lucy Calls the Fire Brigade	Reading 360 Upstarts	Ginn	Level 3	5
Lucy loses Red Ted	Storyworlds	Heinemann	Stage 4 Our World	3
Lucy Meets a Dragon	Literacy Links Plus	Kingscourt	Fluent B	10
Lucy the Tiger	Reading 360 Upstarts	Ginn	Level 1	3
Lucy's Box	Cambridge Reading	CUP	Becoming a R Stage A	4
Lucy's Rooster	Sunshine Spirals	Heinemann	Set 6	4
Luke's First Day	Pathways	Collins	Stage 2 Set A	3
Lunch at the Pond	Foundations for Reading	Folens	Level 4 Emergent	3
Lydia and her cat	Oxford RT Branch Library	OUP	Lydia Bks Stage 3A	4
Lydia and her garden	Oxford RT Branch Library	OUP	Lydia Bks Stage 3A	4
Lydia and the ducks	Oxford RT Branch Library	OUP	Lydia Bks Stage 3A	4
Lydia and the letters	Oxford RT Branch Library	OUP	Lydia Bks Stage 3A	3
Lydia and the present	Oxford RT Branch Library	OUP	Lydia Bks Stage 3A	4
Lydia at the shops	Oxford RT Branch Library	OUP	Lydia Bks Stage 3A	4
M				
Magic Bean	Book Project Fiction 1	Longman	Band 2 Read On	4
Magic Boots	Reading 360 New	Ginn	Little Bks L 5 Set 3	7
Magic boots, The	Storyworlds	Heinemann	Stage 7 Fantasy World	6
Magic carpet, The	Storyworlds	Heinemann	Stage 9 Fantasy World	9
Magic Carrot, The	Reading 360 Upstarts	Ginn	Level 4	7
Magic coat, The	Storyworlds	Heinemann	Stage 7 Fantasy World	6
Magic hat, The	Storyworlds	Heinemann	Stage 7 Fantasy World	6
Magic Key, The	Oxford Reading Tree	OUP	Stage 5 Playscripts	4
Magic Key, The	Oxford Reading Tree	OUP	Stage 5 Storybooks	4
Magic Machine, The	Sunshine Spirals	Heinemann	Set 3	3
Magic Porrige Pot, The	All Aboard	Ginn	Stage 3 Set B Patt & Rh	4
Magic shoes, The	Storyworlds	Heinemann	Stage 7 Fantasy World	6
Magic Smell, The	All Aboard	Ginn	Stage 7 Sam & Rosie	10

TITLE	SERIES	PUBLISHER	SET (OR AUTHOR)	BAND
Magic Tree, The	Sunshine Spirals	Heinemann	Set 4	4
Magic Trick, A	Pathways	Collins	Stage 1 Set A	1
Magic Wood, The	One, Two, Three & Away	Collins	Blue Platform 7-10	4
Magician's Lunch, The	Tiddlywinks	Kingscourt	Stage 2	7
Magpie's Baking Day	PM Storybooks	Nelson	Blue Set A	4
Magpie's Tail, The	Ready to Read	Nelson	Fluent Set C	8
Mai Ling In The Toy Shop	Book Project Fiction 1	Longman	Band 1 Read On	2
Mai Ling plays monsters	Book Project Fiction 1	Longman	Band 1 Read On Specials	2
Mai Ling's castle	Book Project Fiction 1	Longman	Band 1 Read On Specials	2
Mai Ling's Friend	Book Project Fiction 1	Longman	Band 1 Read On	2
Maisie Middleton		Collins Pict Lions	Sowter	7
Major Jump	Sunshine	Heinemann	Level 1 Set B	1
Make a Book Book, The	Pathways	Collins	Stage 3 Set A	7
Make a Lei	Ready to Read	Nelson	Early Set C	3
Make it spin	Ready to Read	Nelson	Emergent Set B	2
Making a Chapati	Pathways	Collins	Stage 1 Set B	3
Making a Salad	Foundations for Reading	Folens	Level 1 Emergent	1
Making Caterpillars and Butterflies	Literacy Links Plus	Kingscourt	Early C	6
Making Faces	Oxford Reading Tree	OUP	Stage 2 More Wrens	1
Making Friends	Foundations for Reading	Folens	Level 11 Early	5
Making Masks	All Aboard Non Fiction	Ginn	Stage 4	5
Making Music	Wonder World	Badger	Set 3	2
Making Pictures	Foundations for Reading	Folens	Level 2 Emergent	1
Making Things	Foundations for Reading	Folens	Level 6 Early	3
Mamba and the crocodile bird	Storyworlds	Heinemann	Stage 7 Animal World	5
Man Who Didn't Do His Dishes, The	Scholastic Books	Ashton Scholastic	Krasilovsky, Phyllis	7
Man Who Enjoyed Grumbling, The	Sunshine	Heinemann	Level 6	8
Man, his Son and the Ass, The	Fables from Aesop	Ginn	Books 7-12	5
Mango tree, The	Storyworlds	Heinemann	Stage 5 Our World	4
Maps	Discovery World	Heinemann	Stage E	7
Marco Saves Grandpa	Foundations for Reading	Folens	Level 10 Early	4
Maria Goes to School	Foundations for Reading	Folens	Level 10 Early	4
Market Day for Mrs Wordy	Sunshine New	Heinemann	Level 1 Set J	4
Marmalade's Nap		Piccadilly	Wheeler, Cindy	4
Marvellous Treasure, The	Sunshine New	Heinemann	Level 4	7
Mary's Meadow	Book Project Fiction 1	Longman	Band 3 Read On	4
Masks	Wonder World	Badger	Set 3	3
Materials	Discovery World	Heinemann	Stage C	3
Maths is everywhere	Sunshine	Heinemann	Level 1 Non-fiction	3
Maui and the Sun	Ready to Read	Nelson	Fluent Set D	9
Max and the apples	Storyworlds	Heinemann	Stage 4 Animal World	3
Max and the cat	Storyworlds	Heinemann	Stage 4 Animal World	3
Max and the drum	Storyworlds	Heinemann	Stage 4 Animal World	3
Max makes breakfast	Oxford Reading Tree	OUP	Stage 6 More Robins	8
Max wants to fly	Storyworlds	Heinemann	Stage 4 Animal World	3
Me	PM Storybook Starters	Nelson	Set 1	1
Meanies	Story Chest	Kingscourt	Large Read-tog Set 2	3
Medal for Nicky, A	Sunshine New	Heinemann	Level 2	7
Meg and Mog		Picture Puffin	Pienkowski, Jan	7
Meg at Sea		Picture Puffin	Pienkowski, Jan	7
Meg on the Moon		Picture Puffin	Pienkowski, Jan	7
Meg's Car		Picture Puffin	Pienkowski, Jan	7
Meg's Eggs		Picture Puffin	Pienkowski, Jan	8
Merry Go Round, The	PM Storybooks	Nelson	Red Set A	2
Merry-go-round, The	Sunrise	Heinemann		2
Mice	Literacy Links Plus	Kingscourt	Early D	6
Mice	PM Animal Facts	Nelson	Pets	6
Microscope	Story Chest	Kingscourt	Get-ready Set DD	3

TITLE	SERIES	PUBLISHER	SET (OR AUTHOR)	BAND
Midge and the Eggs	Oxford Reading Tree	OUP	Stage 4 Sparrows	4
Midge in Hospital	Oxford Reading Tree	OUP	Stage 3 Sparrows	3
Milk	Ginn Science Info Bks	Ginn	Year 1 Second Set	6
Milk Oh!	Reading World	Longman	Level 2: More Books	8
Milking	Wonder World	Badger	Set 2	4
Milton the Early Riser		Picture Puffin	Kraus, Robert	7
Minibeast Encyclopaedia	Discovery World	Heinemann	Stage C	8
Minibeasts	Discovery World	Heinemann	Stage C	5
Minnie and the Champion Snorer	Book Project Fiction 1	Longman	Band 3 Read Aloud	6
Minnie meets a monkey	Book Project Fiction 1	Longman	Band 3 Read On	5
Minnie's bike	Book Project Fiction 1	Longman	Band 3 Read On	5
Minnie's kite	Book Project Fiction 1	Longman	Band 3 Read On	5
Miranda and the Dragon	One, Two, Three & Away	Collins	Introductory W-Z	4
Miranda and the Flying Broomstick	One, Two, Three & Away	Collins	Blue Platform 17-20	5
Miranda and the Magic Stones	One, Two, Three & Away	Collins	Blue Platform 17-20	5
Mirrors		Nelson	Redhead, J S	3
Misha Disappears	Literacy Links Plus	Kingscourt	Fluent D	8
Mishi-na	Sunshine	Heinemann	Level 1 Set I	7
Miss Blossom	Pathways	Collins	Stage 3 Set A	6
Miss Popple's Pets	Literacy Links Plus	Kingscourt	Emergent A	1
Missing Bear	Book Project Fiction 1	Longman	Band 4 Read On	8
Mister Magnolia		Collins Pict Lions	Blake, Quentin	6
Mitch to the Rescue	PM Storybooks	Nelson	Orange Set B	6
Moana's Island	Sunshine New	Heinemann	Level 3	8
Model, The	Sunshine Spirals Starters	Heinemann	Set B	1
Mog and Me		Collins Pict Lions	Kerr, Judith	2
Mog and the Baby		Collins Pict Lions	Kerr, Judith	7
Mog at the Zoo		Picture Puffin	Pienkowski, Jan	8
Mog's Mumps		Picture Puffin	Pienkowski, Jan	8
Molly And The Giant	Reading 360 Upstarts	Ginn	Level 4	8
Molly, the Guide Dog	Pathways	Collins	Stage 0 Set D	3
Monarch Butterfly, The	Foundations for Reading	Folens	Level 15 Experienced	5
Monday, Fun Day		Sainsbury	Sharratt, Nick	1
Monkey And Fire	Literacy Links Plus	Kingscourt	Early D	7
Monkey and the Fisherman, The	Fables from Aesop	Ginn	Books 13-18	7
Monkey bridge, The	Sunshine	Heinemann	Level 1 Set E	3
Monkey Tricks	Oxford Reading Tree	OUP	Stage 3 Wrens	2
Monkey Tricks	PM Storybooks	Nelson	Turquoise Set A	7
Monkeys	Pathways	Collins	Stage 3 Set D	10
Monkeys and Apes	PM Animal Facts	Nelson	Animals in the Wild	8
Monkey's banana	Book Project Fiction 1	Longman	Band 1 Read On Specials	2
Monkey's Friends	Literacy Links Plus	Kingscourt	Early A	2
Monster	Tiddlywinks	Kingscourt	Stage 2	6
Monster and the Magic Umbrella	Cook, Ann	Longman	Monster Books	7
Monster at School	Cook, Ann	Longman	Monster Books	8
Monster Cleans His House	Cook, Ann	Longman	Monster Books	6
Monster Comes to the City	Cook, Ann	Longman	Monster Books	5
Monster Feast, The	Book Project Fiction 1	Longman	Band 3 Read On	7
Monster Goes to School	Cook, Ann	Longman	Monster Books	8
Monster Goes to the Museum	Cook, Ann	Longman	Monster Books	8
Monster Goes to the Zoo	Cook, Ann	Longman	Monster Books	8
Monster has a Party	Cook, Ann	Longman	Monster Books	8
Monster in the Box, The	Reading 360 Upstarts	Ginn	Level 1 Extension	3
Monster in the Cupboard, The	Reading 360 Upstarts	Ginn	Level 2 Extension	4
Monster Looks for a Friend	Cook, Ann	Longman	Monster Books	6
Monster Looks for a House	Cook, Ann	Longman	Monster Books	6
Monster Meets Lady Monster	Cook, Ann	Longman	Monster Books	6
Monster Mistake, A	Oxford Reading Tree	OUP	Stage 5 More Stories A	4

TITLE	SERIES	PUBLISHER	SET (OR AUTHOR)	BAND
Monster on the Bus	Cook, Ann	Longman	Monster Books	7
Monster Sandwich, A	Story Chest	Kingscourt	Get-ready Set B	2
Monster Who Loved Cameras, The	Book Project Fiction 1	Longman	Band 4 Read On	5
Monster Who loved Telephones, The	Book Project Fiction 1	Longman	Band 4 Read On	4
Monster Who Loved Toothbrushes, The	Book Project Fiction 1	Longman	Band 4 Read On	6
Monsters	Pathways	Collins	Stage 2 Set A	2
Monster's Baking Day	Pathways	Collins	Stage 2 Set B	5
Monsters' Party, The	Story Chest	Kingscourt	Large Read-tog Set 2	3
Monty and the ghost train	Storyworlds	Heinemann	Stage 2 Fantasy World	2
Monty at McBurgers	Storyworlds	Heinemann	Stage 2 Fantasy World	2
Monty at the party	Storyworlds	Heinemann	Stage 2 Fantasy World	2
Monty at the seaside	Storyworlds	Heinemann	Stage 2 Fantasy World	2
Monty the Monster Mouse	Reading 360 Upstarts	Ginn	Level 4 Extension	7
Moon Story	Sunshine Spirals	Heinemann	Set 4	3
Moonlight	Literacy Links Plus	Kingscourt	Early A	5
Moonlit Owl, The	Cambridge Reading	CUP	Becoming a R Stage B	5
More Spaghetti I Say	Scholastic Books	Ashton Scholastic	Gelman, Rita	5
Morning Bath	Sunshine	Heinemann	Level 5	7
Morning Dance	Tiddlywinks	Kingscourt	Stage 3	7
Morning Star	Literacy Links Plus	Kingscourt	Fluent A	10
Mo's Photo	All Aboard	Ginn	Stage 3 Booster Bks	4
Mosque School	Oxford Reading Tree	OUP	Stage 4 More Sparrows	3
Most Scary Ghost, The	Tiddlywinks	Kingscourt	Stage 3	7
Most Terrible Creature in the World, The	Ready to Read	Nelson	Fluent Set B	5
Mother Hippopotamus	Foundations for Reading	Folens	Level 1 Emergent	1
Mother Hippopotamus Gets Wet	Foundations for Reading	Folens	Level 14 Experienced	5
Mother Hippopotamus Goes Shopping	Foundations for Reading	Folens	Level 5 Emergent	2
Mother Hippopotamus's Dry Skin	Foundations for Reading	Folens	Level 9 Early	4
Mother Hippopotamus's Hiccups	Foundations for Reading	Folens	Level 11 Early	4
Mother Sea Turtle	Foundations for Reading	Folens	Level 15 Experienced	6
Motorway, The	Oxford Reading Tree	OUP	Stage 7 More Owls	7
Mountain Gorillas	Wonder World	Badger	Set 4	8
Mountain Rescue	All Aboard	Ginn	Stage 8 Sam & Rosie	9
Mouse	Story Chest	Kingscourt	Get-ready Set B	2
Mouse Box, The	Sunshine Spirals	Heinemann	Set 8	6
Mouse Monster	Tiddlywinks	Kingscourt	Stage 4	8
Mouse Paint		Orchard Books	Walsh, Ellen Stoll	5
Mouse Tales		Heinemann	Lobel, Arnold	7
Mouse Train	Story Chest	Kingscourt	Get-ready Set CC	1
Mouse Wedding, The	Tiddlywinks	Kingscourt	Stage 6	8
Mouse, The	Ready to Read	Nelson	Emergent Set B	1
Move It	Wonder World	Badger	Set 2	3
Moving Day	Foundations for Reading	Folens	Level 2 Emergent	1
Moving In	Foundations for Reading	Folens	Level 7 Early	3
Mr Archimedes' Bath		Collins Pict Lions	Allen, Pamela	8
Mr Beep	Tiddlywinks	Kingscourt	Stage 4	8
Mr Bumbleticker	Foundations for Reading	Folens	Level 1 Emergent	1
Mr Bumbleticker Goes Shopping	Foundations for Reading	Folens	Level 13 Experienced	5
Mr Bumbleticker Likes to Cook	Foundations for Reading	Folens	Level 10 Early	4
Mr Bumbleticker Likes to Fix Machines	Foundations for Reading	Folens	Level 12 Early	5
Mr Bumbleticker's Apples	Foundations for Reading	Folens	Level 14 Experienced	6
Mr Bumbleticker's Birthday	Foundations for Reading	Folens	Level 4 Emergent	3
Mr Crawford	Foundations for Reading	Folens	Level 6 Early	3
Mr Grump	Sunshine	Heinemann	Level 1 Set E	2
Mr Gumpy's Motor Car		Picture Puffin	Burningham, John	8
Mr Gumpy's Outing		Picture Puffin	Burningham, John	8
Mr Marvel and the cake	Storyworlds	Heinemann	Stage 3 Fantasy World	2
Mr Marvel and the car	Storyworlds	Heinemann	Stage 3 Fantasy World	2

TITLE	SERIES	PUBLISHER	SET (OR AUTHOR)	BAND
Mr Marvel and the lemonade	Storyworlds	Heinemann	Stage 3 Fantasy World	2
Mr Marvel and the washing	Storyworlds	Heinemann	Stage 3 Fantasy World	2
Mr Snow	All Aboard	Ginn	Stage 2 Set B Patt & Rh	3
Mr Whisper	Sunshine	Heinemann	Level 1 Set H	7
Mr Wumple's Travels	Tiddlywinks	Kingscourt	Stage 3	8
Mr. Brown's Goat	One, Two, Three & Away	Collins	Red Platform 1-6	5
Mrs Always Goes Shopping	Sunshine New	Heinemann	Level 4	7
Mrs Barmy	Pathways	Collins	Stage 2 Set A	4
Mrs Barnett's Birthday	Sunshine New	Heinemann	Level 1 Set J	5
Mrs Blue-hat and the Little Black Cat	One, Two, Three & Away	Collins	Introductory Q-V	3
Mrs Blue-hat and the Little Brown Mouse	One, Two, Three & Away	Collins	Introductory M-P	3
Mrs Bold	Literacy Links Plus	Kingscourt	Early B	4
Mrs Grimble's Grapevine	Sunshine Spirals	Heinemann	Set 7	5
Mrs Grindy's shoes	Sunshine	Heinemann	Level 1 Set I	6
Mrs Harriet's Hairdo	Sunshine Spirals	Heinemann	Set 7	6
Mrs MacDonald And The Mayor's Tea Party	Reading 360 New	Ginn	Little Bks L.5 Set 3	6
Mrs Pepperpot's Pet	Literacy Links Plus	Kingscourt	Fluent B	8
Mrs Pye's Pool	Sunshine Spirals	Heinemann	Set 6	4
Mrs Rig and the Little Black Cat	One, Two, Three & Away	Collins	Introductory Q-V	3
Mrs Spider's Beautiful Web	PM Storybooks	Nelson	Green Set A	5
Mrs Wishy Washy	Story Chest	Kingscourt	Large Read-tog Set 1	3
Mrs Wishy-Washy's Tub	Story Chest	Kingscourt	Get-ready Set BB	1
Mud		Nelson	Wagstaff, Alan	4
Mud Cake	Bangers and Mash	Longman	Books 1A-6A	6
Mum	PM Storybook Starters	Nelson	Set 1	1
Mum and Dad Went Out	All Aboard	Ginn	Stage 1 Sam & Rosie	2
Mum Paints the House	Foundations for Reading	Folens	Level 10 Early	4
Mum to the Rescue	Oxford Reading Tree	OUP	Stage 5 More Stories B	5
Mumps	PM Storybooks	Nelson	Yellow Set A	3
Mums and Dads	PM Storybook Starters	Nelson	Set 1	1
Mum's Birthday	Sunshine	Heinemann	Level 1 Set I	6
Mum's diet	Sunshine	Heinemann	Level 1 Set J	7
Mum's Getting Married	Sunshine New	Heinemann	Level 4	7
Mum's New Car	Foundations for Reading	Folens	Level 6 Early	3
Mum's new car	Oxford Reading Tree	OUP	Stage 7 More Robins	9
Mum's New Car	Reading 360 Upstarts	Ginn	Level 2 Extension	4
Mum's Surprise Ride	Reading 360 New	Ginn	Little Bks L 4 Set 1	6
Muppy's Ball	Sunshine	Heinemann	Level 7	9
Museum, The	Sunshine Spirals	Heinemann	Set 7	6
Mushrooms For Dinner	PM Storybooks	Nelson	Blue Set A	4
My Pet	All Aboard	Ginn	Stage 1 Pattern & Rhyme	1
My Accident	PM Storybook Starters	Nelson	Set 2	1
My Bad Mood		Nelson	Cowley, Joy	3
My Bean Diary	Discovery World	Heinemann	Stage C	4
My Big Brother	PM Non-fiction	Nelson	Yellow Level	4
My Big Family	Sunshine New	Heinemann	Level 6	7
My Bike	Foundations for Reading	Folens	Level 1 Emergent	1
My Bike	Ready to Read	Nelson	Early Set A	3
My Bike Can Fly	Sunshine Spirals	Heinemann	Set 2	2
My Birthday Surprise	Foundations for Reading	Folens	Level 8 Early	3
My boat	Sunshine	Heinemann	Level 1 Set G	5
My Body	Discovery World	Heinemann	Stage B	2
My Book	Sunshine New	Heinemann	Level 1 Set A	1
My Book		Picture Puffin	Maris, Ron	1
My Box	Sunshine Spirals Starters	Heinemann	Set C	1
My Brown Cow	Story Chest	Kingscourt	Ready-set-go Set BB	3
My Cat Likes to Hide in Boxes		Picture Puffin	Sutton, Eve	7
My Chair	Ready to Read	Nelson	Emergent Set B	1

TITLE	SERIES	PUBLISHER	SET (OR AUTHOR)	BAND
My Clothes	Foundations for Reading	Folens	Level 4 Emergent	3
My Computer	Wonder World	Badger	Set 2	4
My Dad	PM Non-fiction	Nelson	Yellow Level	4
My Day	Link Up	Collins	Level 1	3
My Day	Pathways	Collins	Stage 1 Set C	3
My Dog Jessie		Frances Lincoln	Bryant, Donna	6
My Dog's Party	Cambridge Reading	CUP	Begin to Read Stage B	4
My Dream	Oxford RT Branch Library	OUP	Wildsmith Bks St 2A	2
My Family	Sunrise	Heinemann		1
My Fish Bowl	Foundations for Reading	Folens	Level 1 Emergent	1
My Friend	Foundations for Reading	Folens	Level 4 Emergent	3
My Friend	Sunrise	Heinemann		2
My Friend Jess	Wonder World	Badger	Set 2	5
My Friend Trent	Foundations for Reading	Folens	Level 11 Early	4
My Gran and Grandad	PM Non-fiction	Nelson	Yellow Level	4
My Hat	Pathways	Collins	Stage 2 Set B	3
My History	Discovery World	Heinemann	Stage B	1
My Holiday Diary	Discovery World	Heinemann	Stage F	9
My Home	Story Chest	Kingscourt	Ready-set-go Set B	2
My Home	Sunrise	Heinemann		2
My home	Sunshine	Heinemann	Level 1 Set C	2
My House	Literacy Links Plus	Kingscourt	Early D	5
My Jigsaw	Pathways	Collins	Stage 0 Set C	1
My Letter	Wonder World	Badger	Set 3	3
My Little Dog	PM Storybook Starters	Nelson	Set 2	1
My Little Sister	PM Non-fiction	Nelson	Yellow Level	4
My Monster Friends	Literacy Links Plus	Kingscourt	Early B	5
My Mum and Dad	Story Chest	Kingscourt	Ready-set-go Set CC	3
My Nest is Best	Foundations for Reading	Folens	Level 3 Emergent	2
My New Bike	Pathways	Collins	Stage 2 Set B	3
My Old Cat	Foundations for Reading	Folens	Level 4 Emergent	3
My Old Cat and the Computer	Foundations for Reading	Folens	Level 8 Early	3
My Old Teddy		Walker	Mansell, Dom	4
My Perfect Pet	Pathways	Collins	Stage 2 Set E	3
My Pet	Cambridge Reading	CUP	Begin to Read Stage B	1
My Picture	Story Chest	Kingscourt	Get-ready Set CC	2
My Planet	Sunshine Spirals Starters	Heinemann	Set D	1
My Puppy	Sunshine	Heinemann	Level 1 Set B	1
My Rabbit Bobbie		Frances Lincoln	Bryant, Donna	5
My Ride	Foundations for Reading	Folens	Level 1 Emergent	1
My Secret Pet	Pathways	Collins	Stage 3 Set B	8
My Secret Place	Wonder World	Badger	Set 4	6
My Shadow	Foundations for Reading	Folens	Level 2 Emergent	1
My Shadow	Sunrise	Heinemann		1
My Sister's Getting Married	Foundations for Reading	Folens	Level 17 Experienced	7
My Skin	Wonder World	Badger	Set 2	3
My sloppy tiger	Sunshine	Heinemann	Level 1 Set H	6
My sloppy tiger goes to school	Sunshine	Heinemann	Level 1 Set J	6
My Special Job	Ready to Read	Nelson	Early Set D	5
My Story	Wonder World	Badger	Set 4	1
My Two Mums	Sunshine New	Heinemann	Level 2	6
N				
Nancy and the Giant Spotted Newt	Reading 360 Upstarts	Ginn	Level 4 Extension	7
Nancy No Size		Little Mammoth	Hoffman, M/Northway, J	5
Nandy's Bedtime		Red Fox	Lloyd, Errol	5
Naughty Ann, The	PM Storybooks	Nelson	Green Set A	5
Naughty Children	Oxford Reading Tree	OUP	Stage 3 Wrens	2
Naughty Joe	Storyworlds	Heinemann	Stage 2 Our World	2

TITLE	SERIES	PUBLISHER	SET (OR AUTHOR)	BAND
Naughty Kitten	Sunshine Spirals Starters	Heinemann	Set B	1
Naughty Nick's Book	Link Up	Collins	Level 4	5
Naughty Nog	All Aboard	Ginn	Stage 4 Set B Sam & Ros	5
Naughty Norman	Reading 360 Upstarts	Ginn	Level 3	6
Naughty Patch	Foundations for Reading	Folens	Level 5 Emergent	3
Nelson, the Baby Elephant	PM Storybooks	Nelson	Turquoise Set A	7
Nest, The	Oxford RT Branch Library	OUP	Wildsmith Bks St 1A	1
Nest, The	Story Chest	Kingscourt	Get-ready Set CC	2
Nesting Place, The	PM Storybooks	Nelson	Turquoise Set C	7
Nests	Literacy Links Plus	Kingscourt	Emergent C	4
Nests	Wonder World	Badger	Set 1	1
New Baby, The	Oxford Reading Tree	OUP	Stage 5 More Stories B	5
New Baby, The	PM Storybooks	Nelson	Yellow Set A	3
New Bed, A	Sunshine Spirals	Heinemann	Set 5	4
New Bike, The	Reading 360 Upstarts	Ginn	Level 2	4
New Bike, The	Sunshine New	Heinemann	Level 4	6
New Boy At School, A	Reading 360 New	Ginn	Little Bks L 4 Set 2	5
New boy, The	Storyworlds	Heinemann	Stage 7 Our World	6
New building, The	Sunshine	Heinemann	Level 1 Non-fiction	4
New Cat, The	Ready to Read	Nelson	Emergent Set B	1
New Classroom, A	Oxford Reading Tree	OUP	Stage 5 More Stories B	5
New Dog, A	Oxford Reading Tree	OUP	Stage 2 Storybooks	2
New Glasses	Pathways	Collins	Stage 0 Set A	1
New House, The	Oxford Reading Tree	OUP	Stage 4 Playscripts	3
New House, The	Oxford Reading Tree	OUP	Stage 4 Storybooks	4
New House, The	Sunshine New	Heinemann	Level 1 Set A	1
New Nest, The	Foundations for Reading	Folens	Level 9 Early	4
New Pants	Story Chest	Kingscourt	Get-ready Set AA	2
New Shoes	Wonder World	Badger	Set 2	2
New Trainers	Oxford Reading Tree	OUP	Stage 2 Storybooks	3
New Trees	Oxford Reading Tree	OUP	Stage 3 More Wrens	2
Newts	All Aboard Non Fiction	Ginn	Stage 5	8
Next door neighbour, The	Storyworlds	Heinemann	Stage 7 Our World	6
Nick's Glasses	Ready to Read	Nelson	Early Set A	3
Nicky's Noisy Night		Picture Puffin	Zeifert, Harriet	4
Night	Sunshine Spirals	Heinemann	Set 2	2
Night Noises	Sunshine New	Heinemann	Level 1 Set H	4
Night Train, The	Story Chest	Kingscourt	Ready-set-go Set C	3
Night-time	Story Chest	Kingscourt	Get-ready Set B	1
Nine on a String	Reading 360	Ginn	Magic Circle Level 5	6
Nishal's Box	Cambridge Reading	CUP	Becoming a R Stage C	6
No	Open Door	Nelson	Red Fun Books	1
No Dogs Allowed	Reading 360 Upstarts	Ginn	Level 2 Extension	4
No Extras	Literacy Links Plus	Kingscourt	Early C	5
No Lunchbox	All Aboard	Ginn	Stage 1 Sam & Rosie	2
No Sam!	All Aboard	Ginn	Stage 2 Sam & Rosie	2
No School Today	Reading 360 New	Ginn	Little Bks L 3 Set 1	5
No You Can't!	Sunshine New	Heinemann	Level 1 Set C	2
No! Percy Green	One, Two, Three & Away	Collins	Pre-reader 5a-8a	2
No, No	Story Chest	Kingscourt	Ready-set-go Set D	3
Noah's Ark	Reading 360 New	Ginn	Little Bks L 3 Set 3	5
Noah's Ark	Sunshine	Heinemann	Level 1 Non-fiction	5
Noah's Ark Adventure	Oxford Reading Tree	OUP	Stage 5 More Stories B	5
Nobody	Reading World	Longman	Level 2 Pack A	2
Nobody Got Wet	Oxford Reading Tree	OUP	Stage 4 More Stories A	4
Nobody Got Wet	Oxford Reading Tree	OUP	Stage 4 Playscripts	3
Nobody Knew My Name	Foundations for Reading	Folens	Level 14 Experienced	5
Nobody Laughed	Pathways	Collins	Stage 1 Set D	4

TITLE	SERIES	PUBLISHER	SET (OR AUTHOR)	BAND
Nobody Wanted to Play	Oxford Reading Tree	OUP	Stage 3 Storybooks	2
Nog	All Aboard	Ginn	Easy Start Sam & Rosie	1
Nog's Dinner	All Aboard	Ginn	Stage 1 Intro Sam & Ro	2
Noise	Sunshine	Heinemann	Level 1 Set G	6
Noises	Literacy Links Plus	Kingscourt	Emergent D	4
Noises in the Night	All Aboard	Ginn	Stage 7 Sam & Rosie	7
Noisy		Walker	Hughes, Shirley	7
Noisy Nora		Collins Pict Lions	Wells, Rosemary	6
Norma's Notebook	Book Project Fiction 1	Longman	Band 2 Read On	2
Nose Book, The	Bright and Early Books	Collins	Perkins, Al	5
Noses	Literacy Links Plus	Kingscourt	Emergent D	4
Not Like That, Like This		Little Mammoth	Bradman, T/Boroughs, J	6
Not Now Bernard		Red Fox	McKee, David	5
Not so Quiet Evening, A	Tiddlywinks	Kingscourt	Stage 5	9
Not Yet Nathan!	Cambridge Reading	CUP	Becoming a R Stage A	4
Not yet! Ben Biggins said	Book Project Fiction 1	Longman	Band 1 Read On	2
Not-so-Silly Billy	Reading 360 Upstarts	Ginn	Level 4	7
Now We Can Go		Walker	Jonas, Ann	2
Nowhere and Nothing	Sunshine	Heinemann	Level 1 Set H	5
Number Plates	PM Storybooks	Nelson	Turquoise Set B	7
Numbers		Picture Puffin	Pienkowski, Jan	1
Nyamia and the Bag of Gold	Book Project Fiction 2	Longman	Band 3	7

O

TITLE	SERIES	PUBLISHER	SET (OR AUTHOR)	BAND
Obadiah	Story Chest	Kingscourt	Small Read-together	5
Obstacle Course, The	Foundations for Reading	Folens	Level 16 Experienced	6
Odd Socks	Literacy Links Plus	Kingscourt	Early B	5
Off We Go!	Ready to Read	Nelson	Emergent Set A	1
Oh Dear		Lothian	Campbell, Rod	3
Oh, Columbus!	Literacy Links Plus	Kingscourt	Fluent B	8
Oh, jump in a sack	Story Chest	Kingscourt	Ready-set-go Set D	3
Oh, Stanley!	Reading World	Longman	Level 3	8
Old Blue Bus, The	One, Two, Three & Away	Collins	Blue Platform 1-6	2
Old Bones	Sunshine New	Heinemann	Level 5	8
Old Dad Cunningham	Reading 360 New	Ginn	Little Bks L 5 Set 3	7
Old Green Machine, The	Sunshine Spirals	Heinemann	Set 8	5
Old Grizzly	Sunshine	Heinemann	Level 1 Set G	6
Old Hat New Hat		Collins Pict Lions	Berenstain, Stan	6
Old Man and the Seven Mice, The	One, Two, Three & Away	Collins	Blue Platform 17-20	4
Old Man and the Wind, The	One, Two, Three & Away	Collins	Main Books 1-2B	4
Old Man, The	One, Two, Three & Away	Collins	Introductory A-D	3
Old Mother Hubbard		Little Mammoth	Hawkins, Colin & Jacqui	4
Old Oak Tree, The	Tiddlywinks	Kingscourt	Stage 1 Large Books	3
Old Red Bus, The	One, Two, Three & Away	Collins	Red Platform 1-6	5
Old Tales	Reading 360	Ginn	Level 5	7
Old Tales	Reading 360 New	Ginn	Level 5	7
Old Teeth, New Teeth	Wonder World	Badger	Set 1	5
Old Truck, The	Sunshine Spirals	Heinemann	Set 5	4
Old Tuatara	Ready to Read	Nelson	Emergent Set D	2
Old Vase, The	Oxford Reading Tree	OUP	Stage 7 Robins	8
Old Woman and the Hen, The	Storyworlds	Heinemann	Stage 2 Once Upon a Time	2
Oliver Takes a Bow		Collins Pict Lions	Kraus, Robert	4
On a Chair	Story Chest	Kingscourt	Get-ready Set B	2
On Friday Something Funny Happened		Red Fox	Prater, John	4
On My Bike	Reading 360 New	Ginn	Little Bks L 1 Set 2	2
On Safari	Sunshine Spirals Starters	Heinemann	Set C	1
On the Beach	Sunshine Spirals Starters	Heinemann	Set D	1
On the Farm	Literacy Links Plus	Kingscourt	Emergent B	2
On the Move	Wonder World	Badger	Set 3	3

TITLE	SERIES	PUBLISHER	SET (OR AUTHOR)	BAND
On the Run	Pathways	Collins	Stage 2 Set A	3
On the Sand	Oxford Reading Tree	OUP	Stage 3 Storybooks	3
Once There Were Giants		Walker	Waddell, Martin	7
Once Upon a Time	Reading 360	Ginn	Level 4	6
One Bird Sat on the Fence	Wonder World	Badger	Set 1	2
One Blue Hen	Cambridge Reading	CUP	Becoming a R Stage A	4
One Cold Wet Night	Story Chest	Kingscourt	Small Read-together	4
One Jumping Kangaroo	Open Door	Nelson	Blue Fun Books	2
One Puzzled Parrot	Pathways	Collins	Stage 3 Set B	6
One Sock	All Aboard	Ginn	Stage 2 Sam & Rosie	2
One Teddy All Alone	Cambridge Reading	CUP	Begin to Read Stage B	2
One thousand currant buns	Sunshine	Heinemann	Level 1 Set G	7
One, one is the sun	Story Chest	Kingscourt	Get-ready Set C	2
One, Two, Three	One, Two, Three & Away	Collins	Pre-reader 5-8	2
Only An Octopus	Literacy Links Plus	Kingscourt	Early C	6
Oogly Gum Chasing Gum, The	Literacy Links Plus	Kingscourt	Fluent B	9
Oops	Scholastic Books	Ashton Scholastic	Mayer, Mercer	4
Open It!	Ready to Read	Nelson	Emergent Set D	2
Optometrist, The	PM Non-fiction	Nelson	Blue Level	5
Oriki and the monster who hated balloons	Book Project Fiction 1	Longman	Band 4 Read Aloud	8
Oscar Got the Blame		Red Fox	Ross, Tony	6
Osprey (whole text)	Cambridge Reading	CUP	Becoming a R Stage A	7
Ouch!	Literacy Links Plus	Kingscourt	Emergent A	2
Our Baby	Foundations for Reading	Folens	Level 11 Early	5
Our Baby	Literacy Links Plus	Kingscourt	Emergent B	2
Our Baby	PM Non-fiction	Nelson	Yellow Level	4
Our Car	Sunshine New	Heinemann	Level 1 Set B	2
Our Cat	Foundations for Reading	Folens	Level 7 Early	3
Our Dog	Pathways	Collins	Stage 0 Set D	3
Our Dog Sam	Literacy Links Plus	Kingscourt	Emergent C	2
Our Garden	Literacy Links Plus	Kingscourt	Emergent B	2
Our Grandad	Sunrise	Heinemann		2
Our Granny	Sunshine	Heinemann	Level 1 Set B	2
Our Mum	PM Non-fiction	Nelson	Yellow Level	4
Our Parents	PM Non-fiction	Nelson	Blue Level	5
Our Place	Pathways	Collins	Stage 2 Set D	5
Our Rocket	Ready to Read	Nelson	Emergent Set C	1
Our street	Sunshine	Heinemann	Level 1 Set D	2
Our Teacher, Miss Pool	Ready to Read	Nelson	Early Set A	2
Out In The Weather	PM Storybook Starters	Nelson	Set 2	1
Out of the House	Open Door	Nelson	Blue Fun Books	2
Outing, The	Oxford Reading Tree	OUP	Stage 6 Owls	7
Over and Under and Up and Around	Reading World	Longman	Level 1 Pack B	3
Over in the Meadow	Cambridge Reading	CUP	Becoming a R Stage B	5
Owl	Pathways	Collins	Stage 3 Set B	8
Owl and the Pussy Cat, The		Collins Pict Lions	Lear, Edward	7
Owliver	Picture Puffin		Kraus, Robert	5
Owls	Ginn Science Info Bks	Ginn	Year 1 Second Set	5
Owl's Party	Pathways	Collins	Stage 2 Set D	7
P				
Pack It Up, Ben	Pathways	Collins	Stage 2 Set B	5
Packing	Foundations for Reading	Folens	Level 1 Emergent	1
Packing My Bag	PM Storybook Starters	Nelson	Set 2	1
Paint the Sky	Sunshine New	Heinemann	Level 1 Set A	1
Painting	Story Chest	Kingscourt	Get-ready Set A	2
Pancake Day	Reading 360 Upstarts	Ginn	Level 3 Extension	6
Pancake, The	Oxford Reading Tree	OUP	Stage 1 First Words	1
Pancakes	All Aboard	Ginn	Stage 1 Intro Sam & Ro	2

TITLE	SERIES	PUBLISHER	SET (OR AUTHOR)	BAND
Pancakes	Foundations for Reading	Folens	Level 9 Early	3
Pancakes	Reading World	Longman	Level 1 Pack A	3
Papa's Spaghetti	Literacy Links Plus	Kingscourt	Early D	5
Paper Birds, The	Foundations for Reading	Folens	Level 16 Experienced	6
Paper Patchwork	Ready to Read	Nelson	Early Set C	3
Parade The	Reading 360 New	Ginn	Little Bks L 1 Set 2	2
Park Street	Link Up	Collins	Level 1	3
Park, The	All Aboard	Ginn	Stage 1 Sam & Rosie	2
Park, The	Reading 360	Ginn	Level 3	3
Park, The Park, The	Reading 360	Ginn	Magic Circle Level 2	3
Parrot, The	All Aboard	Ginn	Stage 1 Intro Sam & Ro	1
Party Games	Foundations for Reading	Folens	Level 16 Experienced	6
Party, The	Story Chest	Kingscourt	Get-ready Set A	1
Paru Has a Bath	Ready to Read	Nelson	Fluent Set B	8
Pat the Cat		Picture Puffin	Hawkins, Colin	5
Patrick		Picture Puffin	Blake, Quentin	8
Patterns	Literacy Links Plus	Kingscourt	Early B	4
Paul and the Robber	Reading 360 Upstarts	Ginn	Level 1	3
Paul Bunyan	Sunshine New	Heinemann	Level 7	8
Peas in a Pod	Cambridge Reading	CUP	Becoming a R Stage B	5
Pedal Power	Ready to Read	Nelson	Emergent Set D	2
Peg and the Fair	Reading 360 Upstarts	Ginn	Level 1 Extension	3
Pelican, The	Sunshine Spirals	Heinemann	Set 7	6
Pencil, The	PM Storybook Starters	Nelson	Set 2	1
Penguin's Chicks	Ready to Read	Nelson	Early Set C	3
Penguins, The	Sunshine Spirals	Heinemann	Set 3	3
People at Work	Ginn Geography Topic Bks	Ginn	Year 1	4
People at Work	Link Up	Collins	Starter Books	1
People Dance	Wonder World	Badger	Set 3	5
Pepper Goes to School	Foundations for Reading	Folens	Level 13 Experienced	4
Pepper's Adventure	PM Storybooks	Nelson	Green Set A	5
Percy Green	One, Two, Three & Away	Collins	Introductory M-P	2
Percy Green and Mr Red-hat's Car	One, Two, Three & Away	Collins	Introductory Q-V	3
Percy Green and Mrs Blue-hat	One, Two, Three & Away	Collins	Blue Platform 11-16	3
Person from Planet X, The	Sunshine	Heinemann	Level 3	6
Pet Parade, The	Literacy Links Plus	Kingscourt	Emergent C	2
Pet Shop	Story Chest	Kingscourt	Ready-set-go Set CC	3
Pet Shop, The	Oxford Reading Tree	OUP	Stage 2 Wrens	1
Pete Little	PM Storybooks	Nelson	Green Set A	5
Peter and the Wolf	Read It Yourself	Ladybird	Level 4	5
Pete's New Shoes	Literacy Links Plus	Kingscourt	Early B	5
Pets	Link Up	Collins	Starter Books	1
Pets	Literacy Links Plus	Kingscourt	Emergent D	3
Pets	PM Storybook Starters	Nelson	Set 1	1
Pets	Ready to Read	Nelson	Fluent Set A	6
Pets Need Vets	Reading 2000	Longmans	Storytime Reds	6
Philippa and the Dragon	Literacy Links Plus	Kingscourt	Early C	6
Photo Book, The	PM Storybooks	Nelson	Red Set A	2
Photograph, The	Oxford Reading Tree	OUP	Stage 9 Robins	9
Picnic For Tortoise, A	Reading 360	Ginn	Level 3	5
Picnic in the Sky, The	Foundations for Reading	Folens	Level 3 Emergent	2
Picnic, The	Cambridge Reading	CUP	Begin to Read Stage A	2
Picnic, The	Reading World	Longman	Level 1 Pack A	2
Picnic, The	Wonder World	Badger	Set 4	5
Picture for Harold's Room, A		Heinemann	Johnson, Crockett	5
Pied Piper of Hamelin, The	Read It Yourself	Ladybird	Level 4	8
Pied Piper, The	Storyworlds	Heinemann	Stage 7 Once Upon a Time	6
Pig in Pyjamas, A	Open Door	Nelson	Yellow Fun Books	3

TITLE	SERIES	PUBLISHER	SET (OR AUTHOR)	BAND
Pig in the Pond, The		Walker	Waddell, Martin	7
Pig Pig Rides		Heinemann	McPhail, D	6
Pig That Learned to Jig, The	Wonder World	Badger	Set 1	6
Piggle		Heinemann	Bonsall, Crosby	8
Pigs	PM Animal Facts	Nelson	Farm Animals	9
Pile in Pete's Room, The	Sunshine New	Heinemann	Level 5	8
Pink Pink		Gerrard Publish'g	DeLage, Ida	7
Pip and the Little Monkey	Oxford Reading Tree	OUP	Stage 4 Sparrows	4
Pip at the Zoo	Oxford Reading Tree	OUP	Stage 3 Sparrows	4
Pippa and the Witch	Reading 360 Upstarts	Ginn	Level 3	6
Pippo Gets Lost		Walker	Oxenbury, Helen	7
Pirate Adventure	Oxford Reading Tree	OUP	Stage 5 Playscripts	4
Pirate Adventure	Oxford Reading Tree	OUP	Stage 5 Storybooks	5
Pirate Pete and the monster	Storyworlds	Heinemann	Stage 4 Fantasy World	3
Pirate Pete and the treasure island	Storyworlds	Heinemann	Stage 4 Fantasy World	3
Pirate Pete keeps fit	Storyworlds	Heinemann	Stage 4 Fantasy World	3
Pirate Pete loses his hat	Storyworlds	Heinemann	Stage 4 Fantasy World	3
Pirate Treasure	Reading 360 New	Ginn	Little Bks L 1 Set 3	2
Pirate, The	Sunshine Spirals	Heinemann	Set 3	3
Pirates, The	Story Chest	Kingscourt	Stage 2	6
Pizza	All Aboard	Ginn	Easy Start Sam & Rosie	1
Pizza		Wayland	Moses, Brian	10
Pizza For Dinner	Literacy Links Plus	Kingscourt	Early C	6
Pizza Princess	All Aboard	Ginn	Stage 4 Set A Patt & Rh	5
Pizza, The	Foundations for Reading	Folens	Level 3 Emergent	2
Places We Visit	All Aboard Non Fiction	Ginn	Stage 1	2
Planets, The	Wonder World	Badger	Set 3	7
Plants of my Aunt, The	Tiddlywinks	Kingscourt	Stage 5	7
Plants to Eat	Ginn Science Info Bks	Ginn	Year 1	4
Play a Play	Reading 360 New	Ginn	Little Bks L 3 Set 1	4
Play Book		Picture Puffin	Turner, Gwenda	3
Play Tunnel, The	All Aboard	Ginn	Easy Start Sam & Rosie	1
Play with Me	All Aboard	Ginn	Stage 2 Set B Patt & Rh	3
Play, The	All Aboard	Ginn	Stage 1 Sam & Rosie	2
Play, The	Oxford Reading Tree	OUP	Stage 4 Storybooks	4
Playhouse for Monster, A		Picture Puffin	Mueller, Virginia	4
Playing	Link Up	Collins	Starter Books	1
Playing	PM Storybook Starters	Nelson	Set 1	1
Playing Football	Foundations for Reading	Folens	Level 12 Early	5
Playing with Dad	Foundations for Reading	Folens	Level 7 Early	3
Playtime	Book Project Fiction 1	Longman	Band 1 Read On Specials	2
Please Miss!	Cambridge Reading	CUP	Becoming a R Stage B	5
Plop!	Story Chest	Kingscourt	Ready-set-go Set B	2
Plum Magic	All Aboard	Ginn	Stage 6 Sam & Rosie	6
Pocketful of gold	Book Project Fiction 1	Longman	Band 3 Read On	6
Polar Bear, Polar Bear, What Do You Hear		Picture Puffin	Martin, Bill	7
Police Car The	Link Up	Collins	Starter Build-Up	2
Pollution	Wonder World	Badger	Set 2	5
Polly's Puffin		Picture Puffin	Garland, Sarah	6
Pond Monster	Bangers and Mash	Longman	Books 1A-6A	7
Poor Bobby	All Aboard	Ginn	Stage 3 Booster Bks	4
Poor Old Mum!	Oxford Reading Tree	OUP	Stage 4 More Stories A	3
Poor Old Polly	Story Chest	Kingscourt	Small Read-together	4
Poor Rabbit	Reading World	Longman	Level 3	8
Poor sore paw, The	Sunshine	Heinemann	Level 1 Set H	6
Pop Group, The	Sunshine	Heinemann	Level 6	7
Pop!	Pathways	Collins	Stage 1 Set C	2
Popcorn	Sunshine Spirals	Heinemann	Set 5	4

TITLE	SERIES	PUBLISHER	SET (OR AUTHOR)	BAND
Poppy, The	Ready to Read	Nelson	Fluent Set B	9
Porcupine, A	Wonder World	Badger	Set 2	2
Porridge	Wonder World	Badger	Set 1	7
Potatoes, Potatoes	Wonder World	Badger	Set 4	5
Potter in Fiji, A	Wonder World	Badger	Set 4	10
Praying Mantis, The	Ready to Read	Nelson	Early Set B	3
Pre-historic Record Breakers	Discovery World	Heinemann	Stage E	9
Presents	Storyworlds	Heinemann	Stage 5 Our World	4
Princess and the Pea, The	Favourite Tales	Ladybird		8
Printing Machine, The	Literacy Links Plus	Kingscourt	Early B	4
Priscilla and the Dinosaurs	Sunshine New	Heinemann	Level 2	7
Processed Food	Wonder World	Badger	Set 3	2
Proper Bike, A	Oxford Reading Tree	OUP	Stage 9 Robins	8
Prudence Bunting and her Bike		Nelson	Cartwright, Pauline	6
Pterosaur's Long Flight	PM Storybooks	Nelson	Orange Set B	6
Pudding	Book Project Fiction 1	Longman	Band 2 Read On	4
Pumpkin, The	Story Chest	Kingscourt	Ready-set-go Set C	3
Pumpkin House, The	Literacy Links Plus	Kingscourt	Fluent B	7
Puppet Show, The	Literacy Links Plus	Kingscourt	Emergent D	2
Push!	Oxford Reading Tree	OUP	Stage 2 Wrens	2
Puss in Boots	Read It Yourself	Ladybird	Level 2	5
Pussy and the Birds	PM Storybooks	Nelson	Red Set A	2
Put Me In the Zoo	Beginner Books	Collins	Lopshire, Robert	5
Pyjama Party, The	Sunshine New	Heinemann	Level 1 Set D	2
Q				
Quack, Quack		Walker	Casey, Patricia	2
Quack, quack, quack!	Sunshine	Heinemann	Level 1 Set I	7
Queen and the Cabbage, The	Reading 360 Upstarts	Ginn	Level 1 Extension	3
Queen's Parrot, The	Literacy Links Plus	Kingscourt	Early D	6
Quest, The	Oxford Reading Tree	OUP	Stage 9 Magpies	9
Quilt for Kiri, A	Ready to Read	Nelson	Fluent Set D	7
R				
Rabbit said Miaow, The	Reading 360 Upstarts	Ginn	Level 1	3
Rabbit, The		Red Fox	Burningham, John	5
Race to Green End, The	PM Storybooks	Nelson	Turquoise Set C	7
Race, The	Sunshine	Heinemann	Level 1 Set D	2
Race, The	Reading 360 Upstarts	Ginn	Introductory	1
Rachel and the Difference Thief	Book Project Fiction 2	Longman	Band 4	10
Rachel versus Bonecrusher the Mighty	Book Project Fiction 2	Longman	Band 4	10
Racing Pigeons	All Aboard Non Fiction	Ginn	Stage 5	6
Raft Ride	Pathways	Collins	Stage 0 Set A	2
Rags in Trouble	Reading 2000	Longman	Storytime Reds	6
Rain and the Sun, The	Wonder World	Badger	Set 1	5
Rain Arrow, The	Pathways	Collins	Stage 3 Set B	10
Rain Puddle, The		Picture Puffin	Holl, Adelaide	7
Rain, Rain	Ready to Read	Nelson	Early Set B	3
Rain, The	Foundations for Reading	Folens	Level 11 Early	4
Rainbow Adventure, The	Oxford Reading Tree	OUP	Stage 8 Magpies	8
Rainy Day	Pathways	Collins	Stage 2 Set D	6
Ramu and Sita and the Robber	One, Two, Three & Away	Collins	Introductory W-Z	4
Rap Party, The	Foundations for Reading	Folens	Level 14 Experienced	6
Rapunzel	Literacy Links Plus	Kingscourt	Fluent D	8
Rapunzel	Read It Yourself	Ladybird	Level 4	6
Rat a Tat Tat	Tiddlywinks	Kingscourt	Stage 1 Large Books	5
Rat's Funny Story	Story Chest	Kingscourt	Get-ready Set BB	2
Rats, Bats, and Black Puddings	Ready to Read	Nelson	Fluent Set D	9
Rattlesnake Looks for Food, The	Foundations for Reading	Folens	Level 4 Emergent	3
Ratty-tatty	Sunshine	Heinemann	Level 1 Set H	6

TITLE	SERIES	PUBLISHER	SET (OR AUTHOR)	BAND
Raven and the Fox, The	Cambridge Reading	CUP	Becoming a R Stage A	5
Reading is everywhere	Sunshine	Heinemann	Level 1 Non-fiction	2
Ready Steady Go		Red Fox	Watanabe, Shigeo	4
Ready, Steady, Jump!	Ready to Read	Nelson	Early Set B	3
Rebecca and the Concert	PM Storybooks	Nelson	Orange Set C	6
Red	One, Two, Three & Away	Collins	Pre-reader 1-4	1
Red and Blue and Yellow	PM Non-fiction	Nelson	Red Level	3
Red Bird	Pathways	Collins	Stage 2 Set C	4
Red nose	Bangers and Mash	Longman	Books 1A-6A	5
Red Planet	Oxford Reading Tree	OUP	Stage 7 Owls	7
Red Planet	Oxford Reading Tree	OUP	Stage 7 Playscripts	6
Red Riding Hood	Pathways	Collins	Stage 3 Set A	6
Red Riding Hood	Read It Yourself	Ladybird	Level 2	5
Red Rose, The	Story Chest	Kingscourt	Large Read-tog Set 2	3
Red socks and yellow socks	Sunshine	Heinemann	Level 1 Set H	5
Red Ted at the beach	Storyworlds	Heinemann	Stage 4 Our World	3
Red Ted goes to school	Storyworlds	Heinemann	Stage 4 Our World	3
Red, Green, Blue, Yellow and Brown	One, Two, Three & Away	Collins	Pre-reader 1a-4a	2
Reindeer, The	Reading 360 New	Ginn	Little Bks L 3 Set 1	5
Rescue at sea	Storyworlds	Heinemann	Stage 8 Our World	7
Rescue, The	PM Storybooks	Nelson	Green Set B	5
Rescuing Nelson	PM Storybooks	Nelson	Turquoise Set B	7
Rhyming Riddles	Cambridge Reading	CUP	Becoming a R Stage C	6
Rice Cakes	Literacy Links Plus	Kingscourt	Early D	6
Riddles	Literacy Links Plus	Kingscourt	Early A	4
Ride! Ride! Ride!	Reading 360	Ginn	Magic Circle Level 2	3
Riding	Foundations for Reading	Folens	Level 3 Emergent	2
Riding	Wonder World	Badger	Set 3	7
Riding to Craggy Rock	PM Storybooks	Nelson	Turquoise Set C	7
Rip's Bath	One, Two, Three & Away	Collins	Blue Platform 1-6	2
River Rapids Ride, The	Sunshine New	Heinemann	Level 3	6
River Run	Reading 2000	Longmans	Storytime Reds	7
River, The	Foundations for Reading	Folens	Level 2 Emergent	1
Road Robber	Sunshine	Heinemann	Level 2	7
Road Signs	All Aboard Non Fiction	Ginn	Stage 4	7
Robber Pig and The Ginger Bee, The	Tiddlywinks	Kingscourt	Stage 5	8
Robber Pig and The Green Eggs, The	Tiddlywinks	Kingscourt	Stage 5	8
Robber, The	Sunshine Spirals Starters	Heinemann	Set C	1
Robbie's First Day at School	Reading 2000	Longmans	Storytime Yellows	4
Robbie's Trousers	Reading 2000	Longmans	Storytime Yellows	7
Robert, the Rose Horse	Beginner Books	Collins	Heilbroner, Joan	6
Roberto's Smile	Story Chest	Kingscourt	Ready-set-go Set BB	2
Robin Hood	Oxford Reading Tree	OUP	Stage 6 Owls	6
Robin Hood	Oxford Reading Tree	OUP	Stage 6 Playscripts	5
Robot, The	Sunshine Spirals Starters	Heinemann	Set D	1
Robots, The	Storyworlds	Heinemann	Stage 3 Our World	2
Rock in the Road, The	Ready to Read	Nelson	Fluent Set B	5
Rock Pools, The	PM Storybook Starters	Nelson	Set 2	1
Roger and Mrs Blue-hat	One, Two, Three & Away	Collins	Introductory I-L	2
Roger and Rip	One, Two, Three & Away	Collins	Introductory E-H	3
Roger and the Ball	One, Two, Three & Away	Collins	Pre-reader 1a-4a	2
Roger and the Bus	One, Two, Three & Away	Collins	Pre-reader 1a-4a	2
Roger and the Cats	One, Two, Three & Away	Collins	Yellow Platform 1-6	6
Roger and the Frog	One, Two, Three & Away	Collins	Pre-reader 9b-12b	2
Roger and the Ghost	One, Two, Three & Away	Collins	Main Books 1-2B	4
Roger and the Little Mouse	One, Two, Three & Away	Collins	Introductory I-L	3
Roger and the Pond	One, Two, Three & Away	Collins	Introductory E-H	3
Roger and the School Bus	One, Two, Three & Away	Collins	Green Platform 1-6	5

TITLE	SERIES	PUBLISHER	SET (OR AUTHOR)	BAND
Roger at the Fair	One, Two, Three & Away	Collins	Pre-reader 9b-12b	3
Roger has a Ride	One, Two, Three & Away	Collins	Blue Platform 17-20	4
Roger Red-hat	One, Two, Three & Away	Collins	Introductory A-D	2
Roger Red-hat and Mrs Green's Hat	One, Two, Three & Away	Collins	Pre-reader 1b-4b	2
Roger Rings the Bell	One, Two, Three & Away	Collins	Red Platform 1-6	5
Roger,Billy, Jennifer and Johnny	One, Two, Three & Away	Collins	Pre-reader 5-8	2
Roll Over	Literacy Links Plus	Kingscourt	Early B	3
Roller Blades	Foundations for Reading	Folens	Level 8 Early	3
Roller Blades for Luke	PM Storybooks	Nelson	Orange Set C	6
Roller Coaster	All Aboard Non Fiction	Ginn	Stage 5	7
Roller Coaster	Pathways	Collins	Stage 1 Set D	2
Roly-Poly	Story Chest	Kingscourt	Stage 2	6
Roman adventure	Oxford Reading Tree	OUP	Stage 7 More Owls	7
Roof and a Door, A	PM Non-fiction	Nelson	Red Level	3
Room Full of Light, A	Pathways	Collins	Stage 2 Set A	5
Rope Swing, The	Oxford Reading Tree	OUP	Stage 3 Storybooks	3
Rosa at the Zoo	Ready to Read	Nelson	Fluent Set A	4
Rosie and the Dinosaurs	All Aboard	Ginn	Stage 1 Intro Sam & Ro	1
Rosie and the Wasp	All Aboard	Ginn	Stage 1 Sam & Rosie	2
Rosie the Nosey Goat	Sunshine New	Heinemann	Level 1 Set G	3
Rosie Wanted to Play	All Aboard	Ginn	Stage 1 Sam & Rosie	2
Rosie's Babies		Walker	Waddell, Martin	9
Rosie's Family	All Aboard	Ginn	Easy Start Sam & Rosie	1
Rosie's New Pet	Reading World	Longman	Level 3	9
Rosie's Walk		Picture Puffin	Hutchins, Pat	4
Rotten Apples	Oxford Reading Tree	OUP	Stage 6 More Owls	6
Round and Round	Story Chest	Kingscourt	Ready-set-go Set A	2
Round and Round the Garden		Simon & Schust'r	Kemp, Moira	3
Rounders	Sun Rise	Heineman		2
Row Your Boat	Literacy Links Plus	Kingscourt	Early A	2
Roy and the Budgie	Oxford Reading Tree	OUP	Stage 3 Sparrows	3
Roy at the Fun Park	Oxford Reading Tree	OUP	Stage 4 Sparrows	4
Roy G. Biv	Story Chest	Kingscourt	Ready-set-go Set CC	3
Rubbish	Wonder World	Badger	Set 3	5
Rumpelstiltskin	Reading 360	Ginn	Once Upon a Time 1-4	6
Rum-Tum-Tum	Reading 360 Upstarts	Ginn	Level 2	4
Rum-Tum-Tum	Story Chest	Kingscourt	Ready-set-go Set C	3
Run!	Sunrise	Heinemann		1
Runaway Pram, The	Reading 360 Upstarts	Ginn	Level 2	4
Runaway Van, The	Link Up	Collins	Level 3	5
Running	Foundations for Reading	Folens	Level 3 Emergent	2
S				
S Book, The	Pathways	Collins	Stage 0 Set A	1
Sadie Spider	Reading World	Longman	Level 1 Pack B	4
Sadie Spider Moves In	Reading World	Longman	Level 1: More Books	3
Sadie Spider Strikes Again	Reading World	Longman	Level 1 Pack B	4
Safe Place, The	Ready to Read	Nelson	Fluent Set A	5
Salad	Story Chest	Kingscourt	Get-ready Set BB	1
Sally and the Daisy	PM Storybooks	Nelson	Red Set A	2
Sally and the Elephant	Wonder World	Badger	Set 1	3
Sally and the Sparrows	PM Storybooks	Nelson	Yellow Set B	3
Sally's Beans	PM Storybooks	Nelson	Yellow Set A	3
Sally's Day	Pathways	Collins	Stage 2 Set A	3
Sally's Friends	PM Storybooks	Nelson	Blue Set A	4
Sally's New Shoes	PM Storybook Starters	Nelson	Set 2	1
Sally's Picture	Literacy Links Plus	Kingscourt	Early A	5
Sally's Red Bucket	PM Storybooks	Nelson	Red Set A	4
Sam and Sue at the Seaside	Reading 360 New	Ginn	Little Bks L 4 Set 1	6

TITLE	SERIES	PUBLISHER	SET (OR AUTHOR)	BAND
Sam and Sue at the Zoo	Reading 360 New	Ginn	Little Bks L 4 Set 1	5
Sam and the Firefly	Beginner Books	Collins	Eastman, P.D.	7
Sam and the Tadpoles	All Aboard	Ginn	Stage 5 Set A Sam & Ros	7
Sam hides Red Ted	Storyworlds	Heinemann	Stage 4 Our World	3
Sam Went In	All Aboard	Ginn	Easy Start Sam & Rosie	1
Sammy the Seal		Heinemann I	Hoff, Syd	6
Sam's Bike	All Aboard	Ginn	Stage 2 Booster Bks	3
Sam's Bus	Pathways	Collins	Stage 2 Set C	4
Sam's Family	All Aboard	Ginn	Easy Start Sam & Rosie	1
Sam's Mask	Ready to Read	Nelson	Emergent Set D	2
Sand		Nelson	Cartwright, Pauline	2
Sandwich Person, A	Wonder World	Badger	Set 3	4
Sandwich, The	Pathways	Collins	Stage 0 Set C	2
Sandwich, The	Reading World	Longman	Level 1 Pack A	1
Sandy and the Snowball	Reading 360 Upstarts	Ginn	Level 4 Extension	6
Sarah and the Barking Dog	PM Storybooks	Nelson	Orange Set B	6
Sarah, The Bear and the Kangaroo	Tiddlywinks	Kingscourt	Stage 6	8
Sausage, The	Sunshine Spirals	Heinemann	Set 2	1
Sausages	PM Storybooks	Nelson	Red Set A	2
Say It Fast	Reading 360	Ginn	Magic Circle Level 5	4
Scarecrow, The	Literacy Links Plus	Kingscourt	Emergent C	7
Scarecrows	Oxford Reading Tree	OUP	Stage 5 More Stories B	5
Scaredy Cat	Pathways	Collins	Stage 1 Set D	5
Scare-kid	Literacy Links Plus	Kingscourt	Fluent A	9
Scarf, The	Oxford Reading Tree	OUP	Stage 4 More Stories B	4
Scat Cat!	All Aboard	Ginn	Stage 3 Sam & Rosie	4
Scat! said the cat	Sunshine	Heinemann	Level 1 Set D	3
School Fair, The	Reading 360 New	Ginn	Little Bks L 1 Set 3	2
School, The		Red Fox	Burningham, John	3
Science Dictionary	Discovery World	Heinemann	Stage F	9
Scit, Scat Scaredy Cat!	Sunshine New	Heinemann	Level 1 Set F	3
Scots Pine, The (whole text)	Cambridge Reading	CUP	Becoming a R Stage C	9
Scratch My Back	Foundations for Reading	Folens	Level 6 Early	2
Screech!	Literacy Links Plus	Kingscourt	Early A	3
Scrumptious Sundae, A	Literacy Links Plus	Kingscourt	Emergent A	1
Sea Wall, The	Foundations for Reading	Folens	Level 16 Experienced	6
Seagull is Clever	PM Storybooks	Nelson	Yellow Set A	3
Seagull Sweaters	Book Project Fiction 2	Longman	Band 4	10
Seal (whole text)	Cambridge Reading	CUP	Becoming a R Stage A	5
Seals, The	Sunshine Spirals	Heinemann	Set 3	3
Seasons	Discovery World	Heinemann	Stage A	1
Seat Belt Song, The	PM Storybooks	Nelson	Turquoise Set B	7
Secret of Spooky House, The	Sunshine	Heinemann	Level 1 Set J	8
Secret Plans, The	Oxford Reading Tree	OUP	Stage 10 Robins	8
Secret Room, The	Oxford Reading Tree	OUP	Stage 4 Playscripts	3
Secret Room, The	Oxford Reading Tree	OUP	Stage 4 Storybooks	4
Secret Soup	Literacy Links Plus	Kingscourt	Early A	4
Secret, The	Reading World	Longman	Level 2 Pack B	6
Seed, The	Sunshine	Heinemann	Level 1 Set F	3
Seed, The	Wonder World	Badger	Set 1	1
Seeds	Ginn Science Info Bks	Ginn	Year 1 Second Set	5
See-saw, The	Storyworlds	Heinemann	Stage 3 Our World	2
Selfish Dog, The	Storyworlds	Heinemann	Stage 3 Once Upon a Time	2
Seven Geese	One, Two, Three & Away	Collins	Pre-reader 5b-8b	2
Shadow Dance, The	Book Project Fiction 2	Longman	Band 1	9
Shadows	Literacy Links Plus	Kingscourt	Emergent D	3
Shadows	Wonder World	Badger	Set 1	8
Shapes	Discovery World	Heinemann	Stage A	1

TITLE	SERIES	PUBLISHER	SET (OR AUTHOR)	BAND
Shapes		Picture Puffin	Pienkowski, Jan	1
Sharing	Literacy Links Plus	Kingscourt	Emergent A	2
Shark in a Sack	Sunshine	Heinemann	Level 1 Set D	2
Shark with no teeth, The	Storyworlds	Heinemann	Stage 8 Animal World	6
Sharks	Sunshine Spirals	Heinemann	Set 4	3
Sharks	Wonder World	Badger	Set 4	8
Sheep	PM Animal Facts	Nelson	Farm Animals	9
Shiny Key, The	Oxford Reading Tree	OUP	Stage 6 More Owls	6
Ships	Wonder World	Badger	Set 3	10
Shipwreck at Old Jelly's Farm	All Aboard	Ginn	Stage 5 Set A Patt & Rh	5
Shoe Grabber, The	Tiddlywinks	Kingscourt	Stage 3	6
Shoes	Pathways	Collins	Stage 3 Set C	7
Shoes had Spots, The	Reading 360 Upstarts	Ginn	Level 1	3
Shoo!	Sunshine	Heinemann	Level 1 Set C	2
Shoo, Fly!	Story Chest	Kingscourt	Get-ready Set AA	1
Shopping	All Aboard	Ginn	Easy Start Sam & Rosie	1
Shopping	Discovery World	Heinemann	Stage A	1
Shopping	Link Up	Collins	Level 2	4
Shopping	Literacy Links Plus	Kingscourt	Emergent D	2
Shopping	Oxford Reading Tree	OUP	Stage 2 More Wrens	2
Shopping	Sunrise	Heinemann		1
Shopping at the Supermarket	Foundations for Reading	Folens	Level 1 Emergent	1
Shopping Mall, The	PM Storybook Starters	Nelson	Set 1	1
Shops	Ginn Geography Topic Bks	Ginn	Year 1	5
Show and Tell	Foundations for Reading	Folens	Level 15 Experienced	6
Show-and-Tell	Cambridge Reading	CUP	Becoming a R Stage B	5
Shush!	Ready to Read	Nelson	Early Set B	2
Sick Lion, The	Fables from Aesop	Ginn	Books 13-18	6
Signs	Journeys in Reading	Schofield & Sims	Level 1	3
Signs	Literacy Links Plus	Kingscourt	Emergent A	2
Signs	Sunshine Spirals	Heinemann	Set 6	5
Silly Billy		Julia MacRae	Hutchins, Pat	7
Silly Billys	Sunshine	Heinemann	Level 3	6
Silly Children	Link Up	Collins	Level 3	5
Silly Elephant, The	Reading 360 Upstarts	Ginn	Level 2 Extension	4
Silly Goose		Walker	Ormerod, Jan	4
Silly old possum	Story Chest	Kingscourt	Get-ready Set C	2
Silly Old Story, A	Tiddlywinks	Kingscourt	Stage 4	9
Silly Willy and Silly Billy	Foundations for Reading	Folens	Level 12 Early	5
Sing a Song	Story Chest	Kingscourt	Large Read-tog Set 1	3
Sinking Feeling, A	Oxford Reading Tree	OUP	Stage 3 Wrens	2
Sita and Ramu	One, Two, Three & Away	Collins	Introductory I-L	3
Sita and the Little Old Woman	One, Two, Three & Away	Collins	Blue Platform 7-10	3
Sita and the Robin	One, Two, Three & Away	Collins	Red Platform 7-10	6
Sita Climbs the Wall	One, Two, Three & Away	Collins	Green Platform 1-6	5
Sitting	Literacy Links Plus	Kingscourt	Emergent D	4
Sitting in my Box		Faber and Faber	Lillegard, Dee	5
Six in a Bed	Oxford Reading Tree	OUP	Stage 1 First Words	1
Six Little Pigeons	Sunshine Spirals	Heinemann	Set 8	6
Sizes	Discovery World	Heinemann	Stage B	2
Sizes		Picture Puffin	Pienkowski, Jan	1
Skateboard, The	Reading World	Longman	Level 1: More Books	3
Skating	Story Chest	Kingscourt	Ready-set-go Set AA	2
Skeleton on the Bus, The	Literacy Links Plus	Kingscourt	Fluent B	8
Skier, The	PM Storybook Starters	Nelson	Set 1	1
Skin	Literacy Links Plus	Kingscourt	Early B	4
Skin,Skin	Wonder World	Badger	Set 2	4
Sky Diver, The	Sunshine Spirals	Heinemann	Set 3	3

TITLE	SERIES	PUBLISHER	SET (OR AUTHOR)	BAND
Sky People	Reading 2000	Longmans	Storytime Yellows	6
Sleep Tight	Cambridge Reading	CUP	Becoming a R Stage C	7
Sleeping	Literacy Links Plus	Kingscourt	Early B	3
Sleeping Beauty	Read it Yourself	Ladybird	Level 3	5
Sleeping Giant, The	One, Two, Three & Away	Collins	Yellow Platform 1-6	6
Sleeping Out	Story Chest	Kingscourt	Ready-set-go Set C	2
Sleepy Bear	Foundations for Reading	Folens	Level 5 Emergent	3
Sleepy Bear	Literacy Links Plus	Kingscourt	Early A	4
Slinky Malinky		Picture Puffin	Dodd, Lynley	8
Slugs	All Aboard Non Fiction	Ginn	Stage 5	6
Slugs and Snails	Wonder World	Badger	Set 1	6
Sly Fox and the Red Hen, The	Read It Yourself	Ladybird	Level 1	4
Small Pig		Heinemann	Lobel, Arnold	7
Small world, A	Sunshine	Heinemann	Level 1 Non-fiction	5
Smallest Tree, The	Literacy Links Plus	Kingscourt	Fluent D	7
Smarty pants	Story Chest	Kingscourt	Large Read-tog Set 1	3
Smile! said Dad	Ready to Read	Nelson	Early Set B	2
Smile, The	Ready to Read	Nelson	Early Set A	2
Smile, The	Tiddlywinks	Kingscourt	Stage 4	7
Snail Song	Book Project Fiction 1	Longman	Band 1 Read On	2
Snails	Foundations for Reading	Folens	Level 6 Early	4
Snake that couldn't hiss, The	Storyworlds	Heinemann	Stage 8 Animal World	6
Snakes	Foundations for Reading	Folens	Level 17 Experienced	7
Snap!	Sunshine	Heinemann	Level 1 Set B	2
Snap! Splash!	Ready to Read	Nelson	Early Set D	4
Snap! Splat!	Sunshine New	Heinemann	Level 1 Set C	1
Snatch and Grab	Bangers and Mash	Longman	Supplementary Books	8
Sneezes	Literacy Links Plus	Kingscourt	Early A	4
Snoopy Bear		Nelson	Redhead, J S	3
Snow on the hill	PM Storybooks	Nelson	Green Set B	5
Snow Race, The	Sunshine Spirals	Heinemann	Set 3	3
Snow White and the Seven Dwarfs	Read It Yourself	Ladybird	Level 2	8
Snow, The		Red Fox	Burningham, John	5
Snowball Fight!	Wonder World	Badger	Set 1	3
Snowman	Story Chest	Kingscourt	Get-ready Set AA	2
Snowman, A	Foundations for Reading	Folens	Level 3 Emergent	2
Snowman, The	Oxford Reading Tree	OUP	Stage 3 More Stories A	3
Snowman, The	Sunshine Spirals Starters	Heinemann	Set A	1
Snowy gets a wash	PM Storybooks	Nelson	Yellow Set B	3
So Do I	Journeys in Reading	Schofield & Sims	Level 1	3
So You Want to Move a Building?	Ready to Read	Nelson	Fluent Set D	9
Socks	Sunshine Spirals Starters	Heinemann	Set B	1
Soil	Pathways	Collins	Stage 3 Set D	9
Something in the Fridge	All Aboard	Ginn	Stage 3 Set A Patt & Rh	3
Sometimes	Literacy Links Plus	Kingscourt	Emergent A	2
Sometimes	Wonder World	Badger	Set 4	1
Sonic Sid	All Aboard	Ginn	Stage 7 Sam & Rosie	6
Sophie's Box	Cambridge Reading	CUP	Becoming a R Stage B	5
Sophie's Singing Mother	Tiddlywinks	Kingscourt	Stage 5	7
Soup	Sunshine	Heinemann	Level 2	6
Souvenirs	Literacy Links Plus	Kingscourt	Fluent A	7
Space	Sunshine	Heinemann	Level 1 Non-fiction	5
Space Ark, The	Sunrise	Heinemann		2
Space Journey	Sunrise	Heinemann		1
Space race	Sunshine	Heinemann	Level 1 Set J	6
Spacegirl Sue	All Aboard	Ginn	Stage 2 Set B Patt & Rh	3
Sparky the Dragon	Reading 360 New	Ginn	Little Bks L 3 Set 3	4
Special Clothes	All Aboard Non Fiction	Ginn	Stage 4	6

TITLE	SERIES	PUBLISHER	SET (OR AUTHOR)	BAND
Special Clothes	Discovery World	Heinemann	Stage A	1
Speed Boat, The	Sunshine Spirals	Heinemann	Set 3	2
Speedy's Day Out	All Aboard	Ginn	Stage 5 Set A Sam & Ros	6
Spider		BBC Books	Ralph, Graham	5
Spider	Literacy Links Plus	Kingscourt	Fluent C	9
Spider, Spider	Sunshine	Heinemann	Level 1 Set E	2
Spiders	Wonder World	Badger	Set 2	4
Spinning Top	Wonder World	Badger	Set 4	6
Splash!	Foundations for Reading	Folens	Level 1 Emergent	1
Splish, Splash	Pathways	Collins	Stage 0 Set A	2
Splosh	Story Chest	Kingscourt	Ready-set-go Set A	2
Spooky Old Tree, The	Bright and Early Books	Collins	Berenstain, Stan & Jan	4
Spooky Riddles	Beginner Books	Collins	Brown, Marc	6
Spot Goes on Holiday		Picture Puffin	Hill, Eric	4
Spots	Oxford Reading Tree	OUP	Stage 2 More Stories A	3
Spots	Sunshine New	Heinemann	Level 1 Set C	1
Spots	Sunshine Spirals Starters	Heinemann	Set C	1
Spot's Birthday Party		Picture Puffin	Hill, Eric	6
Spot's First Christmas		Picture Puffin	Hill, Eric	7
Spot's First Walk		Picture Puffin	Hill, Eric	5
Squeak in the Gate	Tiddlywinks	Kingscourt	Stage 6	9
Squeak-a-lot		Walker	Waddell, Martin	4
Squirrel is lonely	Reading World	Longman	Level 2: More Books	4
Stamps	Wonder World	Badger	Set 3	5
Stanley		Mammoth	Hoff, Syd	7
Stanley Goes to School	Reading World	Longman	Level 2 Pack B	6
Stars	All Aboard	Ginn	Stage 5 Set B Patt & Rh	5
Stars and Spots	All Aboard	Ginn	Easy Start Patt & Rhyme	1
Starting School		Picture Puffin	Ahlberg, Janet & Allen	7
Stepping Stones	Sunshine New	Heinemann	Level 1 Set C	1
Stepping-stones, The	One, Two, Three & Away	Collins	Main Books 5-8	7
Stone Soup	PM Traditional Tales	Nelson	Turquoise Level	7
Stone Works	Wonder World	Badger	Set 4	7
Stop It Bobby!	All Aboard	Ginn	Stage 4 Set A Sam & Ros	5
Stop it! Percy Green	One, Two, Three & Away	Collins	Pre-reader 9a-12a	2
Stop it, Webster!	Book Project Fiction 1	Longman	Band 1 Read On Specials	3
Stop that Noise!	Ready to Read	Nelson	Emergent Set B	2
Stop!	PM Storybook Starters	Nelson	Set 2	1
Stop!	Story Chest	Kingscourt	Ready-set-go Set D	2
Stop!	Wonder World	Badger	Set 4	2
Stop! Cried Alex	One, Two, Three & Away	Collins	Pre-reader 9b-12b	3
Stop! Look!	Reading 360	Ginn	Magic Circle Level 3	2
Storm Castle	Oxford Reading Tree	OUP	Stage 9 Magpies	7
Storm!	Wonder World	Badger	Set 2	6
Storm, The	Foundations for Reading	Folens	Level 8 Early	3
Storm, The	Literacy Links Plus	Kingscourt	Emergent D	3
Storm, The	Oxford Reading Tree	OUP	Stage 4 Playscripts	3
Storm, The	Oxford Reading Tree	OUP	Stage 4 Storybooks	5
Storm, The	Story Chest	Kingscourt	Get-ready Set A	2
Storm, The	Sunrise	Heinemann		1
Storm, The	Sunshine Spirals	Heinemann	Set 1	1
Stormalong's Great Sea Adventure	Sunshine New	Heinemann	Level 7	8
Story of Running Water, The	Cambridge Reading	CUP	Becoming a R Stage C	7
Story of You, The	Sunshine New	Heinemann	Level 5 Non-fiction	10
Story without end	Book Project Fiction 1	Longman	Band 3 Read On	5
Straw House, The	Storyworlds	Heinemann	Stage 5 Once Upon a Time	4
Strawberry Jam	Oxford Reading Tree	OUP	Stage 3 More Stories A	3
Sun and the Wind, The	Storyworlds	Heinemann	Stage 4 Once Upon a Time	3

TITLE	SERIES	PUBLISHER	SET (OR AUTHOR)	BAND
Sun smile	Story Chest	Kingscourt	Stage 2	6
Sun, A Flower, A	Foundations for Reading	Folens	Level 2 Emergent	1
Sunflower named Bert, A	Reading World	Longman	Level 2: More Books	4
Sunflower Seeds	Story Chest	Kingscourt	Get-ready Set DD	3
Sunflower that Went Flop, The	Story Chest	Kingscourt	Stage 5	8
Sunil's Bad Dream	Reading 360 Upstarts	Ginn	Level 3 Extension	5
Sunrise	Literacy Links Plus	Kingscourt	Emergent C	2
Sunshine Street	Sunshine	Heinemann	Level 1 Non-fiction	5
Super Hero	Sunshine New	Heinemann	Level 1 Set B	1
Superdog	Oxford Reading Tree	OUP	Stage 9 Magpies	7
Supermarket Chase, The	Sunshine New	Heinemann	Level 3	7
Supper For a Troll	Journeys in Reading	Schofield & Sims	Level 1	4
Surfer, The	Wonder World	Badger	Set 1	3
Surprise Cake	Literacy Links Plus	Kingscourt	Emergent C	2
Surprise Party, The		Picture Puffin	Hutchins, Pat	8
Surprise, Surprise!	Book Project Fiction 1	Longman	Band 4 Read On	8
Surprise, The	Oxford Reading Tree	OUP	Stage 8 More Robins	9
Surprise, The	Reading 360 Upstarts	Ginn	Level 2 Extension	4
Surprise, The	Story Chest	Kingscourt	Get-ready Set AA	1
Survival Adventure	Oxford Reading Tree	OUP	Stage 9 Magpies	8
Swamp Hen	Ready to Read	Nelson	Early Set C	4
Swan Rescue	All Aboard	Ginn	Stage 6 Sam & Rosie	6
Swap!	Oxford Reading Tree	OUP	Stage 4 More Stories B	3
Swim in the Park, A	Reading 360 New	Ginn	Little Bks L 2 Set 2	3
Swimming	All Aboard	Ginn	Stage 1 Sam & Rosie	1
Swimming	All Aboard Non Fiction	Ginn	Stage 1	1
Swing	Story Chest	Kingscourt	Get-ready Set AA	1

T

TITLE	SERIES	PUBLISHER	SET (OR AUTHOR)	BAND
T J's Tree	Literacy Links Plus	Kingscourt	Early B	4
T Shirts	Ready to Read	Nelson	Early Set D	4
Tabby In The Tree	PM Storybooks	Nelson	Blue Set A	4
Tadpoles	Pathways	Collins	Stage 2 Set D	7
Tail of the Mouse, The	Reading 360	Ginn	Magic Circle Level 5	7
Tails	Literacy Links Plus	Kingscourt	Emergent D	5
Tails	Wonder World	Badger	Set 1	5
Tails And Claws	Wonder World	Badger	Set 2	3
Tails Can Tell	Wonder World	Badger	Set 4	8
Tale Of Peter Rabbit, The		Picture Puffin	Potter, Beatrix	8
Tale on the Turnip, The	PM Traditional Tales	Nelson	Orange Level	6
Talk,Talk,Talk	Literacy Links Plus	Kingscourt	Early A	2
Tall Things	PM Non-fiction	Nelson	Red Level	3
Tap Tap Tap	All Aboard	Ginn	Stage 1 Intro Patt & Rh	2
Tea break	Bangers and Mash	Longman	Supplementary Books	6
Teacher, The	PM Non-fiction	Nelson	Blue Level	5
Teasing Dad	PM Storybooks	Nelson	Blue Set B	4
Teatime	Reading World	Longman	Level 1 Pack A	3
Teddy Goes Swimming	Book Project Fiction 1	Longman	Band 1 Read On	3
Teddy in the garden	Book Project Fiction 1	Longman	Band 1 Read On Specials	3
Teddy liked the little one	Book Project Fiction 1	Longman	Band 1 Read On Specials	2
Teddy plays hide and seek	Book Project Fiction 1	Longman	Band 1 Read On Specials	2
Teddybears 1-10		A & C Black	Gretz, Suzanna	3
Teeny Tiny		Picture Corgi	Rosato, A	6
Teeny Tiny Tina	Literacy Links Plus	Kingscourt	Emergent A	2
Teeny Tiny Woman	Scholastic Books	Ashton Scholastic	Seuling, Barbara	6
Teeth	Story Chest	Kingscourt	Ready-set-go Set CC	4
Teeth	Wonder World	Badger	Set 1	2
Ten Apples Up on Top	Beginner Books	Collins	Le Seig, Theo	7
Ten in the Bed		Walker	Dale, Penny	5

TITLE	SERIES	PUBLISHER	SET (OR AUTHOR)	BAND
Ten Jolly Jumpers	All Aboard	Ginn	Stage 2 Set B Patt & Rh	3
Ten Little Caterpillars	Literacy Links Plus	Kingscourt	Early C	4
Ten Little Crocodiles		Walker	West, Colin	6
Ten Little Garden Snails	PM Storybooks	Nelson	Green Set A	5
Ten Loopy Caterpillars	Tiddlywinks	Kingscourt	Stage 1 Small Books	7
Ten Sleepy Sheep		Hippo	Keller, Holly	6
Terrible Armadillo, The	Tiddlywinks	Kingscourt	Stage 2	6
Terrible Fright, The	All Aboard	Ginn	Stage 2 Sam & Rosie	2
Terrible tiger, The	Sunshine	Heinemann	Level 1 Set G	5
Terrible,Terrible Tiger		Walker	Hawkins, Colin & Jacqui	5
Tess and Paddy	Sunshine	Heinemann	Level 1 Set J	6
That Dog!	Foundations for Reading	Folens	Level 14 Experienced	5
That's Just Fine and Who-o-o Did It		Gerrard Publish'g	Lexau, Joan	8
That's Me	Cambridge Reading	CUP	Begin to Read Stage B	2
That's Mine, That's Yours		Picture Puffin	Sage, A & C	6
That's Really Weird	Tiddlywinks	Kingscourt	Stage 2	5
Then And Now	Pathways	Collins	Stage 3 Set C	10
There is a Carrot in my Ear	Scholastic Books	Ashton Scholastic	Schwart, Alvin	7
There is a Planet	Sunshine New	Heinemann	Level 1 Set D	2
There's A Dragon In My Garden	Sunshine Spirals	Heinemann	Set 7	6
There's a Hippopotomus Under my Bed		Avon Camelot	Thaler, Mike	7
There's a Monster	Reading 360 Upstarts	Ginn	Level 1	3
There's No One Like Me!	Sunshine New	Heinemann	Level 1 Set F	3
There's Paul	Reading 360 Upstarts	Ginn	Introductory	1
Things at Home	Link Up	Collins	Starter Books	1
Things in School	Link Up	Collins	Starter Books	2
Things in the Street	Link Up	Collins	Starter Books	1
Things on Wheels	Link Up	Collins	Starter Books	1
Things People Do for Fun	Foundations for Reading	Folens	Level 12 Early	5
Things to Eat	Link Up	Collins	Starter Books	1
Things We Read	Link Up	Collins	Starter Books	1
This is the Bear		Walker	Hayes, Sarah	6
This is the House Where Jack Lives		Heinemann	Heilbroner, Joan	7
This is the Register	Cambridge Reading	CUP	Becoming a R Stage A	5
This Mouth	Wonder World	Badger	Set 3	2
This Week	All Aboard Non Fiction	Ginn	Stage 1 Intro	1
Three Bears	Scholastic Books	Ashton Scholastic	Galdone, Paul	7
Three Billy Goats Gruff, The	PM Traditional Tales	Nelson	Orange Level	6
Three Billy Goats, The	Storyworlds	Heinemann	Stage 3 Once Upon a Time	2
Three by the Sea		Red Fox	Marshall, James	7
Three Friends		Viking/Kestrel	Kraus, Robert	6
Three Little Ducks	Story Chest	Kingscourt	Small Read-together	3
Three Little Pigs, The	PM Traditional Tales	Nelson	Orange Level	6
Three Little Pigs, The	Reading 360	Ginn	Once Upon a Time 1-4	6
Three Magicians, The	Literacy Links Plus	Kingscourt	Fluent D	9
Three Muddy Monkeys	Foundations for Reading	Folens	Level 8 Early	3
Three Robbers, The	One, Two, Three & Away	Collins	Main Books 9-12	7
Three Robbers, The		Methuen	Ungerer,Toni	8
Three Sillies, The	Literacy Links Plus	Kingscourt	Fluent C	10
Three Silly Monkeys	Foundations for Reading	Folens	Level 9 Early	4
Three Silly Monkeys Go Fishing	Foundations for Reading	Folens	Level 11 Early	4
Three Spotty Monsters	Cambridge Reading	CUP	Begin to Read Stage B	2
Three Wishes, The	Pathways	Collins	Stage 2 Set F	5
Three Wishes, The	Storyworlds	Heinemann	Stage 8 Once Upon a Time	7
Tick Tock	All Aboard	Ginn	Stage 1 Pattern & Rhyme	2
Tick-Tock	Story Chest	Kingscourt	Get-ready Set DD	1
Tidy-Up Story, The		Methuen	Erickson and Roffey	5
Tiger and the Jackal, The	Storyworlds	Heinemann	Stage 8 Once Upon a Time	7

133

TITLE	SERIES	PUBLISHER	SET (OR AUTHOR)	BAND
Tiger Dreams	Cambridge Reading	CUP	Becoming a R Stage C	8
Tiger runs away	PM Storybooks	Nelson	Blue Set B	4
Tiger, Tiger	PM Storybooks	Nelson	Red Set A	2
Tilak and the Digger	All Aboard	Ginn	Stage 2 Booster Bks	3
Tilak's Tooth	All Aboard	Ginn	Stage 3 Sam & Rosie	4
Tim	Sunshine Spirals	Heinemann	Set 7	6
Time for a Party	Discovery World	Heinemann	Stage D	3
Time for Bed	Sunshine Spirals Starters	Heinemann	Set B	1
Time for Dinner	Sunshine Spirals Starters	Heinemann	Set A	1
Time for Sleep	Sunshine New	Heinemann	Level 1 Set C	2
Timmy	Literacy Links Plus	Kingscourt	Emergent D	3
Timothy Goes to School		Picture Puffin	Wells, Rosemary	7
Tim's favourite toy	PM Storybooks	Nelson	Blue Set B	4
Tim's Paintings	Sunshine Spirals Starters	Heinemann	Set C	2
Tin Can Telephone	Wonder World	Badger	Set 4	5
Tinny Tiny Tinker	Tiddlywinks	Kingscourt	Stage 6	9
Tiny and the big wave	PM Storybooks	Nelson	Yellow Set B	3
Tiny woman's coat, The	Sunshine	Heinemann	Level 1 Set H	6
Titch		Picture Puffin	Hutchins, Pat	5
To New York	Story Chest	Kingscourt	Ready-set-go Set A	2
To School	Sunrise	Heinemann		1
To Town	Story Chest	Kingscourt	Large Read-tog Set 2	4
To Work	Sunshine New	Heinemann	Level 1 Set D	2
Toad Crossing	All Aboard	Ginn	Stage 8 Sam & Rosie	8
Toad Road	Reading World	Longman	Level 3	8
Toby and BJ	PM Storybooks	Nelson	Orange Set A	6
Toby and the Accident	PM Storybooks	Nelson	Turquoise Set A	7
Toby and the Big Red Van	PM Storybooks	Nelson	Orange Set B	6
Toby and the Big Tree	PM Storybooks	Nelson	Orange Set A	6
Toby and the Space Cats	Reading 360 Upstarts	Ginn	Level 4	7
Together	Sunshine	Heinemann	Level 1 Non-fiction	2
Tom and Sam		Picture Puffin	Hutchins, Pat	7
Tom and the Monster	One, Two, Three & Away	Collins	Red Platform 1-6	5
Tom is Brave	PM Storybooks	Nelson	Red Set A	2
Tom Looks for a Home	Reading 360 New	Ginn	Little Bks L 3 Set 3	4
Tom Turtle	Reading 360	Ginn	Magic Circle Level 5	4
Tomato Sauce	Pathways	Collins	Stage 1 Set D	3
Tommy's Treasure	Literacy Links Plus	Kingscourt	Fluent A	6
Tommy's Tummy Ache	Literacy Links Plus	Kingscourt	Emergent A	1
Tomorrow You Can		Whitman & Co	Corey, Dorothy	4
Tom's Box	Cambridge Reading	CUP	Becoming a R Stage C	6
Tom's Handplant	Literacy Links Plus	Kingscourt	Fluent B	10
Tongues	Literacy Links Plus	Kingscourt	Fluent A	10
Tony and the Butterfly	Literacy Links Plus	Kingscourt	Fluent D	8
Too Big for Me	Story Chest	Kingscourt	Ready-set-go Set C	3
Too Busy for Pets!	Sunshine New	Heinemann	Level 3	7
Too Late!	Foundations for Reading	Folens	Level 9 Early	4
Too Little	Foundations for Reading	Folens	Level 5 Emergent	3
Too Many Clothes	Literacy Links Plus	Kingscourt	Emergent A	2
Too Many Steps	Foundations for Reading	Folens	Level 15 Experienced	6
Too Much Noise	Literacy Links Plus	Kingscourt	Early D	6
Too Much Noise	Scholastic Books	Ashton Scholastic	McGovern, Ann	6
Toot Toot	Oxford RT Branch Library	OUP	Wildsmith Bks St 1A	2
Tooth Book, The	Bright and Early Books	Collins	Le Seig, Theo	7
Toothday and birthday	Bangers and Mash	Longman	Books 7-12 Pack B	8
Tortoise and the Hare, The	Cambridge Reading	CUP	Becoming a R Stage B	5
Tortoise, The	Reading 360	Ginn	Level 3	4
Town Cat, The	Reading 360 New	Ginn	Little Bks L.5 Set 3	6

TITLE	SERIES	PUBLISHER	SET (OR AUTHOR)	BAND
Town Mouse and Country Mouse	All Aboard	Ginn	Stage 3 Set B Patt & Rh	3
Town Mouse and Country Mouse	Fables from Aesop	Ginn	Books 1-6	6
Town Mouse and Country Mouse	Read It Yourself	Ladybird	Level 3	6
Town Mouse and the Country Mouse	Storyworlds	Heinemann	Stage 4 Once Upon a Time	3
Toy Box, A	Literacy Links Plus	Kingscourt	Emergent A	1
Toy Farm, The	PM Storybooks	Nelson	Orange Set A	6
Toys	Foundations for Reading	Folens	Level 1 Emergent	1
Toys Now and Then	All Aboard Non Fiction	Ginn	Stage 2	1
Toy's Party, The	Oxford Reading Tree	OUP	Stage 2 Storybooks	2
Toyshop, The	Reading 360 Upstarts	Ginn	Level 2 Extension	4
Traffic Lights	Pathways	Collins	Stage 0 Set C	1
Train Ride Story	Sunshine	Heinemann	Level 2	6
Train Ride, The	Literacy Links Plus	Kingscourt	Emergent C	3
Train that Ran Away, The	Tiddlywinks	Kingscourt	Stage 4	7
Tramping with Dad	Wonder World	Badger	Set 3	6
Traveller and the Farmer, The	Sunshine Spirals	Heinemann	Set 8	6
Treasure Chest	Oxford Reading Tree	OUP	Stage 6 Owls	7
Treasure House, The	Reading 2000	Longmans	Storytime Reds	7
Treasure hunt, The	Oxford Reading Tree	OUP	Stage 9 More Robins	9
Treasure Hunt, The	Sunshine Spirals Starters	Heinemann	Set A	1
Tree Doctor, The	Sunshine	Heinemann	Level 7	8
Tree House, The	Reading 2000	Longmans	Storytime Yellows	6
Tree, The	Sunshine	Heinemann	Level 1 Non-fiction	4
Tree-House, The	Story Chest	Kingscourt	Get-ready Set A	1
Trees	Literacy Links Plus	Kingscourt	Early D	7
Tricking Tracy	Tiddlywinks	Kingscourt	Bargain Book	3
Trip to the Park, The	Foundations for Reading	Folens	Level 14 Experienced	5
Trip to the Video Store, A	Foundations for Reading	Folens	Level 8 Early	3
Trog	Sunshine New	Heinemann	Level 3	6
Trojan Horse, The	Literacy Links Plus	Kingscourt	Fluent C	8
Trouble for Lelang and Julie	Book Project Fiction 2	Longman	Band 2	9
Trouble in the Ark		Picture Puffin	Rose, Gerald	7
Trouble in the Sandpit	Foundations for Reading	Folens	Level 16 Experienced	7
Trouble with Babies, The		Picture Puffin	Sage, A & C	5
Trouble with Gran, The		Collins Pict Lions	Cole, Babette	7
Trouble with Heathrow, The	Sunshine	Heinemann	Level 6	7
Trucks	Foundations for Reading	Folens	Level 12 Early	5
Trucks	Literacy Links Plus	Kingscourt	Early A	3
Trumpet, The	Reading World	Longman	Level 1 Pack A	2
Trunk, The	Oxford RT Branch Library	OUP	Wildsmith Bks St 1A	1
Try again, Hannah	PM Storybooks	Nelson	Green Set B	5
T-shirt Triplets, The	Literacy Links Plus	Kingscourt	Fluent B	8
Tug of War, The	Storyworlds	Heinemann	Stage 7 Once Upon a Time	6
Turnips for Dinner	Tiddlywinks	Kingscourt	Stage 1 Large Books	5
Turtle and the Crane, The	Book Project Fiction 1	Longman	Band 4 Read On	9
Turtle Flies South	Literacy Links Plus	Kingscourt	Fluent A	8
Turtle, The	Foundations for Reading	Folens	Level 5 Emergent	2
Tusk Tusk		Red Fox	McKee, David	7
Twiga and the moon	Storyworlds	Heinemann	Stage 7 Animal World	5
Two Babies	Cambridge Reading	CUP	Begin to Read Stage A	2
Two Bears and the Fireworks	Oxford RT Branch Library	OUP	Two Bears Bks St 7A	7
Two Bears at the Party	Oxford RT Branch Library	OUP	Two Bears Bks St 7A	8
Two Bears at the Seaside	Oxford RT Branch Library	OUP	Two Bears Bks St 7A	8
Two Bears find a Pet	Oxford RT Branch Library	OUP	Two Bears Bks St 7A	6
Two Bears go Fishing	Oxford RT Branch Library	OUP	Two Bears Bks St 7A	6
Two Bears in the Snow	Oxford RT Branch Library	OUP	Two Bears Bks St 7A	7
Two by Two	Cambridge Reading	CUP	Becoming a R Stage A	5
Two Can Toucan		Red Fox	McKee, David	8

TITLE	SERIES	PUBLISHER	SET (OR AUTHOR)	BAND
Two Eyes, Two Ears	PM Non-fiction	Nelson	Red Level	3
Two Giants, The	One, Two, Three & Away	Collins	Main Books 3-4b	5
Two Giants, The	Storyworlds	Heinemann	Stage 9 Once Upon a Time	10
Two little dogs	Story Chest	Kingscourt	Ready-set-go Set D	3
Two Little Goldfish	PM Storybooks	Nelson	Orange Set C	6
Two Little Mice, The	Literacy Links Plus	Kingscourt	Early D	5
Two Monsters		Red Fox	McKee, David	8
Two Shoes, New Shoes		Walker	Hughes, Shirley	7
Two silly stories	Book Project Fiction 1	Longman	Band 3 Read On	5
Two Wheels Two Heads		Collins	Ahlberg, Allan	7
Tyres	Foundations for Reading	Folens	Level 10 Early	5
U				
Ugly Duckling, The	PM Traditional Tales	Nelson	Turquoise Level	7
Ugly Duckling, The	Storyworlds	Heinemann	Stage 5 Once Upon a Time	5
Umbrella	Story Chest	Kingscourt	Ready-set-go Set AA	2
Umbrellas	Sunshine New	Heinemann	Level 2 Non-fiction	9
Uncle Buncle's house	Sunshine	Heinemann	Level 1 Set C	2
Uncle Carlos's Barbecue	Foundations for Reading	Folens	Level 10 Early	5
Uncle Elephant	Scholastic Books	Ashton Scholastic	Lobel, Arnold	8
Uncle Joe	Ready to Read	Nelson	Fluent Set A	7
Underground Adventure	Oxford Reading Tree	OUP	Stage 5 More Stories A	5
Underwater journey	Sunshine	Heinemann	Level 1 Non-fiction	5
Unhappy Giant, The	Reading 360 Upstarts	Ginn	Level 2 Extension	4
Up and Down	Oxford Reading Tree	OUP	Stage 3 More Wrens	2
Up and Down	Pathways	Collins	Stage 1 Set A	1
Up in a tree	Sunshine	Heinemann	Level 1 Set D	2
Up the Wall	Open Door	Nelson	Blue Fun Books	2
Up We Go	Reading 360 New	Ginn	Little Bks L 2 Set 1	2
Upside Down Harry Brown	All Aboard	Ginn	Stage 5 Set A Patt & Rh	6
Use Your Hanky, Hannah	Pathways	Collins	Stage 2 Set F	6
Using Tools	Discovery World	Heinemann	Stage C	3
V				
Vagabond Crabs	Literacy Links Plus	Kingscourt	Early D	7
Valentine's day	Story Chest	Kingscourt	Ready-set-go Set AA	2
Vanishing Cream	Oxford Reading Tree	OUP	Stage 5 More Stories A	5
Very Busy Spider, The		Picture Puffin	Carle, Eric	7
Very Clever Clown, The	All Aboard	Ginn	Stage 4 Set B Sam & Ros	5
Very Hot Day, A	Cambridge Reading	CUP	Begin to Read Stage A	2
Very Hungry Caterpillar, The		Picture Puffin	Carle, Eric	6
Vicky the High Jumper	Literacy Links Plus	Kingscourt	Fluent C	9
Vicky's Box	Cambridge Reading	CUP	Becoming a R Stage C	8
Victor and the computer cat	Oxford RT Branch Library	OUP	Victor Bks Stage 5A	5
Victor and the kite	Oxford RT Branch Library	OUP	Victor Bks Stage 5A	4
Victor and the martian	Oxford RT Branch Library	OUP	Victor Bks Stage 5A	5
Victor and the sail-kart	Oxford RT Branch Library	OUP	Victor Bks Stage 5A	5
Victor the champion	Oxford RT Branch Library	OUP	Victor Bks Stage 5A	5
Victor the hero	Oxford RT Branch Library	OUP	Victor Bks Stage 5A	5
Victorian Adventure	Oxford Reading Tree	OUP	Stage 8 Magpies	8
Viking Adventure	Oxford Reading Tree	OUP	Stage 8 Magpies	7
Village in the Snow	Oxford Reading Tree	OUP	Stage 5 Playscripts	4
Village in the Snow	Oxford Reading Tree	OUP	Stage 5 Storybooks	5
Village Show, The	Oxford Reading Tree	OUP	Stage 9 Robins	9
Village with Three Corners, The	One, Two, Three & Away	Collins	Main Books 1-2B	3
Visit to the Library, A	Foundations for Reading	Folens	Level 7 Early	3
Visiting the Vet	Foundations for Reading	Folens	Level 13 Experienced	6
Visitors	Literacy Links Plus	Kingscourt	Emergent D	3
Vosper's Boat, The	Sunshine Spirals	Heinemann	Set 8	7
Voyage into space	Storyworlds	Heinemann	Stage 9 Fantasy World	9

TITLE	SERIES	PUBLISHER	SET (OR AUTHOR)	BAND
W				
Wait and See		Little Mammoth	Bradman, Tony	6
Waiting	Story Chest	Kingscourt	Get-ready Set AA	2
Waiting for the Rain	Foundations for Reading	Folens	Level 17 Experienced	7
Wake Up	Open Door	Nelson	Red Fun Books	1
Wake Up Mr B		Walker	Dale, Penny	3
Wake Up!	Book Project Fiction 1	Longman	Band 4 Read On	4
Wake Up, Dad!	PM Storybooks	Nelson	Red Set A	2
Wake up, Mum!	Sunshine	Heinemann	Level 1 Set E	2
Wake Up, Webster!	Book Project Fiction 1	Longman	Band 1 Read On	3
Walk with Grandpa, A	Tiddlywinks	Kingscourt	Stage 3	8
Walk, Robot, Walk	Reading 360	Ginn	Magic Circle Level 1	1
Walking in the Autumn	PM Non-fiction	Nelson	Green Level	6
Walking in the Jungle	Cambridge Reading	CUP	Begin to Read Stage A	2
Walking in the Spring	PM Non-fiction	Nelson	Green Level	6
Walking in the Summer	PM Non-fiction	Nelson	Green Level	6
Walking in the Winter	PM Non-fiction	Nelson	Green Level	6
Washing	All Aboard	Ginn	Stage 1 Pattern & Rhyme	2
Washing	Foundations for Reading	Folens	Level 8 Early	3
Wasp, The	Reading World	Longman	Level 1: More Books	2
Waste	Pathways	Collins	Stage 2 Set B	3
Watch Out	Pathways	Collins	Stage 2 Set F	6
Watching the Whales	Foundations for Reading	Folens	Level 17 Experienced	7
Watching TV	Foundations for Reading	Folens	Level 9 Early	3
Watching TV	Sunshine Spirals	Heinemann	Set 1	1
Water	Ginn Geography Topic Bks	Ginn	Year 2	6
Water	Literacy Links Plus	Kingscourt	Emergent B	2
Water	Wonder World	Badger	Set 4	6
Water Boatman, The	Ready to Read	Nelson	Early Set B	3
Water Falling	Literacy Links Plus	Kingscourt	Early A	6
Water Fight, The	Oxford Reading Tree	OUP	Stage 2 More Stories A	3
Water, Water	Book Project Fiction 1	Longman	Band 4 Read On	4
Waving Sheep, The	PM Storybooks	Nelson	Green Set A	5
Way I Go to School, The	PM Storybook Starters	Nelson	Set 1	1
Wayne's Box	Cambridge Reading	CUP	Becoming a R Stage A	4
We All Play Sports	Ready to Read	Nelson	Emergent Set C	1
We Can Run	PM Storybook Starters	Nelson	Set 2	1
We Dance	Ready to Read	Nelson	Emergent Set C	2
We Go Out	PM Storybook Starters	Nelson	Set 1	1
We Like	Foundations for Reading	Folens	Level 2 Emergent	1
We Like Animals	Sunshine Spirals Starters	Heinemann	Set C	1
We Like Fish!	PM Storybook Starters	Nelson	Set 2	1
We need a bigger Zoo	Reading 360	Ginn	Magic Circle Level 1	1
We never get to do anything		Picture Puffin	Alexander, Martha	6
Wearing Glasses	All Aboard Non Fiction	Ginn	Stage 5	7
Weather	All Aboard Non Fiction	Ginn	Stage 2	2
Weather	Pathways	Collins	Stage 2 Set E	7
Weather		Picture Puffin	Pienkowski, Jan	1
Weather Chart, The	Sunshine New	Heinemann	Level 1 Set B	2
Weather Forecast, The	Ginn Science Info Bks	Ginn	Year 1	4
Weather Forecast, The	Pathways	Collins	Stage 0 Set C	1
Weather Vane, The	Oxford Reading Tree	OUP	Stage 4 More Stories A	4
Weather, The	Sunshine Spirals	Heinemann	Set 6	5
Weather, The	Sunshine Spirals Starters	Heinemann	Set A	1
Webster and the Treacle Toffee	Book Project Fiction 2	Longman	Band 1	9
Webster's Week	Book Project Fiction 1	Longman	Band 1 Read On	3
We'd better make a List	Story Chest	Kingscourt	Ready-set-go Set DD	4
Wedding, The	Literacy Links Plus	Kingscourt	Emergent D	3

137

TITLE	SERIES	PUBLISHER	SET (OR AUTHOR)	BAND
Wedding, The	Oxford Reading Tree	OUP	Stage 4 More Stories A	4
Wedding, The	Sunshine	Heinemann	Level 4	8
Well Done, Sam!	Cambridge Reading	CUP	Becoming a R Stage C	5
Well I Never	Story Chest	Kingscourt	Stage 5	8
We're Going on a Bear Hunt		Walker	Rosen, Michael	6
Wet Day at School, A	Sunshine	Heinemann	Level 1 Set E	5
Wet Grass	Story Chest	Kingscourt	Stage 2	6
Wet paint	Bangers and Mash	Longman	Books 7-12 Pack B	8
Wet Paint	Oxford Reading Tree	OUP	Stage 4 More Stories B	3
Whale, The	Sunshine Spirals	Heinemann	Set 4	3
Whales	Foundations for Reading	Folens	Level 17 Experienced	6
Whales	Wonder World	Badger	Set 4	10
What a bad dog!	Oxford Reading Tree	OUP	Stage 2 Storybooks	3
What a Mess!	Oxford Reading Tree	OUP	Stage 2 More Wrens	2
What a Mess!	Story Chest	Kingscourt	Ready-set-go Set C	2
What a Mess!	Sunshine Spirals Starters	Heinemann	Set A	1
What a Surprise!	Reading 360	Ginn	Level 4	5
What a Tale!	Oxford RT Branch Library	OUP	Wildsmith Bks St 1A	3
What Am I?	Foundations for Reading	Folens	Level 9 Early	4
What Am I?	Pathways	Collins	Stage 1 Set A	2
What am I?	Sunshine	Heinemann	Level 1 Non-fiction	5
What Are You Doing?	Foundations for Reading	Folens	Level 3 Emergent	2
What Are You?	Literacy Links Plus	Kingscourt	Emergent A	1
What Can I See?	Foundations for Reading	Folens	Level 1 Emergent	1
What Can Jigarees do?	Story Chest	Kingscourt	Get-ready Set CC	2
What Can This Animal Do?	Foundations for Reading	Folens	Level 1 Emergent	1
What Did Baby Say?	Reading 360 New	Ginn	Little Bks L.5 Set 3	6
What Did Ben Want?	Sunshine Spirals Starters	Heinemann	Set D	1
What did I use?	Discovery World	Heinemann	Stage B	2
What Did Kim Catch?	Literacy Links Plus	Kingscourt	Emergent D	2
What Do I See in the Garden?	Wonder World	Badger	Set 1	5
What Do We Drive?	All Aboard Non Fiction	Ginn	Stage 1	2
What do You Like to Eat?	Foundations for Reading	Folens	Level 3 Emergent	2
What Does Greedy Cat Like?	Ready to Read	Nelson	Emergent Set D	1
What else?	Sunshine	Heinemann	Level 1 Non-fiction	5
What For?	Cambridge Reading	CUP	Begin to Read Stage B	2
What Goes in the Bathtub?	Literacy Links Plus	Kingscourt	Emergent C	2
What Happens Next?	All Aboard Non Fiction	Ginn	Stage 1 Intro	1
What has Spots?	Literacy Links Plus	Kingscourt	Emergent B	1
What I Would Do	Tiddlywinks	Kingscourt	Stage 2	6
What If a Bear Comes?	Reading World	Longman	Level 2 Pack A	3
What is a huggles?	Sunshine	Heinemann	Level 1 Set B	2
What is Bat?	Literacy Links Plus	Kingscourt	Early C	5
What Is It?	Foundations for Reading	Folens	Level 8 Early	3
What is it?	Oxford Reading Tree	OUP	Stage 3 More Wrens	2
What is it? said the Dog	Reading 360	Ginn	Magic Circle Level 4	4
What is Red?	Literacy Links Plus	Kingscourt	Emergent C	2
What is This?	Pathways	Collins	Stage 0 Set A	1
What Season is This?	Wonder World	Badger	Set 1	1
What Shall I Do?	Sunshine New	Heinemann	Level 5	7
What Tommy Did	Literacy Links Plus	Kingscourt	Early B	7
What Was This?	Wonder World	Badger	Set 3	5
What Webster wants!	Book Project Fiction 1	Longman	Band 1 Read On Specials	3
What would you like?	Sunshine	Heinemann	Level 1 Set E	2
Whatever Will These Become?	Literacy Links Plus	Kingscourt	Early C	5
What's Around the Corner	Literacy Links Plus	Kingscourt	Early B	4
What's for Dinner, Dad?	Sunshine New	Heinemann	Level 3	7
What's for lunch?	Story Chest	Kingscourt	Get-ready Set C	2

TITLE	SERIES	PUBLISHER	SET (OR AUTHOR)	BAND
What's for Lunch?		Philomel Books	Carle, Eric	2
What's For Tea?	Reading World	Longman	Level 1: More Books	3
What's In The Box?	Cambridge Reading	CUP	Begin to Read Stage A	2
What's in this Egg?	Sunrise	Heinemann		1
What's Inside?	Foundations for Reading	Folens	Level 3 Emergent	2
What's Inside?	Wonder World	Badger	Set 4	8
What's That?	Book Project	Longman	Beginner Band 1	2
What's that?	Sunrise	Heinemann		1
What's the time Mr Wolf?		Little Mammoth	Hawkins, Colin	3
What's the time, Mai Ling?	Book Project Fiction 1	Longman	Band 1 Read On Specials	2
What's the Time?	Cambridge Reading	CUP	Becoming a R Stage A	5
What's the Weather?		MacMillan	Roffey, Maureen	3
What's There?	Pathways	Collins	Stage 2 Set A	2
What's Underneath	Discovery World	Heinemann	Stage D	8
Whatsit, The	Oxford Reading Tree	OUP	Stage 5 More Stories A	5
Wheels	Literacy Links Plus	Kingscourt	Emergent A	1
Wheels	Sunshine	Heinemann	Level 1 Non-fiction	2
When Dad did the Washing		Picture Puffin	Armitage, Ronda	7
When Dad went to playschool	Sunshine	Heinemann	Level 1 Set I	6
When Gran Was A Girl	All Aboard Non Fiction	Ginn	Stage 2	2
When I Left My House	Pathways	Collins	Stage 3 Set A	5
When I Look Up	Foundations for Reading	Folens	Level 2 Emergent	1
When I Pretend	Literacy Links Plus	Kingscourt	Emergent D	4
When I was Sick	Literacy Links Plus	Kingscourt	Emergent C	3
When I'm Big		Methuen	Bruna, Dick	2
When I'm Older	Literacy Links Plus	Kingscourt	Early C	5
When it Rains	Foundations for Reading	Folens	Level 2 Emergent	1
When Itchy Witchy sneezes	Sunshine	Heinemann	Level 1 Set C	2
When Jose Hits That Ball	Ready to Read	Nelson	Fluent Set A	5
When Nan Came to Stay	All Aboard	Ginn	Stage 5 Set A Sam & Ros	6
When the Balloon Went Pop!	Sunshine Spirals	Heinemann	Set 5	4
When the School Door was Shut	One, Two, Three & Away	Collins	Green Platform 1-6	5
When the Sun Goes Down	Wonder World	Badger	Set 3	6
When the Volcano Erupted	PM Storybooks	Nelson	Turquoise Set A	7
When we went to the Park		Walker	Hughes, Shirley	4
Where are My Socks?	Ready to Read	Nelson	Emergent Set C	3
Where are the Babies?	PM Storybook Starters	Nelson	Set 2	1
Where Are the Seeds?	Wonder World	Badger	Set 3	2
Where are the Sun Hats?	PM Storybooks	Nelson	Yellow Set A	3
Where are they Going?	Story Chest	Kingscourt	Ready-set-go Set A	2
Where are you going, Aja Rose?	Sunshine	Heinemann	Level 1 Set F	3
Where are you Going?	Reading 360	Ginn	Level 3	5
Where Can Teddy Go?	Foundations for Reading	Folens	Level 6 Early	3
Where does the Sun go at Night?		Walker	Ginsberg, Mirra	6
Where is Fred Dragon?	Reading 360 Upstarts	Ginn	Level 1 Extension	3
Where is Hannah?	PM Storybooks	Nelson	Red Set B	2
Where is It?	Reading 360 New	Ginn	Little Bks L 1 Set 1	2
Where is Jill?	Reading 360 New	Ginn	Little Bks L 2 Set 2	3
Where is Little Ted?	Reading 360 New	Ginn	Little Bks L 3 Set 3	4
Where is Lunch?	Ready to Read	Nelson	Emergent Set B	1
Where is Miss Pool?	Ready to Read	Nelson	Early Set B	3
Where Is My Ball?	Book Project	Longman	Beginner Band 1	1
Where is My Bone?	Reading 360 New	Ginn	Little Bks L 1 Set 1	2
Where is my Bone?	Sunshine New	Heinemann	Level 1 Set D	1
Where is my Caterpillar?	Wonder World	Badger	Set 1	8
Where is My Dad?	Sunshine Spirals	Heinemann	Set 1	1
Where is My Grandma?	Foundations for Reading	Folens	Level 3 Emergent	2
Where is My Hat?	Sunshine Spirals	Heinemann	Set 1	2

TITLE	SERIES	PUBLISHER	SET (OR AUTHOR)	BAND
Where is my Pet?	Sunshine Spirals Starters	Heinemann	Set D	1
Where is My Spider?	Story Chest	Kingscourt	Stage 4	7
Where is Skunk?	Story Chest	Kingscourt	Ready-set-go Set CC	3
Where is the Milk?	Foundations for Reading	Folens	Level 6 Early	3
Where Is The Monster?	Reading 360 New	Ginn	Little Bks L 1 Set 3	2
Where Is The Snake?	Book Project	Longman	Beginner Band 1	2
Where is Zip?	Reading 360	Ginn	Magic Circle Level 3	3
Where the Wild Things Are		Collins Pict Lions	Sendak, Maurice	8
Where Will You Sleep Tonight?	Foundations for Reading	Folens	Level 3 Emergent	2
Where's Mai Ling?	Book Project Fiction 1	Longman	Band 1 Read On	3
Where's My Hairy Bear?	Reading World	Longman	Level 1: More Books	3
Where's My Share		Collins Pict Lions	Greeley, Valerie	5
Where's My Teddy?		Walker	Alborough, Jez	5
Where's Spot?		Picture Puffin	Hill, Eric	3
Where's Sylvester's Bed	Wonder World	Badger	Set 2	4
Where's the Fox?	All Aboard	Ginn	Stage 1 Intro Patt & Rh	2
Where's Tim?	Sunrise	Heinemann		2
Where's Woolly?	Cambridge Reading	CUP	Begin to Read Stage B	2
Which is Alive?	Discovery World	Heinemann	Stage A	1
Whiskers	Wonder World	Badger	Set 4	1
Whistle For Willie		Picture Puffin	Keats, Ezra Jack	6
White Horse, The	Literacy Links Plus	Kingscourt	Fluent D	7
White Owls, The	One, Two, Three & Away	Collins	Main Books 5-8	6
Who Am I?	Book Project	Longman	Beginner Band 1	1
Who Asked the Ants?	Reading World	Longman	Level 2 Pack B	8
Who Ate the Bananas?	Sunshine Spirals	Heinemann	Set 1	2
Who Ate the Pizza?	Foundations for Reading	Folens	Level 2 Emergent	1
Who Can See the Camel?	Story Chest	Kingscourt	Ready-set-go Set AA	2
Who did it?	Storyworlds	Heinemann	Stage 5 Our World	4
Who Did That?	Oxford Reading Tree	OUP	Stage 2 More Wrens	2
Who Did That?	Pathways	Collins	Stage 0 Set B	1
Who is it?	Oxford Reading Tree	OUP	Stage 1 First Words	1
Who Likes Icecream?	Literacy Links Plus	Kingscourt	Emergent A	1
Who Made These Tracks?	Literacy Links Plus	Kingscourt	Emergent B	2
Who Sank the Boat?		Picture Puffin	Allen, Pamela	7
Who Sneezed?	Reading World	Longman	Level 1: More Books	3
Who Took My Money?	Reading 360 New	Ginn	Little Bks L 4 Set 1	7
Who Took the Farmer's Hat?	Scholastic Books	Ashton Scholastic	Nodset, Joan	5
Who Will be my Mother?	Story Chest	Kingscourt	Large Read-tog Set 2	4
Who's Afraid?		Picture Puffin	Van-der-Meer, R	5
Who's Coming for a Ride?	Literacy Links Plus	Kingscourt	Emergent A	1
Who's Going to Lick the Bowl?	Story Chest	Kingscourt	Ready-set-go Set A	1
Who's Looking After the Baby?	Foundations for Reading	Folens	Level 13 Experienced	5
Who's There?	Book Project Fiction 1	Longman	Band 1 Read On	3
Whose Eggs Are These?	Sunshine	Heinemann	Level 1 Non-fiction	5
Whose Mouse Are You?		Picture Puffin	Kraus, Robert	4
Whose Shoes?	Oxford RT Branch Library	OUP	Wildsmith Bks St 1A	1
Why Can't I Fly?	Scholastic Books	Ashton Scholastic	Gelman, Rita	5
Why Cats Wash After Dinner	Ready to Read	Nelson	Fluent Set A	6
Why Elephants Have Long Noses	Literacy Links Plus	Kingscourt	Early D	6
Why Rabbits Have Long Ears	Literacy Links Plus	Kingscourt	Fluent D	9
Why the Sea is Salty	Literacy Links Plus	Kingscourt	Fluent C	8
Why There Are Shooting Stars	Ready to Read	Nelson	Fluent Set D	9
Wibble Wobble	Pathways	Collins	Stage 2 Set E	5
Wibble, Wobble, Albatross!	Ready to Read	Nelson	Fluent Set A	5
Wide Mouthed Frog, The	Literacy Links Plus	Kingscourt	Early B	5
Wiggle and Giggle	Cambridge Reading	CUP	Becoming a R Stage B	5
Wiggle, Waggle	Book Project Fiction 1	Longman	Band 1 Read On	2

TITLE	SERIES	PUBLISHER	SET (OR AUTHOR)	BAND
Wiggly Worm	Tiddlywinks	Kingscourt	Stage 1 Large Books	4
Wiggly worms	Bangers and Mash	Longman	Books 1-6 Pack A	6
Wilberforce Goes on a Picnic		Picture Puffin	Gorden, Margaret	8
Wilberforce Goes Shopping		Picture Puffin	Gorden, Margaret	8
Wild Animals	Link Up	Collins	Starter Books	1
Wild Bear	Ready to Read	Nelson	Emergent Set A	1
Wild Woolly Child, The	Tiddlywinks	Kingscourt	Stage 2	8
William and the Dog	Oxford Reading Tree	OUP	Stage 7 Robins	9
William and the Pied Piper	Oxford Reading Tree	OUP	Stage 9 More Robins	9
William's mistake	Oxford Reading Tree	OUP	Stage 8 More Robins	9
William's Wild Wheelchair	Sunshine New	Heinemann	Level 2	7
Wind And Sun	Literacy Links Plus	Kingscourt	Early D	6
Wind and the Sun, The	Reading 360	Ginn	Magic Circle Level 5	7
Wind Blew, The		Picture Puffin	Hutchins, Pat	8
Wind blows strong, The	Sunshine	Heinemann	Level 1 Set F	4
Wind Power	Ready to Read	Nelson	Fluent Set B	5
Wind, The	Ready to Read	Nelson	Emergent Set D	3
Wind, The	Wonder World	Badger	Set 1	5
Windsurfing	Sunshine Spirals	Heinemann	Set 5	4
Windy Day, The	Ginn Science	Ginn		5
Winnie the Witch		OUP	Paul, Korky	8
Wish You Were Here		Red Fox	Selway, Martina	10
Wishing Fishing Tree, The	All Aboard	Ginn	Stage 5 Set A Patt & Rh	6
Witch and the Donkey, The	One, Two, Three & Away	Collins	Blue Platform 7-10	5
Witch Tricks	Reading World	Longman	Level 3	9
Witch Who Lived Next Door, The	One, Two, Three & Away	Collins	Yellow Platform 7-10	7
Wizard of Oz	Read it Yourself	Ladybird	Level 4	8
Wizard, The	All Aboard	Ginn	Stage 1 Intro Patt & Rh	2
Wobbly Tooth, The	Literacy Links Plus	Kingscourt	Early B	4
Wobbly Tooth, The	Oxford Reading Tree	OUP	Stage 2 More Stories B	4
Wolf and the Kids, The	Storyworlds	Heinemann	Stage 5 Once Upon a Time	5
Women at Work	Foundations for Reading	Folens	Level 11 Early	4
Woof!	Literacy Links Plus	Kingscourt	Emergent C	2
Woof!	Pathways	Collins	Stage 0 Set D	1
Woof! Woof!	All Aboard	Ginn	Stage 2 Booster Bks	2
Woolly, Woolly	Literacy Links Plus	Kingscourt	Early B	5
Woosh	Story Chest	Kingscourt	Small Read-together	5
Words	Ready to Read	Nelson	Fluent Set D	9
Words Are Everywhere	Literacy Links Plus	Kingscourt	Early A	4
Working Dogs	Reading 2000	Longmans	Storytime Reds	7
Workshop, The	All Aboard Non Fiction	Ginn	Stage 3	6
Would They Love a Lion?		Kingfisher	Denton, Kady	5
Would you Rather?		Red Fox	Burningham, John	7
Wrinkles	Literacy Links Plus	Kingscourt	Early A	2
Writer's Work, A	Wonder World	Badger	Set 4	8
Y				
Yasmin and the Flood	Oxford Reading Tree	OUP	Stage 4 More Sparrows	4
Yasmin's Box	Cambridge Reading	CUP	Becoming a R Stage B	5
Yasmin's Dress	Oxford Reading Tree	OUP	Stage 4 More Sparrows	3
Yellow	Literacy Links Plus	Kingscourt	Emergent C	1
Yellow	One, Two, Three & Away	Collins	Pre-reader 1-4	1
Yellow Cat and the Brown Dog, The	One, Two, Three & Away	Collins	Pre-reader 5a-8a	2
Yellow Overalls	Literacy Links Plus	Kingscourt	Fluent C	8
Yes Ma'am	Story Chest	Kingscourt	Large Read-tog Set 1	6
Yesterday I lost a Sneaker	Reading 360	Ginn	Magic Circle Level 7	8
Yippy-day-yippy-doo!	Sunshine New	Heinemann	Level 1 Set F	3
You Can Eat My Bicycle	Pathways	Collins	Stage 1 Set B	2
You Can't Park an Elephant	Pathways	Collins	Stage 3 Set C	8

TITLE	SERIES	PUBLISHER	SET (OR AUTHOR)	BAND
You Can't Scare Me!	All Aboard	Ginn	Stage 5 Set A Sam & Ros	6
You'll Soon Grow into Them, Titch		Picture Puffin	Hutchins, Pat	5
Yuk soup	Sunshine	Heinemann	Level 1 Set B	1
Yukadoos, The	Tiddlywinks	Kingscourt	Stage 1 Small Books	7
Yum and Yuk	Story Chest	Kingscourt	Stage 3	5
Yum Yum Gum	Reading World	Longman	Level 1: More Books	3
Yum! Yum!	Storyworlds	Heinemann	Stage 2 Animal World	2
Z				
Zoo		Picture Puffin	Pienkowski, Jan	1
Zoo in our House, A		Walker	Eyles, H & Cooke, A	4
Zoo, A	Literacy Links Plus	Kingscourt	Emergent A	1
Zoo, The	Wonder World	Badger	Set 1	2